The Bonding of Isaac

STORIES AND ESSAYS ABOUT GENDER AND JEWISH SPIRITUALITY

Joel Lurie Grishaver

The Alef Design Group

ALEF DESIGN GROUP • 4423 FRUITLAND AVENUE, LOS ANGELES, CA 90058
(800) 845–0662 • (213) 582-1200 • (213) 585–0327 FAX
E-MAIL MISRAD@TORAHAURA.COM

MANUFACTURED IN THE UNITED STATES OF AMERICA

Dedication

Who is the man
who is satisfied with his life
one who loves each day and sees good…

Psalms 13.12

For my father, and for Carol.

For Kent, Danny, B.J., Brett, and Andy.

For Raph, Michael, Michel, Jesse, etc.

For Earl, Harold, Uncle Seymour and Rabbi Cohan.

For Mark and Harriet.

To Yosi Gordon for teaching and learning with me. To Marc Borovitz for listening and affirming much of this. And especially to Adam Greenman for unrolling the ball of string which led me into and out of this book. And to Julie Goodman, who told me not to abandon it. And to my friends Peter Pitzele, Jack Reimer, and Jeff Salkin whose support assured that I would finish this effort.

Joel Lurie Grishaver

Table of Contents

Before...

This "before-word" is a theological abstract. Here, the entire premise of this work is unfolded from, and then spun around a few verses from, the beginning of Genesis. In this way, we uncover a basic rabbinic vision of male and female who exist with a fundamental and necessary interdependence. This "duality" that stands consistently in need of unification, will be constantly restated throughout this work. Each successive iteration will build the understanding and expand the contextual applications of these simple truths. In other words, this is ground zero...

[1] Here is what I know:

Rabbinic Judaism sees God as having to constantly balance two sides of God's personality: the *Midat ha-Din*—the rule-making, boundry-etching, Divine aspect of Judgment—and the *Midat ha-Rahamin*—the empathic, "womblike," Divine aspect of Mercy.

[2] Here is what I think I know:

The rabbis were telling us that some experiences of God in the world are those of a Patriarchal, Rule-making, Universal King. Other experiences of God in the world are those of a caring, intimate, nurturing Mother. The rabbis tend to be more able to be honest in their male God language than in their female—not an unreasonable weakness given their time frame.

[3] I also know what my friend and teacher, Yosi Gordon, has taught me about creation:

In the beginning there is one only person, ADAM (The Earthling). *ADONAI,* THE GOD, SAID: "IT IS NOT GOOD THAT *ADAM* BE ALONE." (We'll talk about it later, but I really believe that loneliness is an underrated spiritual issue. It, too, will form a major aspect of this work.) To solve the problem, God has a plan. God says: "I WILL MAKE A COMPANION STRENGTH WHO FITS WITH *ADAM*." Now watch the action closely. ADONAI, THE GOD, FORMED FROM THE SOIL ALL THE WILD BEASTS AND ALL THE BIRDS. AND BROUGHT EACH TO THE EARTHLING TO SEE WHAT THE EARTHLING WOULD CALL IT. WHATEVER THE EARTHLING CALLED THE ANIMAL, THAT BECAME ITS NAME... So God, with Adam's help, paired the *KELEV* (dog) with the *KALBAH* (female dog), the *HATUL* (cat) with the *HATULAH* (female cat). Male was matched with female. BUT FOR *ADAM*, NO HELPER WHO FIT COULD BE FOUND. *ADAM* (person) should have been matched with *ADAMAH*—but that word already had been used up; it was already the name for Mother Earth. For the first person, God needed a different solution. So here is what happened: ADONAI, THE GOD, MADE ADAM SLEEP A DEEP SLEEP AND TOOK ONE SIDE AND THEN CLOSED IN THE FLESH. We'll talk about it more later, but the Hebrew makes it clear that God took a side, an aspect of the first person, not just a bone. ADONAI, THE GOD, BUILT THAT SIDE INTO AN Ishah (woman), AND BROUGHT HER TO ADAM. ADAM SAID: "THIS IS THE ONE, BONE FROM MY BONE, FLESH FROM MY FLESH. SHE SHALL BE CALLED Ishah (WO-MAN). BECAUSE SHE WAS TAKEN FROM Ish (MAN)." If you listen closely, first there was an Earthling, one lonely person, whom God splits into two. By creating woman out of Earthling, Ishah out of ADAM, Ish (man), also out of ADAM, comes into being. And then the Torah continues: SO AN Ish WILL LEAVE HIS FATHER AND HIS MOTHER, HE WILL CLING TO HIS Ishah—AND THEY WILL BECOME ONE FLESH. People become whole finding their other half (Genesis 2.18ff).

[4] What I think I also know is this:

What seems obvious to me, but not clearly stated outside of kabalistic sources (perhaps), is that the male echoes the *Midat ha-Din*; the female, the *Midat ha-Raḥamin*.

When God tore ADAM into Ish and Ishah, the split between male and female was intentionally incomplete. The game in life, the search for meaning, is in finding the other half that fits with us to make one flesh. It is the same balance that God constantly seeks, too. This duality plays out in the following verse:

TO THE WOMAN GOD SAID:

YOUR MAN'S CLOSENESS YOU SHALL SEEK AND HE SHALL FIX YOUR LIMITS (Genesis 3.16)."

In this verse, gender difference is first defined in the Torah. It echoes all of the "pop" gender psychology: Women seek intimacy—men establish and enforce boundaries. The verse had been there a long time—perhaps since before creation. I had read by it, as we do with so many things in life, over and over. It took me years to notice it. Then it became self-evidently clear—the dichotomy between "CLOSENESS" and "LIMITS"—shouted. Two truths came together—Carol Gilligan meets Rashi, Robert Bly does midrash—and all of a sudden, in my eyes, they came together, explaining and expanding each other.

1
The Whimshurst Static Generator

For a long time, this book has hovered between two books. It has regularly flipped back and forth (like an electron between states) between being a "men's book" and being a "book about gender" written by a Jewish man. This original first chapter has survived dozens of rewrites, for it has been reworked with each flip. Often I wish I could now retrace the purity of the first draft. But sometimes life doesn't work that way. This prologue to the book tries to state that, like the relationship between me and my father, like the relationship between me and my friend Carol, most true things have two true alternating realities. Male and Female are but another one of these bipolar alternating truths.

The secret to this book is that rabbinic Judaism is very good at the bipolar thing. God has regularly been just and merciful, immanent and transcendent, providing free will and yet completely knowing the future, etc. The rabbis have regularly expressed these contrasting visions of reality in a literature known as midrash. This book, post-modern as it may be, is a work of midrash—the drawing together and stretching out of contrasting bipolar truths...

I t made sparks. That is what it was supposed to do. I had found a picture of the Whimshurst static generator in an old science book, part of that early electricity stuff—like Franklin's kite. My father and I had constructed it out of two old *Mitch Miller Sing-A-Long* records with orbs of aluminum foil that were glued on to serve as collectors. It was seventh grade, or perhaps eighth—memories fade— my big science fair project. Old, outgrown wooden blocks and wooden spools (now emptied of their thread) were called to serve as the frame and gear assembly. There was a crank handle. Strips of bicycle tubing (one with a twist and one without) turned the rotating parallel records in opposite directions. They generated opposite electrical charges. Wire collectors lifted the electric charges off the records and sent them along bent coat hangers that arced over the revolving records and terminated in little round metal globes (globes with world maps), which were taken from pencil sharpeners. The two globes hung a few inches apart. They were dual planets hovering in a shaky and noisy homemade universe. When you turned the crank the charges built up, and then the sparks bridged the gap. We had made our own mini-lightning; lots of little electrons had found their way home.

When my father and I made the Whimshurst static generator for my seventh (or perhaps eighth) grade science fair project, it was one of the classic moments in our relationship. I was in awe of his skill. I had started to build it on my own. Not only was my first model a gonzo—a just-go-for-it thing—with nothing square and dried glue oozing everywhere—but it never could have worked. My translation of the photo into reality had only one record turning in one direction. Then, I didn't understand the nature of bipolar opposites. My father's version was carefully drawn and sketched. Each part was measured, marked, carefully cut and fitted. My father had taken my dream project and made it real. I was grateful. In making it real, I was reduced to the role of scrub nurse, occasionally holding parts while they dried or handing him tools. We had a lot of fights. There were times he worked on it when I was sent to my room. I felt both emasculated and cheated of my fun—my project had been stolen. And, in that jumble of feelings, I was in awe of his mind and hands and patience with things—if not people. I also knew that not every father would give up the kind of time mine had given to help a son and make a dream project actual. To this day, our whole relationship is locked in that science project. It is the spark—jumping a gap between the two worlds—the awe and the anger, the pride and the sense of loss, all there when you turned the crank.

I took the project to school with great pride. I accepted the compliments of my peers with a lot of embarrassment (I felt like the kid who won the soap box derby on his father's engineering skill). I knew it was the best science project ever. A hell of a lot better than the rock collections or the do-it-yourself volcanos (there were three built from the same kit that year). I expected first prize. We won nothing. I thought it was my fault. I had to admit, I was a pain to teach. I was difficult. There was no way the teachers would give me a prize. There is a truth to that. There is also the probability that everyone could see the gap between my work and this piece. And most deeply, I now realize that both truths trace back to my father's inability to help me by empowering me. He's long dead, more than ten years dead, and I've lived past these truths rather than ever really resolving them. The real relationship doesn't stand in a single definition, doesn't have one truth—it lives in the sparks that cross the gap as electrons return home...

This book is a man's Jewish reflection on the meanings of gender. It, in many ways, is a book of midrashim. Midrash is a lot like my relationship with my father. It is the name given to the literature the rabbis (the ones who also wrote the Talmud) created to explain the meaning of the Torah. Midrash is a process. Midrash is a way of stretching the truth taught in the Torah so that it fits and covers our lives. Midrash is a way of digging down to the root of the Torah's truth and isolating the eternal, unchangeable truths revealed there. Midrash, therefore, is two kinds of truth in one: truth that is modernized and truth that is eternal. Midrash is much like the stories found above, a three-dimensional truth built out of two or more individual truths. Midrash is the story of how my father could be simultaneously caring and totally insensitive. Midrash is the story of how Carol and I can be incredibly close and yet never understand each other. This is a book of modern (or perhaps post-modern) midrashim. Midrash is a kind of mini-lightning, too.

Most people who know anything about midrash think that midrashim are "cute" little extra stories told between the lines of the biblical account. Midrash is supposed to be where Judaism does Aesop. That, however, is a very limited understanding. The historical reality is that much of midrash had its origins in sermons that were given to explain the weekly Torah portion. Midrashic sermons, called *petihtot* (openings) in Hebrew and "proems" in English, are built around a very specific structure. As "school figures" are to "ice skating," "proems" are to "midrash."

Each proem has a **"Torah Verse,"** which is the text that comes from the portion being studied, and a **"Proem Verse,"** which is traditionally a piece of text from the rest of the Bible (Prophets or Writings). Over the course of the proem the two verses are woven together and contrasted. The intersecting and conflicting images and contexts slowly help to redefine each other. The makers of midrash arced their sparks and their insights between the two verses. Midrash is always "braided" truth, the learning gleaned from balancing the contrasting bipolar opposites it considers.

11

As this book wrote itself through me, it became more and more a book of midrashim and less and less a collection of polemics. A few of the pieces, like the title piece, emerged full blown as story midrashim—Jewish mythic forms. However, most of the pieces in the book are really "proems," homages to classic midrashic sermons. Like a classical proem, these essays compare and contrast two texts, letting new insight spark across the gap between them. Like the stories of my father, these proems seek to braid and weld together two or more single truths in order to suggest a more dynamic three-dimensional truth.

Davar Aher: Another version of the same truth: I
talk to my friend Carol every night. Almost every night, out of love, I tell her that she is making mistakes. I demand that she solve her life's problems. I am constantly gifting her with solutions. I offer better ways to raise her kids, better ways to cope with her husband's death, better ways to do her job—I constantly open a whole universe of new solutions for her. My solutions are often not what she wants at all—she just needs to "blow steam" and to have someone understand. My understanding is usually a solution. As a way of returning my love, she wants to share my feelings. She questions every statement I make. I think she is doubting and questioning my sincerity—usually she's just trying to understand me, just trying to be close. I often get angry. I want to have my ideas tested, not to have my feelings investigated and affirmed. I reject the aura or illusion of sympathy—I *feel* infantalized (even though I *know* that is not her intent). When I want empirical validity—"Tell me what I am saying is true"—she is offering the gift of empathy—"I know just how you feel." It often infuriates me. This has been going on for more than five years now. We've even gotten good at reversing parts and doing the other's piece. But the gap is still there. Each of us wants to scratch the other's back—but our instincts lead us to scratch the place where we project our own itch. Still it works somehow. We've learned to spark across the gap of gender-oriented tendency and be there in tension and support.

The Braided Truth: Carol and I still talk every night.
Somewhere in my psyche my father and I are still turning the *Mitch Miller Sing-A-Long* records in opposite directions and making sparks. Every day

I struggle with the meaning of my manhood in a world where every aspect of masculinity has been challenged and questioned. This book started out to be a polemic about men's needs and Jewish responses—it wound up being a series of proems about using rabbinic insights to honor gender difference. The proem form both expressed and created that transition. It, too, is a spark across the gap of two worlds, an affirmation of the monotheistic unity of duality. Just turn the crank, read, and be aware. The sparks contained herein are challenging, not dangerous. They are only static electricity, like rubbing your feet on a rug and then touching someone.

2
The Bonding of Isaac

The following midrash, or perhaps short story, is my closest single experience of personal revelation. It got written in one night, without pause, as a kind of vision. The rest of this book has been my attempt to understand and "rationalize" the the insight that came in that all-night meditation before the CRT.

It started this way. (1) It was Thanksgiving, and I stayed in LA, by myself, without friends. I needed the down time. I actually craved the loneliness. (2) It was raining heavily, and I was driving around town, running errands, in a hot, sweaty convertible in the rain. (3) I was listening to a tape of Robert Bly's **Iron John**, which I had previously failed to get past page 10 of—three times, but which people kept quoting to me. (4) The tape got to me, in a way the book didn't, and I found myself driving around LA, in the hot sweaty convertible, crying my eyes out as the rain shielded me from view. I was alone. I was mourning my father and our unresolved relationship. (5) On Sunday night Kent, then 12, called to tell me about how his family had been "trapped" inside a cabin at Yosemite, and his mother had told his brother, "If kids were as easy to divorce as husbands, you'd be long gone." (6) That line triggered the story that follows. I opened a Hebrew Bible with Rashi to Genesis 22 and began to write...

ather and son had fought. The son no longer looked like a child. He stood full height and his beard was tough. He was strong and mature: muscles and stubble and sweat. It was long past the point where the son could have, or perhaps should have, left home for good, but he was still at home, working for Father, eating at Mother's table, still a child of the family. At times he had gone away and been on his own, but in the end he was still at home, still his mother's boy, his father's son. The father and his son had shouted at each other. It was a battle of wills. Somewhere in your heart you know the origins of the fight—perhaps the boy had not cleaned up his space, or played music too loudly, or challenged his mother's authority—it doesn't matter. You know the fight—the raging testosterone, the blood-red blush of angry faces, the emotional lines etched in the sand as both father

14

and son try to become ruler of their own territory—as each needs to be the winner. It was not an adult battle. It was not a struggle for the sake-of-heaven. No Torah was at stake. Rather, the animal urge was marking its prowl, defining the area where one alone should hunt and dominate. The boy went to his space. The mother hid in hers. The father wandered off, looking for something that would appear to be a responsible task, something that could keep him occupied. Silence echoed as the mother tried to slow her nervous shiver, as the men waited for the barometer of their anger to slowly fall; anger can have a very long half-life. But all of them knew the ritual. They had fought this fight often. They had each rehearsed and perfected their parts. Meanwhile, the silence echoed.

AFTER THESE THINGS, GOD TESTED ABRAHAM. Abraham was in no mood for a test. It was a bad time for the Boss to call. He didn't want another responsibility. He wanted his anger, his righteous indignation, his time to convince himself that he was right. Being righteous was the last thing on his mind. But the Boss had called. The time was now. He had no choice. He buried the anger as deeply as he could in the emotional *geniza* of his stomach and put on his best possible face. There was no more time to dwell on family, it was time to do his job.

GOD SAID TO HIM, "ABRAHAM." AND HE SAID, "Yeh, Boss, that's my name, I'm your boy. 'HINENI.' Your wish is my command."

GOD SAID: "PLEASE TAKE YOUR SON," but Abraham whined, "He's just a boy, a kid. Let me do this on my own, or get Eleazer or one of the other men to help me. He is so irresponsible. His mother and I love him—but he just isn't ready to grow up."

God said, "Please take YOUR ONLY ONE." Abraham winced; the memory of leaving Ishmael in the desert was too painful. Now he had only Isaac left. He had failed to raise Ishmael properly and turn that boy into a man. In the end he had no choice but to make the tough decision and kick the boy out. Ishmael had broken the rules too many times—there had been too many "one-more-chances." Sarah had called it "Tough Love." But to Abraham it didn't feel like love at all—except perhaps as an abstraction. It was just his failure. Rather, he had gathered all of the anger and the hurt from the four corners of his being, drawn the line in the sand, and told his boy, "This was for your own good. There is nothing more your

15

mother or I can do." Then he shoved all of the mixed emotions back into his stomach, calling upon his animal urge to assert itself and quell his womb-like empathy. Ishmael was gone. He told his heart, "Perhaps on his own he'll make a man of himself, because he needs to." Inside it still felt like failure and emptiness.

Softly, recognizing the hurt, God said, "If you listen to me, if you'll take the risk, you'll not have to re-live that mistake again." Abraham stared with silent incomprehension.

God said softly, "Please take this son WHOM YOU LOVE." Abraham said, per-haps to himself, "I do love him. It is hard, but I do love him. I always have. Sarah and I waited so long. We had so many dreams and plans of who he could become. We just want the best for him, yet he just can't seem to find a direction. It's my love that gets me so angry. If I didn't love him so much, it would be easier to watch him waste his life and accomplish noth-ing. All of the fights, all of the yelling, all of the hurt is really just loving too much. I know that doesn't make sense. But I just can't seem to make him find himself." God answered him with a voice that seemed to pat him on the back, or perhaps hug his whole being, and said, "You're right, you can't make him find himself—you can only allow him to become what he can become." Again Abraham stared blankly with silent incomprehension.

Then God said, "Please take ISAAC." As soon as God said the name, Abraham teared. His womblike aspect opened the *geniza,* and the memories poured out. He saw the laughter of his boy, his son named "Laughter." The shout-ing faded into the background as all the laughter and hugs came back. The games of catch, the models they built together: the good times. The hugs and times he had wiped the boy's tears and turned the tears back into laughs. He saw his boy Isaac smile at the times he understood some-thing new or important, the silence with which he often just experienced the joy of discovery, the way he could watch and learn and improve— Abraham wiped the tear from his own eye, regained his professional pos-ture, quickly resealed the feelings, and with reestablished dignity said, "HINENI, Boss, what's our mission?"

"GO TO THE LAND OF MORIAH." It is a land of fear and awe and vision and teach-ing—where both of you will learn to see the world anew. There you will turn your heart to him, he will turn his heart to you—a pilgrimage. And

16

you will set him free from his slavery in the boyhood house of bondage, and in turn he will redeem you from all of the anger and hurt. You will both be returned and renewed. "AND YOU WILL CAUSE HIM TO ASCEND—MAKING A SACRIFICE, HIS ASCENT." And Abraham thought he understood. The two of them would go on the quest together. They would walk for days, sharing stories and food cooked on an open fire. They would leave the tents of women behind. It would be men's time. They would hike and hunt and camp—and finish the mission. He would tell the stories and share the secrets, and in the end they would reach the place. There the boy would die and the man would be reborn. The walk, the quest, the ceremony would reestablish their love and let Isaac become a man. A time together outdoors was just what they needed. The boy would die. The man would be born. It would be a time of bonding. The Boss was smart. The Boss really understood the family business. The boy would die—the man would be born. Again Abraham teared just a little. He was sure that no one would notice.

ABRAHAM ROSE EARLY IN THE MORNING. He smiled as he began to pack. Every hunting trip with Terah had started early in the morning. Packing and eating and leaving before dawn was part of the whole experience. All of his own boyhood memories flooded back, the good father–son times. And with them a sweet but profound sadness. He missed his father. So much had happened to him since his death. His father hadn't seen the new country, hadn't known of God's promise or even seen his grandchildren. He had become a man on his own. He had formed a new religion, built a financial empire, established a dynasty as part of his grand partnership—and yet his father was missing. Missing, not only in the present, but in the past. He had died without giving approval, without confirming, without sharing a sense of *nakhas* and affirmation. Abraham had been forced to confirm his own manhood, and that was hard—but he had done it. He had fought the battles, withstood the test of the flames, made the journeys and found his own long-promised place. He missed his father, both the father he had experienced and the father he had never had, but he also knew how to get past these emotions. He folded them carefully and put them away. He then packed and prepared the elements of their journey. HE SADDLED THE ASS. HE TOOK TWO SERVANTS WITH HIM AND HIS SON ISAAC. HE CHOPPED THE WOOD FOR THE FIRE OF SACRIFICE. HE WENT TO THE PLACE WHICH GOD

17

HAD TOLD HIM. Four of them walked together, but Abraham was still walking alone—alone in his mission. The Torah doesn't tell us "They went to the place..." Abraham was going alone with his entourage to the place that God had told him about. He was on his own mission.

It was now THE THIRD DAY. There had been times of silence, times of alienation and doubt. But there had been better moments, too. Working together had helped. The hunt, the camping, the campfires had also helped. It was good to tell the old stories and perhaps better to create the new ones. The telling and the listening were good. The fighting and the yelling and the distance were remembered but were in no way active. There was still distance and caution between them, but this was a better time. Sometimes, too, they just forgot and laughed together. ABRAHAM LOOKED UP AND SAW THE PLACE IN THE DISTANCE. The camping trip was over. The journey, while pleasant, had served its purpose. While they had been together for a few days, Abraham, by himself, looked up and saw the place in the distance. Whatever Isaac saw, he never noticed. Whatever the servants perceived for themselves was beyond his purview. He had responsibilities. He had obligations. He was following the Boss' orders. The Boss knew best. The boy must die to give birth to the man. He shivered for a second as the reality of that statement become clearer as they neared the place. He folded the image of the bloody death of the boy—the real image, not the symbolic meaning—he folded the image of knife, blood and agony—the reality, not the myth of father slaying son—and placed it deep in his stomach. He composed himself and stood erect. ABRAHAM SAID TO HIS SERVANTS, "STAY HERE WITH THE ASS, I AND THE BOY WILL GO THERE." He pointed to the mountaintop. "WE WILL WORSHIP AND RETURN TO YOU."

Abraham said to himself. "I must find the strength to do this for Isaac's sake. If I weaken, he will never leave boyhood. I must be hard and strong. I cannot give in...I must be a man so that he can become a man." Then he said to himself, "Work is good. We must lose ourselves in the task. We'll be too busy to think or question or hesitate. We can lose ourselves in the work and then in the ritual." ABRAHAM TOOK THE WOOD FOR THE SACRIFICE AND HE PUT IT ON ISAAC HIS SON. "He is strong and brave," Abraham thought. "He understands that this is a test for both of us—and yet he has the courage to face it. He does get me angry—but he also makes me proud. He has my temper, my will, my stiff neck—but also his mother's laughter and his

18

own silent sense of profound knowing." He took in his hands the fire and the knife. He carried the flint and iron rocks for fire making and the flint knife. He didn't look at them at all. He saw Isaac, strong and willing, carrying his own heavy load. He thought, "The wood is heavy, and carrying it takes great strength, but that is only physical strength. I am proud that my Isaac is strong. The fire and the knife carry a greater burden—I wonder if my own character is strong enough to let Isaac be reborn as a man." Father and son walked side by side, then one after the other up the path. There was silence, but there was also a shared connection. The distance between man and boy had been shortened. Without saying anything they both took account of how much they shared.

The two of them walked on together. Abraham thought, "It has been a very long time since we have been this together, since we've spent this much time without fighting, since we've liked as well as loved each other."

Isaac spoke to Abraham his father. He often yelled at his father. Traded playful insults with his father. Shared dirty jokes and lewd comments with his father. All kinds of words passed from one to the other, but it had been a long time since they had spoken. It had been a long time since all those bedtime glasses of water, good conversations, and goodnight kisses. He had gotten too old for them—but perhaps not old enough. He said, "My father." He listened as the word "father" echoed: Father. Father. Father. It had many meanings. There was the father he loved but didn't like. The father of demands, disappointments, expectations, and challenges. And there was the father he missed—the father who could have supported, approved, and taken joy in his being. The word "father" echoed: Father. Father. Father. And out of the echo he heard his father's voice. He said, "Hineni, My Son." For Abraham, too, the word son echoed: Son. Son. Son. The lost son of his dreams—the posterity son who would right all his own failures, the innocent son who wanted only a hug and smile and, the angry son who stood in his own confusion, rejecting everything in his father's outstretched hands.

Abraham said, "My son, I am here for you. I am not absent anymore. In fact, I was never really gone. I have always been here for you. I am fully here, ready to be the father you want and need. HINEINI, I love you. I also like you. I am proud of you." Both of them cried just a little, a little more than they thought they should, a lot less than they wanted to...

19

It was silent for a long time. Isaac started to speak several times. Each time the words welled up from his stomach to his heart to his mouth and stopped there. The third or fourth time he found the courage. HE SAID, "Dad, HERE IS THE FIRE AND THE WOOD, BUT WHERE IS THE LAMB FOR THE SACRIFICE?"

There had been the time that his father had said, "If kids were as easy to divorce as wives, you'd have been gone a long time ago." It was said in anger, like the many other times he had shouted aloud and shouted inside at his father, "I wish you were dead." He had meant it as an expression of anger—a use of emotional profanity—not as a potential reality. Yet this was too real. "If kids were as easy to divorce as wives ..." was a joke gone haywire. Ishmael was gone, long gone, now for the second time. Driven away because Abraham wouldn't give in. He thought, "I am just like him." Lot had gone, too. He had been like a son, but they couldn't live together as men. Now we are walking up the mountain. He has the knife. My father—even my angriest, my most maddening father—he couldn't actually do that to me. He is my father—I know that—I must be safe with him. He loves me. He has just told me that. I believe him. I am scared to death. We have never been closer; the gap has never been as great."

Abraham heard the question. He thought, "I love the boy. I want to take him in my arms and hug him, I want to give him horseback rides like when he was nine and make him my joyful burden. BUT, the boy must die so that the man can be born. I need to tell him. There is no way he can understand." ABRAHAM SAID, not to his son, not to anyone in particular, except maybe to God, "GOD WILL SEE THE LAMB FOR THE SACRIFICE." Then there was a long pause. Then he finished the sentence: "MY SON." When the last words had escaped, even Abraham wasn't sure what or how many different things they meant.

They were in love again. They were father and son again. They were ready to fight and kill and hug and forget and forgive. All the possibilities stood before them at this moment: eternal war, reconciliation, death, and transfiguration. And they both understood more than either could put into words. The moment had beauty and horror, and it hung in the balance between powerful symbolism and obscene reality. It made a great movie—it was horrible to live. THE TWO OF THEM WALKED ON TOGETHER.

THEY CAME TO THE PLACE OF WHICH GOD SPOKE. Then Abraham was again alone with his mission. Isaac stood lost and afraid. He watched the flocks of birds migrate across the sky in their pilgrimages. The father, alone, missing his own father, turned to the work at hand. ABRAHAM BUILT THE ALTAR. HE SPREAD OUT THE WOOD. Isaac stood motionless, suspended in the beauty and the horror of the moment. He understood that his father was doing all of this out of love for him—he feared that which his father might do to him out of madness or out of faith. His father said, "It is time for you to meet my God. It is time for the boy to die. It time for the man to be born." Abraham kissed his son on the forehead. He took the rope and asked Isaac to hold one end. With the help of the son, the father wrapped his son—both of them understood that this binding was a shared bond. Isaac started to speak, to question ... Abraham stopped him. They looked deep in each other's eyes. Their last conversation silently echoed. He had asked, "Dad, here is the fire and the wood, but where is the lamb for the sacrifice?" His father had answered: "God will see the lamb for the sacrifice." Then there was a long pause. Abraham had finished the sentence: "My son." HE TIED UP ISAAC, HIS SON. HE PLACED HIM ON THE ALTAR ON TOP OF THE WOOD. There was no struggle. There was no passivity. They both were moving automatically. While they had never been there, together, in that way before, the ritual seemed obvious, and they both played their parts. It was as if each was watching the action from afar—in no way directly involved. Abraham said: "The boy must die so that the man can be born." Isaac hoped that those were just ritual words, a secret initiation rite. Isaac trusted Abraham; after all, fathers just don't kill sons—maybe they kill them with words and silence, but not with knives. Abraham trusted God. He believed literally that the boy would die at his hand and that God would renew him as a man. ABRAHAM SENT OUT HIS HAND TO TAKE THE KNIFE TO KILL HIS SON. The knife hung in the air. The two sets of eyes met. Both questioned and renewed their faith.

ADONAI'S MESSENGER CALLED TO HIM FROM THE HEAVENS, "ABRAHAM!" Abraham said, "What!" His voice challenged the other voice. At first he thought one of the servant boys had followed him against his orders. This was a private moment—it was a family thing. They should be alone. This was hard enough to do at all—it could never be done in front of witnesses. "ABRAHAM," the messenger called for a second time. Both father and son

21

were frozen, suspended—the horror of the almost—hanging too true. They were glad and mad and confused. But for the moment the uncharted journey to Isaac's manhood had been halted. Abraham again sucked in his emotion and gave the ritual answer. HE SAID, "HINENI."

The voice from heaven said, "DO NOT SEND YOUR HAND TO THE BOY!" The voice sounded familiar. Abraham said, "The boy must die so that the man can be reborn." The voice shouted, "No." Then it caught itself and said more gently, "No. No." Then, almost in a whisper, "No." It was then that Abraham realized that the voice from heaven sounded like Terah. "Death is Death— at least in this world. If the boy dies, there will be no man. The child is the father to the man. The boy will grow to manhood when you are ready to allow him to no longer be a child. Jewish fathers must never kill their sons, not in reality, not in ritual, not even with words, not even with silence. They must give them life."

Isaac was no fool. When the knife hesitated he began to struggle. He pulled at the ropes. There were no knots. The only binding was a bonding of will. While Abraham spoke to a voice he could not yet hear for himself, Isaac got up and ran. He knew what he was doing. He was choosing life. His father still looked up to heaven. While Isaac hid behind a rock, listening, Abraham said, "I love my son—I only want to do the best for him. I really want him to find his own happiness. Perhaps I misunderstood God when I was told to bring him up as a sacrifice, an ascent. I was only trying to do for him what no one had ever done for me. My own father was gone; I had grown up the best that I could. I just wanted to make it easier and better for him."

The voice hugged him and wiped his tears. The voice said, "I understand. I am proud of you. You've done everything you could. But now is a time for you to grow up as well. You're the one who must give himself up as a sacrifice at this moment—not Isaac. You're the one who must release Isaac from the dreams and expectations you hold for him. The Isaac who is really you must die, not the real Isaac. You must give him his freedom— he must be freed from the bondage of your needs." Abraham sobbed and picked up the knife again and said, "Thank You. I understand." Then he said, "I must cut my son, give him the warrior's wound, cut the bond, let him stand on his own."

Before he could turn to look at the empty altar the voice shouted, "DON'T EVEN MAKE A MARK ON HIM." Abraham responded, "But how can he become a man without a change? He needs the initiation—he needs the sign." Softly the voice said, "No." "But," Abraham argued, "how can he become a man without the wound? The wound is the focus—the wound is the way he learns to live with pain, to learn that he can master and forgive all the pain of growing up. He can't become a man without the wound." "Listen," the heavenly voice said with great love, "long ago, eight days into his life, you cut the sign of Jewish manhood—long before it could ever be confused with anger or pain. All you need do now is let him go on to his own freedom, to his own promised place. Repeat after me, *BARUKH she-PETURANI....*"

The brakhah was interrupted. Still in a daze, still confused, Abraham asked, "But what about the pain? If he doesn't learn to master the pain of the initiation ritual, how will he ever forgive the other pain I've caused him? How will he ever learn that all of the pain was simply the best I could do— it was the best of my love?" The voice answered with understanding and love, "Because there is more than enough pain involved in the stories he will learn. There is more than enough suffering in the tradition he will pass on. It doesn't take overcoming pain to be a Jewish man, it takes fully feeling it. Someday he will be a slave in Egypt. Someday he will suffer in that house of bondage. Eventually, I will set him free. Every year he will have to live and relive that story. Every year he needs to feel it more and more. When the womblike empathy is no longer locked away, when the animal urge no longer shouts "mine," but rather "ours"—because he can share the pain of others, and walk with them—then he will be a man. The pain must be in the stories he must live and tell—not in what a father does to a son—not in what old men do to boys."

Abraham cried. Isaac cried. In his heart Abraham said, "I love you, son. I respect you. I like you." In his heart Isaac said, "I forgive you." The voice which was Tera<u>h</u>'s said, "Repeat after me: *BARUKH she-PETURANI me'ONESHO she-l'Zeh.*" (Thank God who has freed me from the need to punish this one.) Abraham saw his son was gone. He said, "Isaac, I set you free to be your-self." Isaac said, "Father, I set you free to be yourself. You have raised me well." He stood up behind the rock. The two men's eyes met. He had thought to run away, to spend some time alone, to become himself, before he returned home to formalize the peace. But something held him. They didn't quite run to each other, but father and son hugged and cried for the first time, man to man. Each whispered in the other's ear, "I love you." Abraham let all his memories fill him. No longer would they be locked away. Without speaking a word Isaac walked down the hill. He turned to look back many times, and each time their eyes met. With each turn Isaac feared that he would be called back, that he would be returned to boyhood, but Abraham just smiled with a silent knowing look he had learned from his son. Isaac slowly disappeared.

The voice said, "I am proud of you, My son. You've grown into a wonderful, caring, righteous man. NOW I KNOW THAT YOUR ARE IN AWE OF GOD—YOU DIDN'T HOLD BACK YOUR SON, YOUR ONLY ONE, either from himself or FROM ME. Now he can find his own way to serve Me."

ABRAHAM LOOKED UP AND SAW. HERE, BEHIND HIM IN THE BUSHES, WAS A RAM CAUGHT BY ITS HORNS. ABRAHAM WENT. HE TOOK THE RAM. HE OFFERED IT AS A SACRIFICE for and INSTEAD OF HIS SON. As he killed the ram he understood that he had finally killed his need to own his son's future. ABRAHAM CALLED THE NAME OF THAT PLACE ADONAI-YIREH, meaning "ADONAI sees." He smiled, knowing that there was a witness to that moment. Never again did God speak with him. Abraham didn't need the external voice anymore. He had made peace with his father and peace with his son, and God flowed within him. Abraham had finally accepted himself.

In Tera<u>h</u>'s voice ADONAI'S MESSENGER CALLED TO ABRAHAM A SECOND TIME: "I, MYSELF, PROMISE," ADONAI SAYS, "BECAUSE YOU DID THIS FOR ME, AND DID NOT HOLD BACK YOUR SON, YOUR ONLY remaining SON—I WILL BLESS YOU BY now BLESSING YOU completely. I WILL MAKE YOU MANY, VERY MANY, through Isaac and his sons you will become as many AS THE STARS OF THE SKY, AS THE SAND THAT IS ON THE SEASHORE. YOUR FUTURE-FAMILY SHALL INHERIT THE CITIES OF THEIR ENEMIES. ALL THE NATIONS OF THE EARTH WILL BE BLESSED THROUGH YOUR FUTURE-FAMILY. When darkness came, Abraham sat for a long while, counting the stars and enjoying his old-man dreams. Meanwhile, Isaac, too, was counting the stars as he walked toward his new destiny. He enjoyed the visions and hopes of young men.

ABRAHAM RETURNED TO HIS SERVANTS. THEY GOT UP AND WALKED TOGETHER TO BEER SHEVA. No longer did Abraham ever walk alone, lost in the self-importance of his mission.

Isaac found himself at the Yeshiva of Shem and Eber. He spent much time unlocking the Torah's secrets, coming to understand his father's visions. He loved his teachers, and they mentored him well. After several years he found himself studying this passage in *Bava Metzia*: "IF ONE HAS TO CHOOSE BETWEEN SEARCHING FOR HIS OWN LOST ARTICLE AND HIS FATHER'S LOST ARTICLE, HIS OWN TAKES PRECEDENCE." He smiled his silent, knowing smile and thought, "That is a lesson I almost lost my life learning." IF HE HAS TO CHOOSE BETWEEN SEARCHING FOR HIS FATHER'S LOST ARTICLE AND HIS TEACHER'S LOST ARTICLE, HIS TEACHER'S TAKES PRECEDENCE. BECAUSE WHILE HIS FATHER BROUGHT HIM INTO THIS WORLD, HIS TEACHER, WHO TEACHES HIM WISDOM, BRINGS HIM INTO THE WORLD-TO-COME. Again he smiled his knowing smile. Shem and Eber had taught him many things, things he knew that his father knew, but things that he could never have learned at home. BUT IF HIS FATHER IS A TEACHER, HIS FATHER'S TAKES PRECEDENCE. It was then that Isaac headed home. It was then that he realized that his father had much Torah to teach him. It was then that he understood that home could also be his home, not just his father's house.

AND ISAAC CAME home BY WAY OF BEER-LAH-ROI-BECAUSE HE HAD BEEN LIVING IN THE NEGEV. ISAAC WENT OUT TO WALK IN THE FIELDS—ABOUT EVENING TIME—HE LIFTED UP HIS EYES AND SAW THAT CAMELS WERE COMING—he shielded his eyes from the sun with his left hand, just as his father had done when he had seen the place where they had to go so many years before. Isaac remembered that walk they took together with love—the anger and fear was long gone. RIVKA LIFTED UP HER EYES AND SAW ISAAC. SHE GOT DOWN OFF HER CAMEL AND SAID TO THE SERVANT, "WHO IS THAT MAN WALKING TOWARDS US, THE ONE OUT THERE IN THE FIELD?" Everyone could see that Isaac had grown into a man. THE SERVANT SAID, "HE IS MY MASTER." Even though Abraham was still the father, still the owner, still the master, still the boss, Isaac, too, had found his own place, found the respect of others. ISAAC TOOK HER INTO HIS MOTHER SARAH'S TENT. It was vacant because she had died while he was away. HE TOOK REBEKAH TO BE HIS WIFE. HE LOVED HER. He was ready. Had grown to be a man. He was ready to make his own mistakes with his own family. He was ready to find his own long-promised success. He smiled his silent smile of knowing and understanding.

3
Jewish Men are Spencer Tracy
Rabbinic Images of Manhood

In thinking through the experience of writing **The Bonding of Isaac**, I came up with two basic conceptions: (1) That the duality between male and female seemed to parallel the rabbinic duality between the **Midat ha-Din** (the inner voice of justice) and the **Midat ha-Rahamin** (the inner voice of mercy). There seems to be a high level of congruence here between the gender psychologists and the rabbinic texts. (2) The second insight had to do with the aspects of male behavior that have often been labeled as "evil." It is all rooted in defining aggressive as "wrong" and assertive as "very good." That seemed to make no sense to me, because my life experience had taught me that "there is a time to be aggressive and a time to be 'only' assertive." That led me to look at additional rabbinic sources on the **Yetzer ha-Ra**, the evil urge. My conclusion is that "male" (as we know it) is actually a blend of the **Midat ha-Din** and the **Midat ha-Rahamin**, and that the diffence between **machismo** and **menshlekite** (two contrasting male images—one Hellenistic and one Judaic) is the blend, not the elements.

To trace these insights we will use two text problems from the first chapter of Genesis as our **Torah Texts**, and three memories of **Michael**, one of my former students, as our **Proem texts.**

This is essentially a "male chapter," using "female" only for contrast; in following chapters we will examine the feminine perspective...

Pre-Text One: Researchers at Georgia State University took saliva samples from five fraternities and found that guys in houses with rough and rowdy reputations had higher overall testosterone levels (by 10 to 20 percent) than those in houses with more responsible reputations. The party boys also had worse academic records, did fewer hours of community service, and kept messier rooms. Other studies have linked high testosterone levels with violence, thrill-seeking and domineering, aggressive behavior. Bear this in mind the next time a "frat rat" invites you for tea. ("Side bar." *Sassy Magazine,* March 1994: p. 14.)

Pre-Text Two: Masculinity is supposed to be passed on from father to son. Women, no matter how wonderful, no matter how loving, can't teach it to us. If we don't have fathers, we should have grandfathers, uncles, step-fathers to raise us from boys into men. If we don't have men in our family, then our need for mentors begins early. If the males we know are the other teenage boys or the macho heros from the movies, we may get a distorted, exaggerated concept of masculinity. What we men share is the experience of having been raised by women in a culture that stopped our fathers from being close enough to us to teach us how to be men, in a world in which men were discouraged from talking about our masculinity and questioning its roots and its mystique, in a world that glorified masculinity and gave us impossibly unachievable myths of masculine heroics, but no domestic models to teach us how to do it. So we grew up constantly faking our masculinity, and never knowing quite how much masculinity would be enough. We've all been, to varying degrees, male impersonators—awed by the splendor of the masculine mystique and ashamed of the meager masculinity found in ourselves. (Frank Pittman, M.D., *Man Enough: Fathers, Sons, and the Search for Masculinity.* New York: G.N. Putnam's Sons, 1993, pp. 15–19.)

Prologue: A personal reflection: I am not good at sitting still—I still don't do it well. It is not one of my better behaviors. I have gotten into a lot of trouble because other people have expected me to sit still and keep quiet. In my case, that was too much to expect.

When I was in first grade in public school we had a program where the mothers came to watch us. We were supposed to sit still a lot, keep quiet, and then perfectly perform the lessons we had rehearsed. The big finish was picking up a piece of paper and turning it into a fireman's hat. To make this magic possible the paper had been carefully cut and folded. We had to wait almost an hour before we got to the fireman's hat. I couldn't wait. I played with it a lot. Every time I picked it up the teacher told me to leave it alone, and my mother got embarrassed. It wasn't one of my better days. More than thrity-five years have passed, and I still feel the pain of my mother's embarrassment. It, too, is well-folded away in my *geniza* of excessive emotionalism; even so, the pain of that moment, the pain of not fulfilling her wishes, often leaks out.

Davar Aḥer: **Another first grade memory, similar but different:** In Sunday School they brought us into the sanctuary and showed us the Torah. It was supposed to be another "good behavior time" when they led us up on the bima, but Rabbi Cohan was really friendly, and he broke ranks. He joked and handed us parts of the Torah as he unwrapped it. I wound up with the breastplate. I really was listening to him, and sort of watching, but I was also playing with the heavy silver breastplate. After a while I decided to put my head through the chain and wear it. I remember wanting to know how the Torah felt. Before I could lift the chain my first grade teacher anticipated my move and started to grab me. Rabbi Cohan came to my rescue. He somehow burst through the crowd and lifted the breastplate over my head, explaining to the whole class that originally the high priest had worn the breastplate. I wore my breastplate with pride. "Tommy" Torah (the cartooned living Torah character used in the work by which I have earned my livelihood for the past twenty years) was born that day....

The Torah Text: GOD CREATED MAN IN HIS IMAGE, IN GOD'S IMAGE HE CREATED HIM, MALE AND FEMALE HE CREATED THEM (GENESIS 1.27).

Gender confusion enters the world through this verse. A male God creates man. A male God creates man in His image. A single male God creates people: male and female (in His image). The language here turns in on itself—it demands explanation.[1] As we unlock its encrypted message we will learn the Jewish essence of being a man, a man created in, and living up to, God's image.

To try to unlock this verse's meaning I turn not only to the classical sources; I also think of Michael's performance in class this week. He is the one who—

---

[1] **God created man in His image, in God's image He created him, male and female He created them.** The passage here is a chasm, a reflexive (ABC-CBA) pattern followed by a direct echo. The first two phrases form the chasm (a) *va'Yivrah* (b) *Elohim et ha-Adam* (c) *b'Tzelmo*—(c) *b'tzelem* (b) *Elohim* (a) *Barah oto*. The last phrase is a direct echo of the middle phrase: (x) *b'tzelem Elohim* (y) *Barah* (z) *oto*— (x) *Zakhar u'Nikevah* (y) *Barah* (z) *otam*. A chasm is a device for attracting attention; it is a literary pattern that accomplishes for listeners what a highlighter does for readers. It emphasizes the last clause. We learn by comparing the last two phrases that *b'tzelem Elohim* (God's Image) = *Zakhar u'Nikevah* (male and female) and that *oto* (him/man) = *otam* (them/people).

by example—ultimately teaches me this text's meaning. His actions provide the proem verse that explains, and is explained, by our Torah text.

The Proem Text: Three snapshots of Michael:

Michael is no wimp. He is pure boy, edging into manhood—simultaneously he's both dangerous and kind. Michael is a 14-ish-to-15-ish-year-old I have the privilege of teaching at the Los Angeles Hebrew High School.

[1] Michael always wears an all black (with red and white art) rock-and-roll T-shirt (you know the genre). One of the girls once complained that he wore the same shirt every day. He retorted concisely: "I have lots of them. I wear a different one every day." Then he expanded his commentary: "No one is allowed to wear them at my high school because the stupid faculty thinks they are connected to devil worship." With an eye twinkle and a one-beat pause, he delivers his punch line: "I wear them every day anyway!" This was followed by another short monologue: "All teachers hate me. They always throw me out. They won't listen to anything I say."

[2] Another time, before school, I hear Michael tell one of his peers: "The strangest thing happened this weekend. When I heard that Freddy Mercury (the lead singer of the rock group Queen) died (from AIDS) I began bawling my eyes out. It was really weird. I couldn't stop."

[3] While handing in his midterm today, Michael sincerely apologized. "I'm sorry, but I'm not good at this, I'm stupid." His affect suggested that he felt that he had betrayed me by not doing well. Ironically, not only did he score a solid B, he also wrote a thoughtful, challenging essay.

The Braid: Remember James Dean? Remember *Rebel Without a Cause*? His performance in the film asks the same question about Male and Female He Created Them as do my memories of Michael. How can you cry like a baby over a toy monkey one day and manifest the machismo needed for a drag race to the death the next? "Where is our 'crying place?'" and "Where is the part that goes on 'Chickie Runs?'" And then, when we added in, In God's image, we want to know: "What's God got to do with it?" To solve the problem we need to go more deeply into our Torah text.

TORAH TEXT (Genesis 1.1): In the Beginning God (Elohim) created the Heavens and the Earth....

THIS IS THE FAMILY HISTORY OF THE HEAVENS AND THE EARTH ON THE DAY WHEN ADONAI, THE GOD (*ADONAI ELOHIM*), MADE EARTH AND HEAVEN (Genesis 2.4).

The Problem: When the rabbis read Torah, they become obsessed with each and every word. This is an obsession that the text encourages. Not surprisingly, their close reading of the text often involves the defining of boundaries and the setting of limits of meaning. When they find similar passages—passages which say almost the same thing—rather than emphasizing that they had something in common, they try to explain the differences. They want to learn something different and unique from each example, rather than get a single insight from a shared experience.

In the first story in the Torah, the "Creative Force" is called *Elohim*, God. Here God creates in seven days by the numbers, ending with the creation of people. Beginning in the middle of chapter two, verse four, a second story appears. This is the hands-on creation story with the shaping of mud, the rib, and the garden. Here, people happen right at the beginning. When the story changes, so does the name of the "Creative Force." *Elohim*, God, has become *Adonai-Elohim* (*Adonai*, the God). (God suddenly has a hyphenated name!) The rabbis believed that these two stories must be one, but they also assumed that each half must teach a different thing. They wanted to know the difference the name *Adonai* makes.

The Midrashic Solution: The rabbis then told this midrash (*Genesis Rabbah* 12.15) to explain it: **This can be understood by comparing the situation of a human king who had a beautiful crystal bowl. Said the king: "If I pour hot water into it, it will burst; if I pour cold water into it, it will contract and shatter." So what did the king do? He mixed hot and cold water and poured it into it, so it remained unbroken. This is just what the Holy-One-Who-Is-to-Be-Praised said. "If I create the world on the basis of the *Midat ha-Raḥamin* alone (My attribute of mercy), its sins will be great. If I create it on the basis of the *Midat ha-Din* alone (My attribute of justice), the world cannot exist. Hence I will create it on both the basis of both judgment and mercy, and then it may stand!" Therefore, the Torah teaches ADONAI, THE GOD (*ELOHIM*).**

The Gender-Based Commentary: There is an idea here that echoes in the work of contemporary gender psychologists. In her book *In a Different Voice*, Carol Gilligan explains that men and women solve ethical problems differently. From that insight she proceeds to teach us her take on the essence of manhood and womanhood. She suggests that the central facet in men's thinking is the making and applying of rules. Men's judgment emphasizes boundaries and is a process of dividing people. Men's thinking is a process of individuating, of defining the difference between you and me. In other words, it is mainly *Midat ha-Din*. Women's thought, on the other hand, focuses on commonality. Their analysis of problems emphasizes relationships and the experiences people share. Networking and finding what you and I have in common is the essence of women's problem-solving process. In other words, it is mainly *Midat ha-Ra<u>h</u>amin*.

On the simplest level, a penis does tend to define male behavior—not by its sexual desires, but by the penis' ability to mark territory by urinating on the corners of a field. Carol Gilligan teaches us that rule-making is the extension of marking the corners of the field and calling it "mine."

Virtually the same insight can be found in Deborah Tannen's *You Just Don't Understand*. Where Carol Gilligan found her truth by interviewing children, Deborah Tannen came to the same point by listening to and analyzing the way adult men and women perform ordinary conversations. She says, **"Many men engage in the world as individuals in a hierarchical social order in which they are either one-up or one-down. In this world, conversations are negotiations in which people try to achieve and maintain the upper hand if they can, and protect themselves from others' attempts to put them down and push them around. Life, then, is a contest, a struggle to preserve independence and avoid failure."** In other words, men's primal perceptions, as reflected in their language patterns, essentially involve the making of boundaries, the conquest and defense of territory, and the maintenance of a pecking order. For our purposes, she adds the important word for male perception, **"independence."**

On the other hand, Tannen explains that women approach the world **"as an individual in a network of connections. In this world, conversations are negotiations for closeness in which people try to seek and give confirmation and support, and to reach consensus. They try to protect themselves from others' attempts to push them away. Life, then, is a com-**

31

munity, a struggle to preserve intimacy and avoid isolation." In other words, women's primary motivations involve bringing others closer and building bonds with them. She introduces the new key word for woman's concerns, "**intimacy.**"

Dennis Praeger, a popular Los Angeles talk radio host, likes to define this difference as "macro" versus "micro" thinking. Many men root themselves in global thinking; they generalize everything to a universal rule. In the process they often bury or deny the personal. This is very much a process of emphasizing the *Midat ha-Din*, the attribute of Universal Justice. In contradistinction, many women center themselves in the micro. They personalize everything and see events only in terms of their "personal" connection. They often maximize their full potential when this is balanced with a more global view. In other words, women are not all *Midat ha-Rahamin*, the "womblike attribute of Mercy," but many of them lean in that direction.

The Braided Truth: When Carol Gilligan and Deborah

Tannen's insights, our Torah text, and this midrash are viewed together— the combination suggests a powerful approximation of the truth. The *Midat ha-Din,* God's tendency to make and enforce rules, is the male attribute of God—the attribute of independence, of setting and policing boundaries. We are, in essence, speaking of ethical pecking orders. The *Midat ha-Rahamin* is its bipolar opposite. *Rahamin* comes from the word *Rehem,* womb. This is God's maternal aspect, the feminine attribute—the attribute of celebrating connection, intimacy, and commonality. We are getting in touch with spiritual networks. Once people were created, God's tendencies had to be blended together. For the rabbis, *Adonai Elohim* was not only the God of the second story, but the way God had to be once people were created; the existence of people (which is a fact after the first story) mandates a balance. This is the deeper meaning of MALE AND FEMALE GOD CREATED THEM.

Davar Aher: Another insight. Another Braid:

(GENESIS 1.4) GOD SAW THE LIGHT THAT IT WAS GOOD...

GOD SAW EVERYTHING HE HAD MADE, THAT IT WAS VERY GOOD.

THERE WAS EVENING, THERE WAS MORNING. THE SIXTH DAY (GENESIS 1.31).

The Rabbinic Problem: Six times over the first

six days of creation God looks at His work in progress and sees THAT IT IS GOOD. At the end of the sixth day, just before Shabbat, but after people have been created, God looks at all of creation in total and sees THAT IT IS VERY GOOD. Rather than assuming that this is a culmination, just a networked image, the rabbis believed that there is a difference that can be delineated, a lesson that can be learned by finding a boundary.

The Rabbinic Solution: They believed that the

creation of people made a difference, made things VERY GOOD. In a midrash (*Genesis Rabbah, Bereshit* 9.7), they explained it this way: Man has two urges—*Yetzer ha-Tov*, the tendency to do good, and *Yetzer ha-Ra*, the tendency to do evil. **Rabbi Nahman bar Samuel said the *Yetzer ha-Tov* is good, but the *Yetzer ha-Ra* is very good. "It was very good" means that because of the *Yetzer ha-Ra* men build houses, take wives, father children, and engage in business. As the Torah teaches (Ecclesiastes 4.4): "ALL LABOR AND SKILLFUL WORK COMES FROM COMPETITION BETWEEN MEN."**

The Gender-Based Commentary: If

we take our original Torah text (GOD CREATED MAN IN HIS IMAGE), our insight into God's dual nature (*Midat ha-Din* and *Midat ha-Rahamin*), and this text— blend and stir—another sense of the truth seems to reveal itself. *Yetzer ha-Tov* is like *Midat ha-Rahamin* and *Yetzer ha-Ra* is like *Midat ha-Din*. Just as God had to pour in both into the crystal bowl in order to have a complete image, a man has to blend his *Yetzer ha-Ra* (the animal tendancy to possess and conquer) with his *Yetzer ha-Tov* (his womblike empathy) to become mature.

Listen to Deborah Tannen teach the same truth: "**Each individual works out a unique way of balancing status differences [*Yetzer ha-Ra*] and connection [*Midat ha-Rahamin*] to others. But if we think of these motivations as two ends of a continuum, women and men tend to cluster at the opposite ends.**" Gilligan reaches the same conclusion in this fashion: "**Attachment [*Yetzer ha-Tov*] and separation [*Midat ha-Din*] anchor the cycle of human life, describing the biology of human reproduction and the psychology of human development. The concepts of attachment and separation that depict the** nature and sequence of infant development appear in adolescence as identity and intimacy and then in adult life as love and work."

The Braided Truth: Michael can bawl his eyes out (without the ability to stop) when Freddy Mercury dies and still wear a black rock and roll T-shirt just to anger his teachers (while being hurt that they don't listen to him). No truth goes all the way. That leads us back to the *Yetzer ha-Ra*....

The *Yetzer ha-Ra* is a feral child, a wolf-boy who wants and needs. *Yetzer ha-Ra* is all about gratification and ego. It is good at protection and conquest, but not much else. It is not so much evil as immature and undeveloped. It is pure, unmixed, too much of a strong flavor. You might think of it as Clint Eastwood or Bruce Willis unbound.

The *Yetzer ha-Tov* starts out life as Donna Reed, or perhaps Auntie Mame, but it certainly lived in Rabbi Cohan (*Zakhur l'Tov*), too. Men, too, have their wombs and their empathic womblike nature. But a real Jewish man isn't a feral boy, and he isn't a mother; either, he is a flowing together of the two, a confluence of machismo and menschlekeit.

As much as I like to believe my life is influenced by Jewish metaphors, I am a product of twentieth-century America, too. My soul is filled with two sets of metaphors. I try hard to fill it with a profound sense of deep Jewish imagery, and I pour that into a rich admixture of western images. Any sense of who I am has to meet a deeper test of confluence as well. Therefore, I always need a bunch of cross-cultural tests.

The *Lord of the Flies* Test: Jack, the antagonist, the leader of the choir who becomes the warrior chief, is the embodiment of the *Yetzer ha-Ra*. He is a feral child—pure boy-wolf—with a sense of fun and a propensity toward violence. More wild then evil, he is a boy who can be regulated by the adult society, but whose wildness flows out of control in the wilderness. He totally lacks empathy. Piggy, the fat kid with the glasses, is a male-mother—a creature of pure *Rahamin*. He can give his all—but has no ability to defend himself or others. He can push no boundaries. Ralph, the hero, is our ideal—the flowing together of wolf and mother. Sadly, however, even for our emerging man with the best of intentions and resources, outside forces prove too much. Remember, this is a story about boys—not real men. It is pure *puer* power. It is all about the unblend-ed *Midat ha-Din*. At the end of the story, when the English sea captain is saying, "One would have hoped that a lot of English boys would have done better," the usual critics take it as a statement of how shallow are the reg-imens of civilization—the veneer of English culture wore off quickly. But we know better. *Lord of the Flies* is the story of fourteen-year-olds. It is all about their moment of development. Successfully aged youths, ones who have learned to honor their "*Midat ha-Rahamin,*" would be different. A group of boys would always revert to "wolves." One can believe with great cer-tainly that a group of monks, or an all-male team of Peace Corps volunteers, or probably a group of nineteen-year-old Zionist males on their way to work on a kibbutz would be different. Men easily revert to boys and then to wolves; but, given values and maturity, there are alternatives.

The Peter Pan Test: Peter, too, is pure *Yetzer ha-Ra*—clearly not evil, but with no sense of others. The world is there for his joy, his adventure, his need. Pan's life is all happy thoughts, a celebration of "Christmas, Ice Cream, and Candy." It is all gratification—all "me." He is all want and desire. *Hook*, Steven Spielberg's Peter Pan movie, is really a midrash on the J. M. Barrie story (though it is, to my way of thinking, a better midrash than a movie). Spielberg understands that Captain Hook is nothing more than the dark side of Peter Pan, with the same exact lack of empathy, hardened in unabashed self-aggrandizement. Hook and Pan together are locked eternally into marking out their private boundaries on the same shared playing field—in the endless pursuit of a goal called "adventure." What Spielberg discovers, however, is that Pan becomes a man when he gains the ability to nurture. His "happy thought," his abil-ity to fly, is rooted in fatherhood. In *Peter Pan* there are three nurturers: Wendy and Tinkerbell and Smee. In *Hook*, the aging Pan becomes a real man, not through the loss of virginity, not through the fact of paternity, not through the achievement of power and wealth, but by finding and affirming his ability to parent and nurture. He has found his womb.

The Action Hero Test: Even the two great symbols of American machismo, Sylvester Stallone and Arnold Schwarzenegger, have found their images' wombs. Among all the bullets and punches, the car chases and the macho posturing, both of these super-studs have turned their images' closer to God's image; they have both learned how to mentor and mother. Arnold Swarzenegger's *Terminator II* (after an apprenticeship as *Kindergarten Cop*) achieved the immaculate conception, learning to nurture the future Messiah. *Last Action Hero* is the genre's third attempt to show that "the child is father to the man." Since the original draft of this chapter, Arnold has gone so far at to actually give birth. Meanwhile, if you recall Sylvester Stallone's *Rocky VI*, you've see it all—Rocky is thick-headed, but while punching out the bad guy he learns how to become the father his son never had. There is hope.

The Conclusion: The basic recipe for manhood in the

Jewish tradition is simple. Take one cup of unabashed feral boy, the *Yetzer ha-Ra*, and one cup of pure mother, the *Yetzer ha-Tov*; pour into God's image, and allow the elements to mingle and jell. *Pirke Avot*, a Talmudic book of men's "Zen" wisdom, provides these directions (4.1): Ben Zoma said: "To be wise—learn how to learn from everyone; this is what the Torah teaches when it says, "FROM ALL MY TEACHERS I HAVE GAINED WISDOM" (Psalms 119.99). To be a hero, conquer your own *Yetzer ha-Ra;* this is what the Torah teaches when it says, "HE WHO IS SLOW TO ANGER IS MORE POWERFUL THAN A HERO, AND HE WHO RULES HIS OWN SPIRIT IS MIGHTIER THAN ONE WHO CONQUERS A CITY" (Proverbs 16.32). To be rich, be happy with what you have; this is what the Torah teaches when it says "WHEN YOU EAT OF THE WORK OF YOUR HANDS, YOU SHOULD BE HAPPY AND IT WILL BE GOOD FOR YOU" (Psalms 128.2). To be honored, honor everyone else, this is what the Torah teaches when it says, "THOSE WHO HONOR ME (GOD), I WILL HONOR" (I Samuel 2.30). All the secrets are here: wisdom, power, wealth, and honor—they are all the blending of mother and boy. In the mythos of America, Spencer Tracy knew the secret. He could go fist-to-fist with John Wayne, get the girl Humphrey Bogart couldn't score, say he was sorry and repent, and mentor both Mickey Rooney and Freddie Bartholomew to manhood.

Coda: Today, when Michael confessed his stupidity, I did my best

Spencer Tracy. I made him stand like a man and take it while I graded his paper. After he scored his B and was surprised, I made him stand like a boy and take it when I hugged him and affirmed his abilities and potential in words I had learned from Rabbi Cohan.

4
Adam and Eve and Evil
Reflections on Gender and Evil

This chapter is an extension of the previous chapter. It came with a second insight—that just as **Midat ha-Din** has its shadow, its **Yetzer ha-Ra,** so the **Midat ha-Rahamin** also has a dark side. Just as the tendencies that always draw borders can lead to Jack the Ripper, so can the tendencies to love and cuddle and draw close, create a "Fatal Attraction." Therefore, this chapter explores male and female evil, but it does something else, too. It looks at evil's other side—the possibility of gender difference being redemptive.

This time a piece of Midrash from **Genesis Rabbah** served as the trigger, as the **Torah Text**, while material from Deborah Tannen's **You Just Don't Understand** became the **Proem Text** against which it could be scratched, understood, and made three-dimensional.

Pre-Text: Before you read this chapter, consider this poem by Carl Sandburg. It has regularly become the way I begin my teaching of this material. I ask my students to pick their favorite image and explain its connection to them.

Wilderness

There is a wolf in me…fangs pointed for tearing gashes…a red tongue
    for raw meat…and the hot lapping of blood—I keep this wolf
    because the wilderness gave it to me and the wilderness will not
    let go.

There is a fox in me…a silver-gray fox…I sniff and guess…I pick things
    out of the wind and air…I nose in the dark night and take sleepers
    and eat them and hide the feathers…I circle and loop and double-
    cross.

There is a hog in me…a snout and belly…a machinery for eating and
    grunting…a machinery for sleeping satisfied in the sun—I got this,
    too, from the wilderness and the wilderness will not let it go.

There is a fish in me...I know I came from salt-blue water-gates...I
    scurried with shoals of herring...I blew water spouts with por-
    poises...before land was...before the water went down...before
    Noa<u>h</u>...before the first chapter of Genesis.

There is a baboon in me...clambering-clawed...dog-faced ...yawping a
    galoot's hunger...hairy under the armpits...here are the hawk-
    eyed hankering men...here are the blond and blue-eyed
    women...here they hide curled asleep waiting...ready to snarl and
    kill...ready to sing and give milk...waiting—I keep the baboon
    because the wilderness says so.

There is an eagle in me and a mockingbird...and the eagle flies among the
    Rocky Mountains of my dreams and fights among the Sierra crags of what
    I want...and the mockingbird warbles in the early forenoon before the
    dew is gone, warbles in the underbrush of my Chattanoogas of hope,
    gushes over the blue Ozark foothills of my wishes—And I got the eagle
    and the mockingbird from the wilderness.

O, I got a zoo, I got a menagerie inside my ribs, under my bony head, under
    my red-valve heart—and I got something else: it is a man-child heart,
    a woman child heart, it is a father and mother and lover; it came from
    God-Knows-Where: it is going to God-Knows-Where—For I am the
    keeper of the zoo: I say yes and no: I sing and kill and work: I am a
    pal of the world: I came from the wilderness.

Carl Sandburg, *Cornhuskers*. Orlando, FL: Holt, Reinhart and Winston, Inc., *1918 &1948*.

The Torah Text: AND THE WOMAN SAID TO THE SNAKE (Genesis 3.4)

The Rabbinic Problem: In the midrash on Genesis
there is a better truth than any I could write. It is all contained in this one
sentence—waiting for adults to understand and ask. It spins on a simple
question: **Where was Adam? While Eve was busy fooling around with the
snake—where was Adam?**

The Rabbinic Solution: Two answers are given
in the midrash (*Bereshit Rabbah* 19.3). This meditation will deal only with
the first. The second, the opinion of the Rabbis, says that **Adam was off
working a real estate deal with God**—checking out the property. It under-

stands a whole lot about the absent husband, but that is a different universe.

On the midrash trail we will follow, **Abbal Halfon ben Koriah says: "Right after Eve was created, Adam and Eve consummated their creation**—the first sexual act—**then Adam** (from whose genes W.S. Gilbert would emerge) **fell asleep.**" W.S. Gilbert—the Gilbert of Gilbert and Sullivan—said in the first act of *The Gondoliers,* "Once a king, always a king, but once a night is enough." "**While Adam was sleeping, Eve** (the progenitor of Peggy Lee) **was lonely and restless.**" Peggy Lee sang. "Is That All There Is?" **Eve felt abandoned. It was this sense of abandonment that gave the snake his opening.**"

The Gender-Based Commentary: This
midrash teaches that evil entered the world because Adam fell asleep right after making love. Not only was it love at first sight between me and this text—but even more than that—I loved all my friends' reactions to it. The women loved it and said, "That's just like a man." It was an admission that men had fallen asleep on them, too. My men friends were equally joyous. They exclaimed, "Just like a woman," muttering, not quite completely under their breath, "never satisfied." Either way, everyone laughed a lot, revealing a lot of insight. It was equal-opportunity embarrassment.

The Rabbinic Solution: Look closely and under-
stand something powerful. Sex wasn't to blame. This wasn't sex as original sin, it was just original sex. The first sex act was good clean fun. The midrash explains (*Bereshit Rabbah* 18.6) that this is why the Torah says: "THEY WERE NAKED BUT NOT ASHAMED." Another midrash suggests that all animals learned how to "do it" from watching Adam and Eve (*Bereshit Rabbah* 22.2). Sex was a human creation. The sex was good, great. Adam may have asked, "Was it as VERY GOOD for you as it was for me?" Evil came into the world during the afterglow.

It happened two ways. It happened because Adam fell asleep. And it happened because the snake saw Adam and Eve in action, got horny and jealous—and began to plot. We each have our own deep understanding of both of these truths. To unlock them, consider this **Torah Text:**

GOD SAID:

LET THERE BE A SPACE BETWEEN THE WATERS.

LET IT SEPARATE WATER FROM WATER.

GOD MADE THE SPACE

AND SEPARATED THE WATERS WHICH WERE BELOW THE SPACE

FROM THE WATERS WHICH WERE ABOVE THE SPACE

AND IT WAS SO.

GOD CALLED THE SPACE, "SKY."

THERE WAS EVENING. THERE WAS MORNING.

A SECOND DAY. Genesis 1.6-8

A Commentary on a Torah Text Within This Commentary: Yes, this text has sexual overtones.

At least, that is what a lot of rabbis have seen in it. God saw that it was "Good" at least once on each of the six days of creation. The single exception is the second day. On the second day nothing positive is created; all God makes is a gap, a void, a division, a firmament. **Rabbi Ḥanina said: "This day wasn't considered 'good' because a schism was created." Rabbi Tzabyomi added, "If the Torah doesn't say 'It was good' about a division which makes the world more stable and more orderly, how much the more so to any division which leads to confusion"** (*Bereshit Rabbah 4.6*). All human communication takes place across the firmament—there is a void to cross. Actual sexual relations are only one example. Despite all the macho bravado, most men put everything into one good effort—that one effort, which uses everything up, is required to provide almost endless and ongoing satisfaction. It can be done—but it takes a lot of communication. To understand this, look at our proem text.

Our Proem Text: This conversation is lifted from *You Just Don't Understand.*

Woman: How can you do this when you know it's hurting me?

Man: How can you try to limit my freedom?

Woman: But it makes me feel awful.

Man: You are trying to manipulate me.[2]

40

Rabbinic Commentary: Without even knowing the context—you understand the conversation, because you've been there. Imagine the conversation between Adam and Eve after they wake up.

Eve: You fell asleep and left me alone. You didn't even hold me.

Adam: We had a good time. I was sleepy.

Eve: You don't care about my feelings.

Adam: Jesus, I just fell alseep—I didn't hurt you or anything.

Eve: I felt abandoned.

Adam: Give me a break. Don't try to confine me.

Eve: I'm just telling you how I am feeling.

What's scary is that this conversation is very easy to write. We all know it by heart. It is a by-product of the firmament, and we learn from the Torah that firmaments are never good.

In Leviticus 19.1 we are told, **"You shall be Holy, for I, Adonai, Your God, am Holy."** By way of an explanation the *Targum* (the Aramaic translation) of the text renders this verse, **"You shall be separate—just as I, Adonai, Your God, am separate."** The long and the short of it is that while separations may not be good, they do carry the potential for holiness. Just as God manages to be simultaneously both *immanent* and *transcendant*— worked-at human relations—relationships that reach across the firmament— can allow for both *freedom* and *intimacy*—human *immanence* and *transcendence*.

Mystic Judaism teaches in the Lurianic creation myth that all creation takes place across a gap. God intentionally withdrew in order to allow for free will. This was His act of division. Then God slowly oozed sparks of Herself back into hidden chambers in the world. That was Her act of intimacy. Then something went wrong. Perhaps the contradiction was too great— perhaps the gap wasn't good enough. A cosmic accident took place—the

---

²Consider this quotation from the film *Life With Father* by Lindsay Cross. It is another wonderful expression of the same insight: "Clarence, if a man thinks a certain thing is wrong, then he shouldn't do it. If he thinks it is right, he should do it. Now that has nothing to do with whether he loves his wife or not… Woman! They get stirred up and then they try to get you stirred up, too. If you can keep reason and logic in the argument, well a man can hold his own, of course. But if they *switch* you—pretty soon the argument's about whether you love them or not. I swear I don't know how they do it! Don't you let 'em, Clarence. Don't you let 'em, Clarence. Don't you let 'em."

hidden chambers burst because of the need to make greater connection—or perhaps because the world drew back at the lack of privacy. In any case, what emerged was a jumble of Godly sparks awaiting intimacy—and shattered containers designed to provide insulation and freedom. Man and woman are left to confront this situation, and their job is to reorder the resulting jumble. These mystics call this *tikkun olam;* we can see it as crossing the firmament.

The First Conclusion: The bottom-line gaps between the essential nature of a man's operating system and a woman's operating system are not good. These gaps allow evil to enter through frustration and misunderstanding—but like all good challenges, the very same gap allows for the holiness that comes from meeting the challenge (the kind of challenge the *Yetzer ha-Ra* loves), and through the deeper bond of the shared experience (exactly what gets the *Yetzer ha-Tov* off) from the resulting effort. Both men and woman have a share in both rewards.

MORE OF THE TORAH TEXT: THE SNAKE WAS THE SNEAKIEST OF THE ANIMALS WHICH ADONAI, THE GOD, HAD MADE....

The Rabbinic Problem: What made the snake so sneaky?

The Rabbinic Solution: In various midrashic discussions we learn that the snake looks like a giraffe, a camel, a gorilla, or an orangutan. We also learn that he was the personification of the *Yetzer ha-Ra*. David Eichorn looks at these statements and draws this conclusion: "The Serpent looked like an animal and talked like a man." In other words, he was pure animal urge. In our terms, he was all penis without any womb. He had, and showed, no mercy. The snake was primal—if he saw it and wanted it, he would do what was necessary to get it. There was no connection to others, there was no concern for their feelings. The snake was pure, unfiltered desire. (David Max Eichhorn, *Cain, Son of the Serpent.* Chappaqua: Rossel Books, 1957, p. 15.)

THE SNAKE SAID TO THE WOMAN, "DID GOD REALLY SAY THAT YOU MAY NOT EAT FROM ANY OF THE TREES IN THE GARDEN?" When Adam can't completely satisfy her, when Eve believes that he can't or won't be sensitive to her needs

42

(precisely when she thinks that he only cares about his own desires), Eve turns to the snake for companionship. Companionship is the one thing she doesn't get. This is where evil really enters—not with sex, not even really with the transgression of the first Divine command (that is just a symptom of the problem), but in the misunderstanding and in the acting out.

The Other Question: Where was Mrs. Snake when her husband was making whoopie with Eve?

The Rabbinic Solution: To solve this question, the midrash flips back a few pages and reads the earlier story of creation, where, long before the Garden, the Torah tells us, "MALE AND FEMALE HE CREATED THEM..." In other words, first God created Adam and his first wife, Lilith. Then, when, like a lot of other things in the original creation, that relationship fails, God revises the model and creates Eve. In this parallel universe the midrash constructs, Eve isn't the only one with an outside love interest—Adam has an ex-wife.[3] The Torah understands (especially Torah in broadest midrashic sense) that no relationship is simple—there are always complications, even for the first people, when things were supposed to be primal and simple. The truth is, primal is anything but simple. Lilith, as the folk tales go, was sexually incompatible with Adam. Classically, the traditions suggest that the argument was over who was going to be on top. That's probably why Jewish feminists adopted her as a symbol. I personally think it was a poor choice. I also think that the argument was actually about how long and how often. Contrary to the stories men like to tell, men "have headaches" as often as, if not more often than, women do—women don't have the same performance anxiety. Anyhow, the folk tales about Lilith go downhill from that point. She becomes the anti-heroine of an aggadic version of *Fatal Attraction*. She spends the rest of her life strangling single young men and newborn male infants.

---

[3]In *The Book of Paradise: Adam and Eve in the Garden of Eden*, restored by David Rosenberg (Hyperon, New York, 1993), David Rosenberg picks up on (or invents) a wonderful mythic parallelism. His answer: Mrs. Snake (a.k.a. Lilith) was with Adam. Together they embody the maleness and femaleness of the *Yetzer ha-Ra*. Early in my writing process Alexis Paranei had suggested the existence of many "female" snake images, too, but when I read this one (to quote my friend and teacher, Gail Dorph) "felt true."

As I read the stories—Lilith is as "evil" as the "Snake." In some fables she even becomes the devil's consort; in others she is actually the mythic, midrashic, missing female snake. In these renditions the two seductions, Lilith's of Adam and the Snake's of Eve, are reciprocal and equally invite evil into the world.

The Gender-Based Commentary: The (male) snake is pure penis—obsessive penis, he is all conquest with no intimacy—always on the attack. The pure animal draws boundaries and makes rules so that he has it all. Lilith, on the other hand, is all womb. She needs to be connected to everyone—she cuts no cords. According to her, no one can have independence from her—and live. Every male must be her lover, every son must be her child. If she can't have them—then nobody can! Just ask Michael Douglas. She is the ultimate smothering mother, strangling beyond all hope. Femininity, too, has its dark side. Mythically, every man kills his sons because they are rivals; every mother smothers her children rather than letting them go. Light needs darkness to be light. That is the scary part of truth.

The Second Conclusion: Here is the lesson. A man who doesn't know how to nurture (and make connections) becomes the snake. A woman who doesn't know how to judge (and allow independence) is Lilith, one who smothers her lovers and children. Real men and real women are blends. Human life is a Likert scale: Lilith is on one end and the Snake is on the other. Adam and Eve are in the middle, struggling with finding the right balance. It's not easy to be a person—a man who is not in control can easily "kill" or drive everyone away through aggression. Smothering is every woman's nightmare. If she doesn't know when to let go, she "kills" or drives others away by holding things too close. But men can go overboard and strangle their loved ones with affection, and women can find their anger and go on the attack. Every soul or psyche that is attempting to drive a human being through life's obstacle course faces not only the hazards (of which there are plenty), but also the endless struggle to maintain internal balance.

Listen to the way Adin Steinsaltz confronts this problem: **"In Hebrew good attributes are called "*Midot Tovot*," good measures, which suggests that the excellence of a quality is determined by its proportion, not by** its being what it is in itself, but by its properly related use in particular circumstances. Everything that is not in the right measure, that relates out of proportion to a situation, tends to be bad." (Adin Steinsaltz, *The Thirteen Petalled Rose*. Basic Books, 1980, 104.) He goes on to explain that the rhythm of Jewish life is in constant balance. God is always being immanent and transcendent. Angels are always going up and down Jacob's ladder. The dove is always going back and forth searching the world for the olive branch. To be static is to be dead. Emotions can't be bolted in place. Self-control is always an exercise in fluid dynamics. Living well and fully is a challenge to maintain balance.

If you want to know what it is like to be a man, think of yourself as Indiana Jones driving a truck full of toxic chemicals down a mountain road. The truck, of course, has no brakes. On one side you are threatened with falling off the cliff and having everything volatile explode. Anger does that. On the other side is the bog. Fall off the other side and you sink into the softness, never to move again—permanently imprisoned and trapped. The best part is that there is no end—this juggling is endless. Just getting through every day is an adventure. Meanwhile, while everyone asks, "How are you doing?" the polite answer is always a smile and "Fine." (I invite women to create their own metaphor for this struggle—given the gap—and the reality that I too, tend to fall asleep. I wouldn't presume to speak for them.)

As the descendants of Adam devolve into the generation of the flood, the Torah makes a confession (Genesis 6.5–6): "ADONAI SAW THAT MAN DID A LOT OF EVIL ON THE EARTH. ALL THE IMPULSES OF HIS HEART-THOUGHTS WERE EVIL ALL DAY LONG. ADONAI WAS UNCOMFORTABLE ABOUT HAVING MADE MAN, GOD'S HEART WAS PAINED." God knows that man's operating system is rooted in evil. Every man's soul floats on the snake. Every woman's psyche has much Lilith in the blend. There is great struggle for balance—a struggle that people often lose. It is very hard to reach across the firmament. Relationships inherently fail—families are normatively dysfunctional. The gap and the sense of abandonment it produces are at the core of everyone's essence. People need to be like God and reach back across the void—but that is not easy.

In the Noaḥ story, God does the unthinkable—God saves the experiment rather than washing out the test tubes and starting over again. Our spiritual genetic makeup all comes through Noaḥ. Adam and Eve and all their indiscretions, insensitivities, and obsessions flow in our essences. We own all the weakness and all the potentials for misunderstanding. All God does to rework the experiment is introduce one new tool—the covenant. God doesn't change anything; we have to. But God gives us directions: "Just follow My Image."

The Grace Note: To conquer evil, a man must blend in womb and find intimacy. To be good, a woman must blend in boundaries and grant freedom. That is why the gap represents not just the distance but the potential. Understand this: holiness enters the world just when evil does. It, too, is part of the afterglow.

5
King Solomon Seeks Women's True Desire

This midrashic short story was one of the last pieces written for this book. It is really the warping of an Arthurian myth. When I heard Michael Mead tell this story of Sir Gweyn his was trying to affirm one kind of masculine truth—the importance of honoring the inner king. I, however, realized that this Arthurian myth could be retold as a King Solomon story—and in the process affirm a very different kind of truth. This is a truth which also took me a long time to understand—just like it takes Solomon.

KING SOLOMON LOVED MANY FOREIGN WOMEN IN ADDITION TO PHARAOH'S DAUGH-TER—MOABITE, AMMONITE, EDOMITE, PHOENICIAN AND HITTITE WOMEN, FROM THE NATIONS OF WHICH *ADONAI* HAD SAID TO THE FAMILIES-OF-ISRAEL, "NONE OF YOU SHALL JOIN THEM AND NONE OF THEM SHALL JOIN YOU—LEST THEY TURN YOUR HEART AWAY TO FOLLOW THEIR GODS." SUCH SOLOMON CLUNG TO AND LOVED.

I KINGS 11.1–4

It was a hard night for the king. It was a hard night, in a hard week, in a hard year, in a hard part of his life. Solomon had been singing "Vanity of Vanities" a lot lately. He'd been writing a lot of new verses. It was the same old chorus, "Vanity of Vanities," but it was growing a lot of new verses. A lot of new things were being added to the list of those things that now felt old. It seemed that he had been marrying more lately—but enjoying it less. It seemed that he had been marrying younger and younger—and feeling more and more alone.

Tonight, with a thousand bedrooms to choose from—seven hundred wives, three hundred concubines (and more than a few servant girls)—he had chosen to be alone and feel alone. Alone was better than the entanglements each bedroom offered. Alone, with true memories and a fierce imagination, seemed better than the lies it would take to reassure each and every wife. He did love them, but proving it year after year, wife after wife, got to be a burden. "VANITY OF VANITIES." Yeah, he had it all. Oh, well!

47

Late this night he was hoping for a new season, for a season that finally felt as if it had a purpose. Time was now no problem; purpose was! The river of his life was quickly flowing down into the sea. He could feel it going. He said, "So many vanities, so little time." He said it—but he didn't mean it. It sounded like bravado, but it was just reflex. It was very hard to be an old king after having once been a very good young one. He hadn't even coined a good proverb in a long time. Song of Songs felt like a memory that belonged to someone else.

He went to the stable. He saddled his black horse and pretended that he didn't know where this ride would end up. He had a moment of trying to feel as if he were fifteen and that every time he rode he grew wings. But that didn't work for him tonight. He told himself that he would just loop the streets of his kingdom and see where that led, but he knew all along that he would end up in the shacks at the bottom of the hill. He knew he would be paying a visit to the women who lived on the edge of the forest. He rode through the night. There were few stars. And, while it sounds too manipulated, too much like a self-conscious writer working too hard to force an image, the swaying of the black horse in the hot summer blackness took him back to his first night with the Queen of Sheba. The horse's sweat became her sweat, the undulating muscle suggesting the firm breasts, the hips, the various pieces of her all-embracing and endlessly moving darkness. She had danced for him, a dance of—he lost count how many—veils. It was a night of nakedness and veils. They kissed through the orange gauze that never left her face, tongues meeting in the soaked mesh. They made love over and over in a whirl of darkness, candlelight, nakedness, and her flowing veils.

Sheba had tested him first. There had been riddles: "What comes up like dust from the earth, is spilled out like water, and lights a whole house?" He had wanted to say "women" but had guessed that the right answer was naphtha. Then she had brought a gaggle of forty young boys and girls, all groomed and dressed alike. All looked the same. All sat on benches before him. She asked him to divide them correctly. The solution was simple. It came to him in a moment. Forty servants entered; each was carrying, hidden from view, a ball of nuts and candy. Each servant stood opposite a child. When Solomon said, "A gift for the children," the balls were revealed and thrown in one instant. Solomon knew the secret Mark

48

Twain would later use: the boys spread their legs and caught the balls in their skirts. The girls, trained to modesty, kept their knees pressed tightly together, swung them to one side, and caught the balls. Yes—Solomon smiled—he knew girls. Yes—Solomon smiled—he knew women.

As he rode up, the woman was sitting in the flickering oil light in the window of her shack. They talked. It was banter, not barter. The price was assumed. He did not worry. He hitched his horse, entered, unhitched, and then entered. It was a night to forget. It was an orgasm, not a memory—not bad, not memorable. A relief of tension, he thought. She immediately got up to wash. He felt abandoned. He wanted to hold her for a few minutes, perhaps to doze in her arms a little—while in post-orgasmic daze—before he arose, dressed, paid, and left.

It was all by oil light. It happened in a series of flashes. He sat naked on the edge of the bed, tossing her his money pouch, trusting her to extract the correct amount. He was a King. He was used to being served. She demanded that he make payment directly to her Ashtartai idol as well. He yelled, "I can't go to bed anywhere without going to bed with that damned goddess." She screamed, "All men want to do—" She then hurled his purse at him. He closed his legs, pushed his knees together, swung them to one side, and then caught the purse. Flash. She became a winged serpent, fangs dripping poison. Flash. Ashmedai, Solomon's devil, was standing by her side. She coiled around him; he held her tight. She hissed in his ear; he said, "Sol, my girl Lil here wants to kill you. She wants to fight you and make you die. But I'm a sporting kind of guy. You deserve a chance. I am going to give you a year and a day to answer a riddle." She hissed again. Then he said, "What is it that every woman truly wants from a man?" Then they were gone.

Solomon rode off into the night. He thought and thought and decided how he was going to fight for his life—how he was going to find the freedom to live.

It was a hard year. It was a year of three women a day, each and every day. Even Shabbat. He made the best love he could to each. To each he professed the depth of his love, and beyond. With each, individually, he affirmed the connection, and for each he promised that he would always be there. Then, of each, he asked the question, the life-and-death question: "What is it that every woman truly wants from a man?" There were a thousand women—there were a thousand answers. Love. Respect. Good loving. Wealth. Children. Time. Equality. Good sex. Honesty. When, after a thousand answers, a few days, nights, and afternoon quickies remained, servant girls and professionals were pressed into service. Carrying a long scroll, the scroll of three answers a day, Solomon rode off in the middle of the night to meet his fate.

He entered the oil-lit shack at the edge of the forest. He was anxious to get on with it. But, the serpent hissed and Ashmedai demanded, "Nothing happens unless you settle your debts. You must first pay the goddess and then pay her priestess." Solomon wanted to get this over. He wanted to win. He dropped a talent by the goddess and threw the leather pouch at Ashmedai's head. The serpent caught it in her mouth, and the devil took it from her.

Solomon read and read. He gave more than a thousand answers. To each one they shook their heads. Each one they mocked. Each time he failed their smiles grew bigger. Finally he came to the last one, the one the last girl had said: "eternal love." It did no better than "equality" or "wealth" or "a cute ass." He braced for the attack. He readied himself for the fight. But the snake said for herself, "First things first. First the real answer. What every woman desires of men is for each man to ask that question of only one woman." Solomon literally fell back and found himself sitting on the bed. She then said, "You are too pitiful to fight. Grow older, old man. Grow older and lonelier and more pathetic. Then just die. You are not worth the effort." Then they were gone.

Solomon sat and cried. He cried and cried. No thought—no interpretable feeling—just sobbing tears. "It was all a waste," he said, "my vanity. A thousand times too much is nothing. Hunger is like that." Then he started to pray. "Out of the depths I call to You…" He prayed a long time. He prayed a lot of psalms, some old, some spontaneous. He cried many tears. Just before dawn God spoke to him and said, "So kid, where do we go from here?" Solomon retold the whole story, retold his whole life—and cried. God said, "I know how it feels to be an old king who was once a great young one." God also said, "I know what it is like to be one of seven hundred brides, three hundred concubines, and an uncounted number of servant girls, too. Now go home. Get some sleep. We'll start again tomorrow."

Solomon rode off into the sunrise, hearing the laughter of serpent and devil. His head hung low. He was ready to die. In the shack the idol of Ashtartei exploded; it knocked an oil lamp off the table. The flames began to rise. Solomon thought of his first true love, Bitiah, Pharaoh's daughter. Flames began to rise.

Post-Text: "Men always want to be a woman's first love. We women have a more subtle instinct about things. What we like is to be a man's last romance." (Oscar Wilde, *A Woman of No Importance*.)

6

Why Can't a Woman Gird Her Loins Like a Man?
or A Woman of Valor Reconsidered
The Masculine Side of Strong Jewish Women

This proem is a weaving together of the opening of the **Book of Job** with a song from **My Fair Lady**. The two combine to form a commentary on some verses from the thirty-first chapter of the book of **Proverbs**, a group of verses that Jewish men have classically said on Friday nights to their wives, beginning with the words **Eishet Hayil**.

This proem tells the story of its own creation so there is no need to do that here. The irony, however, is that many feminists have assumed that this is a text that praises a subjugated woman, while this reading suggests just the opposite.

א WHO CAN FIND A WOMAN WHO IS A REAL TROUPER? SHE IS WORTH A LOT MORE THAN RUBIES.

ב HER MAN'S HEART TRUSTS HER COMPLETELY; HE HAS NO LACK OF GAIN.

ג SHE IS GOOD FOR HIM, NOT EVIL—EVERY DAY OF HIS LIFE.

ד SHE SEEKS OUT WOOL AND FLAX AND FINDS SATISFACTION IN WORKING WITH HER HANDS.

ה SHE IS LIKE THE GREAT SAILING VESSELS OF THE MERCHANTS—SHE BRINGS HER BREAD FROM A GREAT DISTANCE.

ו SHE AWAKENS WHEN IT IS STILL NIGHT AND GIVES FOOD TO HER FAMILY; SHE SETS LIMITS FOR HER SERVANT GIRLS.

ז SHE STRATEGIZES THE CONQUEST AND THEN TAKES POSSESSION OF THE FIELD, WITH THE FRUITS OF HER OWN HAND SHE PLANTS A VINEYARD.

ח SHE GIRDS HERSELF WITH STRENGTH AND EMPOWERS HER ARMS.

ט SHE SENSES THAT SHE HAS EARNED A GOOD LIVING—HER LAMP IS NEVER EXTIN-GUISHED AT NIGHT.

י HER HAND IS ON THE WOOF OF THE LOOM, AND HER PALM IS SENDING SPINDLE THROUGH.

כ HER PALM IS STRETCHED OUT TO THE POOR—AND HER HAND IS SENT OUT TO THE NEEDY.

ל HER FAMILY HAS NO FEAR OF SNOW BECAUSE ALL HER FAMILY IS WARMLY CLOTHED.

מ LAYERS SHE MAKES FOR HERSELF—SHE DRESSES IN LINEN AND PURPLE.

נ HER HUSBAND IS KNOWN IN THE GATES—HE SITS WITH THE ELDERS OF THE LAND.

ס SHE MAKES AND SELLS LINEN GARMENTS, AND SHE GIVES GIRDLES TO THE MER-CHANTS.

ע SHE DRESSES IN STRENGTH AND HONOR.

פ HER MOUTH OPENS WITH WISDOM, AND THE TORAH OF KINDNESS IS ON HER TONGUE.

צ SHE IS THE ADVANCE GUARD FOR THE LAWS OF HER FAMILY; SHE NEVER EATS THE BREAD OF THE LAZY.

ק HER CHILDREN GET UP AND PRAISE HER—HER HUSBAND SAYS HALLELUJAH.

ר MANY WOMAN ARE REAL TROUPERS, BUT YOU ARE THE BEST OF ALL.

ש SOPHISTICATION IS A LIE, AND BEAUTY IS EMPTY—BUT THE TRUE GIFT IS A WOMAN WHO HAS FOUND HER AWE OF GOD. SHE DESERVES HALLELUJAH.

ת GIVE HER FROM THE FRUIT OF HER OWN HANDS—AND PRAISE HER IN PUBLIC BECAUSE OF HER WORKS.

The Torah Text: THEN *ADONAI* ANSWERED JOB OUT OF THE WHIRL-WIND AND SAID," WHO IS IT WHO ADVISES FROM DARKNESS—WHO GIVES WORDS WITH-OUT KNOWING? PLEASE, GIRD UP YOUR LOINS LIKE A HERO—AND I WILL MAKE DEMANDS ON YOU—AND IN RESPONDING YOU WILL MAKE YOURSELF KNOWN TO ME" (Job 38.1–3).

The Proem Verse: Why can't a woman be more like a man? (Rogers & Hammerstein, *My Fair Lady.*)

The Prologue: Carol is my best friend. We have the friend-ship Billy Crystal (a.k.a. *Harry*) says can't exist. She is a woman. I am a man. What we fight about a lot is gender. I do my best to be a good girlfriend—

she does her best to be my good buddy. Actually, we are quite good at our parts—but each time we don't completely fulfill our roles, it is a learning experience.

Job is the story of a man falling into a black hole and then being saved by a voice from the whirlwind. Job faces every tragedy imaginable—the loss of family, fortune, and, most significantly, "meaning." He is man alone in the *Twilight Zone*. He is trapped in Kafka's universe with his whole life changed—everything lost—and there is no explanation. His friends want him to take the guilt path, to accept that everything that has gone wrong is his own fault, to assume that bad things just don't happen to good people. Job refuses. He gets his *Midat ha-Din* (his rule-making, justice aspect) in a tizzy. He draws his line in the sand and makes his goal-line stand. Job dares God to justify Himself and make sense of this new warped cosmos. God begins His response this way: "WHO IS IT WHO ADVISES FROM DARKNESS? Job, you think you are tough, but you are speaking from darkness, ignorance. You are claiming insights you don't have—WHO GIVES WORDS WITHOUT KNOWING? You are speaking lots of words and talking yourself in circles—but you don't know anything. You have created the whirlwind out of your quest for meaning. Your struggles for a simple explanation are a dog chasing its tail. There has been enough time in the ashes. It is time to get on with it. PLEASE, GIRD UP YOUR LOINS LIKE A HERO. It is time to be a man and face tomorrow. Yesterday has no explanation. Suffer all you want, continue to suffer all you need, but find the inner strength to go on—AND I WILL ASK OF YOU—because life makes all kinds of demands—endless demands. Life is a river that rarely runs slow and shallow—its rapids are long and seemingly endless—and resting points are hard to find. The vortex seems constant. It takes more strength than anyone has—yet there is no choice. AND YOU WILL MAKE YOURSELF KNOWN TO ME. In your struggle to find and be an answer, you will find yourself, and I will see My image in you."

It is after eleven at night. I have just come home from teaching. I plan on writing for an hour before I call Carol. Tonight is my night to signal. Carol and I talk late almost every night. Almost never will she call me. She "can't handle the rejection when I give the impression of not being excited about the interruption." That is what she claims, but I know, in truth, that she has the strength to handle anything—to handle fears I can't even

54

imagine. So I call Carol every other night and signal her to call me on the alternate nights.

Tonight I come home and run my messages. Carol has called—I can hear her fighting back the tears on the tape. Carol and her husband, Joel, and I have been friends for about five years. A couple of years ago Joel died early one morning in their bedroom. It was the end of a lot of operations and hospitals and struggles—almost twenty years of putting off the implications of inoperable brain tumors. Carol, Joel, and I used to talk three or four nights a week. It started because we were planning a conference together. It continued because it was rewarding for all of us. Now Carol and I keep the tradition alive, not because it is a tradition, but because it continues to be an adventure. I call Carol back. The tears take only two or three sentences. There is an immediate problem. Carol now has a full-time "Jewish" job. She hasn't worked full-time in twenty years. She is in the middle of running a major program. Everything seems to be going wrong. I put on my consultant hat and we diagnose the key issues.

Simply put, Carol has done her job with great sensitivity. She centered herself in her *Midat ha-Rahamin*. She honored the committee process and respected the sanctity of group decisions. She gave those working on the program the room to be responsible. She trusted that everyone in the community would operate out of the best of motivations. And she has willingly invested herself, all of her sense of self, in the program.

There are always two possibilities. The other one had happened. The committee created a camel. The staff was overwhelmed. Some community leaders were letting the program fail because they wouldn't directly benefit. And Carol was over-invested.

We begin to attack the problem. My male language takes over. I talk about it as warfare. I tell Carol the obvious—cut her losses and downsize the area of exposure, full speed ahead—damn the feelings of the staff members; outflank the community agents who are refusing to back the venture (and force them into a position in which they have to come through)—and above all, take your sense of pride from the quality of your struggle, not from the results.

Somewhere in the conversation we hit an old refrain. **"Why can't a woman be more like a man?"** We say it in unison, because Carol has listened to a lot of my diatribes about women who are poor politicians and therefore do their responsibilities a disservice. She has internalized my criticism. She is crying, "I want you to respect me." I tell her to gird up her loins like a man. She says, "You mean I have to piss in the corners of my field." I say, "Yes." She says, "I don't know how." I say, "Bullshit. Don't tell me that a woman who started a day school, was president of a congregation, and ran a CAJE conference for 1800 people doesn't know how to protect her turf and take new ground." We go back and forth. I eventually say, "Women know how to piss on the corners, they just do it sitting down." She laughs, and sort of as the extension of that joke and to provoke the next laugh (as a cute example of turn-about is fair play), I say, "This is a time to honor your masculine side—to be a Woman of Valor." We argue a bit about whether that poem is sexist. She claims it is sexist, subjugating a woman to the home. I argue that it portrays the woman as an economic force to be reckoned with. She counters: "Sure, but she is expected to be a superwoman, both housekeeper and breadwinner." I run and get a siddur, and a radical rereading of the text begins. This rereading and thinking then takes more than a week—but it does burst out. It is as if the text is demanding to be liberated from the stone in which it sits unchiseled. It gets completed later through a lot of conversations, a number of them over a Shabbat with my friend Mark Borovitz.

Eishet Hayil, A Gender-Based Rabbinic Commentary:

The poem is an acrostic (A, B, C, D) found in chapter 31 of Proverbs. It is traditionally said on Erev Shabbat at the dinner table; a husband says it to his wife in anticipation of their later celebration of both the Exodus from Egypt and the Creation of the world, reconsummating their union. Classically, King Solomon is credited with the authorship of **Proverbs**. Since the mid-seventies Eishet Hayil has enjoyed a lot of bad press. It has been viewed as an expression of male subjugation and domination—an enslavement of true womanhood to the needs of husband and family. This running commentary suggests something completely different at work in the text.

א WHO CAN FIND A WOMAN WHO IS A REAL TROUPER? SHE IS WORTH A LOT MORE THAN RUBIES. This text starts out by calling a wife (or lover) a soldier. The Hebrew word is actually *Hiyal*—literally, a soldier. Valor isn't a bad translation—as my friend Carol pointed out, when she reconsidered this text after our discussion, there is nothing soft or weak about valor—nothing that we would normally think of as feminine. Valor is strong and courageous; it is soldiers and football. Even if he wore a pageboy, valor is Prince Valiant. Valor is King Arthur and the crew (not Guinevere and the girls). Valor is John Wayne—it is anything but helpless. See Donna Reed being as brave and strong as John Wayne and you've got *Eishet Hayal*—you don't have to become *Thelma and Louise* and pack a gun. Ironically, in contradiction to conventional post-feminist understanding of this text, which sees a husband demeaning his servile wife—considering her a baby machine bungee-cabled to a microwave (after she comes home from work), in his own way—the poet is celebrating Shabbat (and trying to turn his lover on) by telling her, "You are one tough broad." In better language, "You are a woman who can really honor her masculine aspect." In final words, "I respect you a lot."

ב HER MAN'S HEART TRUSTS HER COMPLETELY; HE HAS NO LACK OF GAIN. I didn't see it, but Mark pointed it out; it is the man who is admitting his feelings—he has the heart. Even in admitting his feelings, he loses nothing. The man has said: "You are strong. You are valuable. You make my heart safe. I can admit my feelings. I lose nothing by letting my heart out. Even if you are strong—from you I need not hold back. I need no protection. If I share my heart with you, I can only profit."

There are two negatives no and lack. But, "no lack" is a positive. It is not "not losing"; rather, it is a gain.

ג SHE IS GOOD FOR HIM, NOT EVIL—EVERY DAY OF HIS LIFE. When I was about sixteen or seventeen my father's drinking buddy, a friend of mine, too, Ralph Rosenfield, taught me two lessons. Lesson One: there is no such thing as a successful relationship—let's face it, men and women cannot work out. After all, you start with the differences. Lesson Two: the secret to lovemaking is to worry about your partner's pleasure more than your own. If you each do that, you each gain. That is what overcomes the impossibility of two sexes—worrying about the other's pleasure. In my own mind, I've always thought of worrying about a woman's pleasure as an "out-of-body experience." It is an act of faith—like praying to an abstract conception of God. There is no way I can ever understand a woman's orgasm. I have nowhere in my own body to find that understanding. There is no parallel. I have to trust my senses—her feedback. I have to trust what I am told—and perhaps what I read. Making love to a woman, caring about her pleasure, has to be an acquired behavior. It not genetic. But it works and it is good—in fact, very good. That is the basic statement here. Two distinct people with independence can be together—and despite the innate struggle, the struggle of two being one (especially two different genders trying to be one), it winds up being good every day. This is not a simple affirmation. It is saying, "You are not my Jewish princess. You are not a smothering Jewish mother. You are not castrating me in any sense. You are woman, and that is good for me—every day. Always! (Even when it is tough.)"

SHE SEEKS OUT WOOL AND FLAX AND FINDS SATISFACTION IN WORKING WITH HER HANDS. The root for "seeks out" is *daresh*. It is saying, in a sense, "She makes a midrash, something meaningful, out of wool and flax; she constructs a sense of purpose out of her work." The Hebrew word for satisfaction is *Hafetz* (as in *Hafetz Hayim*—satisfied in life). The meaning here is profoundly and unabashedly, "You are an Earth Mother. You can not only weave and sew the natural threads together but also fabricate a great sense of meaning and well-being in the process." This is quilting as a spiritual activity.

SHE IS LIKE THE GREAT SAILING VESSELS OF THE MERCHANTS—SHE BRINGS HER BREAD FROM A GREAT DISTANCE. This perfectly makes no sense. No sense is how this verse conveys its meaning. Think about the words. A wife is like a great sailing vessel—an adventurer upon the open seas. A mother brings her bread from a great distance. My mother brought her bread from the grocery store, occasionally the corner market—that didn't make her Wells Fargo. In a

58

couple of verses our Soldier Woman is going to buy a field. She is a farm woman. Bread comes from home. Yet even in making or buying a loaf of bread she is like a great merchant ship going on her voyages of discovery. When I was little and sick and had tomato soup, my mother, to keep me happy, would cut slices of American cheese into shapes and float them in the mystic red broth. Each spoonful was a great act of discovery, uncovering the shapes. This was one food adventure she shared with me, one of many. Even in the basic and foundational act of providing bread, the baseline activity, the poet is saying you are more than a food service—you are an adventure.

SHE AWAKENS WHEN IT IS STILL NIGHT AND GIVES FOOD TO HER FAMILY; SHE SETS LIMITS FOR HER SERVANT GIRLS. In other translations you'll find "She arises while it is yet night and gives food to her household." But that translation is a lie. It is wimped out, subjugated and male dominated language. The translator is the sexist pig, not the poet. The real Eishet Hayil is a lioness. Come and hear.

She wakes up at night and brings "Teref" to her family. This is no four AM bottle-feeding. Teref means food, but it means "torn-food," "hunted-food," "prey." (That is why Treyf food isn't kosher; it is torn, not slaughtered.) Eishet Hayil doesn't get up and go to the refrigerator to have breakfast waiting for her husband (this has nothing to do with housecoats, floppy slippers, and rollers); she is the night stalker. Dangerous, protective, aggressive—but connected to home. (This is not to say she's serving treyf, but to tell us there is a feline nobility to her working style.)

Other translations will tell you "she brings a portion to her servant girls" or "tasks to her maid." One image is worse than the other. Take your choice. Either the woman of valor is supposed to wake up before dawn to serve breakfast to the servants, or the woman of valor wakes the servant girls in the middle of the night, depriving them of sleep and makes them slave away. Either way, she is an obsessive Übermuter, selfless and smothering all at once. This is far from the poet's real truth. Come and hear.

The truth is she gives "Hok" to her maids. "Hok" is law, Hukkim are rules, boundaries, and limits. Take your choice: Is our Eishet Hayil doing early-morning Torah study with the girls? Is she teaching Torah through example? Is she giving secret pre-dawn lectures on proper conduct? Or is she imparting wisdom to her daughters while she combs the snarls out of their hair—getting them ready for the coming day? I don't know. But I do know that boundaries are being set and *hukkim* are being transmitted. Earlier she has made *midrash* out of the flax, now she is setting legal, Torah, boundaries—*Hok* in the pre-dawn hours.

Ahron Soloveichik says, "**A mother usually does not impart Torah through instruction in books or through intellectual reasoning. The mother imparts the purely practical aspects of Torah, through inculcation of ethical qualities, through tender, tolerant, and sympathetic guidance**." (Ahron Soloveichik, *Logic of the Heart, Logic of the Mind.* New York: Genesis Jerusalem Press, 1991, p. 19.)

Maybe she is waking the servant girls up with a glass of juice and a hard roll, but she is also doing a lot more. Maybe, like Sally Fields in *Places in the Heart*, she and the girls are going out to the field to work (just the way they will in the next verse). And there she teaches them real Torah through hard work and example. I don't know, but in any case, *teref* and *hok* are not about serving breakfast in bed. This woman is a hunter, a lioness, a strong and profound rule maker. A boundary setter and enforcer. She is the judge, the teacher of *hukkim*. There is more than a womb here; this woman is in deep connection with her *Midat ha-Din*.

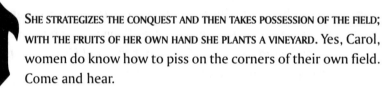 SHE STRATEGIZES THE CONQUEST AND THEN TAKES POSSESSION OF THE FIELD; WITH THE FRUITS OF HER OWN HAND SHE PLANTS A VINEYARD. Yes, Carol, women do know how to piss on the corners of their own field. Come and hear.

The men who are afraid of strong women have translated this verse, "**She examines a field and buys it**," but we know that much more is happening here. After all, we are praising King Solomon's Warrior Woman! Look at the Hebrew: "*Zam-mah*" is not just "examine"; it is really "plot and scheme." We've got Gordon Gecko with two X chromosomes. This is conquest. It is aggressive, well-planned, well-executed expansion. This is manly. This is no *Guiness Book* or *National Enquirer* story about a mother finding the strength to lift the car and save her baby. This is not a woman who when backed in a corner, unsheathes her claws. This is premeditated conquest. And what happens next?

Come and hear. This lady is a gambler. She knows how to leverage her options. She parlays her wealth. She lets it all ride. She plays "bet the company." In other words, WITH THE FRUITS OF HER OWN HAND SHE PLANTS A VINE-YARD—meaning she's reinvesting her profits. This is not some meek farmer's daughter who kept dried apples in a barrel all winter and then personally planted the cores, watering them and praying for them every day—this is a mogul. This is a Warrior Woman. This is a lady who knows how to honor her *Yetzer ha-Rah* and make it very good.

ח SHE GIRDS HERSELF WITH STRENGTH AND EMPOWERS HER ARMS. Mark and I sit in an Italian restaurant having a sports conversation about women. We ask, in the way that men have long debated the ultimate Super Bowl team or the greatest all-star lineup, who are real *Eishet Hayil*. First we reject both Grace Jones and Brigitte Nilsson as steroid fabrications, not women. Then we pick the obvious Warrior Women: Sarah Conners, the fighting mother in *Terminator 2,* and Sigourney Weaver in both *Alien* movies (and, we suppose from the trailer, the third one, too). Then we wonder whether or not they are *Eishet Hayil* or just women who have a moment of *Eishet Hayil* when their children are at risk. We decide that it is a chicken-and-egg problem; either way, they have the strength and courage (and we suspect they will never be the same). Mark adds June Allison to the list—I can't place enough of her movies to know. I nominate Bette Midler and Cher—Mark makes me prove that they are also nurturers and lovers—not just Amazons (because an *Eishet Hayil* is a Warrior Woman with a family)—and I offer up *Mermaids* and *Mask* for Cher, her real life and *For the Boys* for Bette. They make the team. Mark suggests Barbara Streisand based on *The Prince of Tides,* but I haven't seen it. He then suggests Meryl Streep, but I object; I think that I will never forgive her for messing up Alan Alda's life in *The Seduction of Joe Tynan.* I know she's strong, but in her movie roles (not her real life) she doesn't meet my maternal needs. Mark mentions Shirley MacLaine, but I counter with her own clarification: "All the women I've ever played are hookers." Well, maybe in another life, Shirley. I mention Lucille Ball. Mark says, "I was thinking of her, too." We are thinking of the real woman, not the redhead shoving chocolates into her mouth. I tell Mark about a radio interview I had recently heard where the host asked her, **"What do you think of yourself as: a personality, a comedienne, an** actress, what?" And she answered, "A Jewish mother!" The host then asked, "But you're not Jewish, are you?" Then she said, "No, but for me a Jewish mother is a symbol of a woman who can and will do all that their children need." We both agree on Rosalind Russell, but later Carol will clarify: for *Auntie Mame*, not *Gypsy*—in *Gypsy* she is smothering. That leads us to our final and quintessential nomination. As our cappuccino was served, we came up with Tyne Daley. Same caveat: Lacey (as in *Cagney and Lacey*), not *Gypsy*. We want the policewoman who can stand up to any thug and then still cry with Harvey.

Two points: (1) *Eishet Hayil* is a fun game. (2) To be sure, women have depth and strength, and King Solomon knew it. From him we have learned to remind ourselves who we really want to sleep with every Shabbat. Unfortunately, both Katherine Hepburn and Marilyn Monroe fail the test. Hepburn knows how to set limits and live her *Midat ha-Din;* it is her womb-like self that is questionable. Monroe turns us both on; she is our fantasy moment but has no staying power. In the end she is a little girl, not an all-night, all-life Warrior Woman. She is a great sex goddess, but no *Eishet Hayil*. Remember, goddesses are pagan.

SHE SENSES THAT SHE HAS EARNED A GOOD LIVING—HER LAMP IS NEVER EXTINGUISHED AT NIGHT. Don't even think that this verse might be about burning her candle at both ends, that she is up late doing the laundry after a hard day at work. Not a chance. Not my *Eishet Hayil*. This verse teaches us clearly that she knows her own worth. She doesn't have to cry in the dark. She is a constant source of light. She can always get past the darkness.

HER HAND IS ON THE WOOF OF THE LOOM AND HER PALM IS SENDING SPINDLE THROUGH. We already know that weaving is more than weaving. It is not just arts and crafts. It is far more than women's work. Weaving is meditation. Weaving is making whole. Weaving is drawing together. Weaving is tracing and recreating the matrix of the universe. As we have already learned—weaving is *midrash,* and weaving is also the making of *halakhah*, the setting of *Hukkim*. Weaving is the Torah of life—the making concrete of the abstract. A woman may be muscles, but she also has the delicate ability to draw threads together.

Another explanation: When Sinclair Lewis introduces Babbitt we are told, "**He made nothing in particular, neither butter nor shoes nor poetry, but he was nimble in the calling of selling houses for more than people can afford.**" *Eishet Hayil* may be a real estate empress, but she is about more than just acquisition—she is strong and powerful and still makes something useful and beautiful.

כ HER PALM IS STRETCHED OUT TO THE POOR—AND HER HAND IS SENT OUT TO THE NEEDY. In the previous verse the "hand" and the "palm" weave—in this verse the "palm" and the "hand" give tzedakah. This, too, is a weaving. We are being told that knowing that she is worthwhile, being a lamp, and girding her own strength is directly interwoven with the doing of justice—the *Midat ha-Din* practice of Tzedakah.

ל HER FAMILY HAS NO FEAR OF SNOW BECAUSE ALL HER FAMILY IS WARMLY CLOTHED. She is strong, but that does not make her cold or distant. Her strength is a source of warmth and protection. This lioness can weave. In her family there may be blizzards, there may be struggles, but our Warrior Weaver has protected her family, given them the resources to radiate their inner warmth and withstand the cold. She has made them secure, made them garments in which they can find their own warmth.

מ LAYERS SHE MAKES FOR HERSELF—SHE DRESSES IN LINEN AND PURPLE. *Eishet Hayil* is deep. She dresses in layers. She is fine linen—the weave of her own hands. She is mystic purple majesty—queen of deep mystery.

נ HER HUSBAND IS KNOWN IN THE GATES—HE SITS WITH THE ELDERS OF THE LAND. You might think that this verse is the bottom line—that *Eishet Hayil* can do what she wants, but her husband is the big man. That everything we have said so far is just a facade for the truth: she has to stand behind her man. But read the next verse and know the real truth.

ע SHE MAKES AND SELLS LINEN GARMENTS, AND SHE GIVES GIRDLES TO THE MERCHANTS. She knows how to weave meaning into her life and makes it available to others. She has learned to gird her own loins and is not threatened by others who can also make themselves strong. Maybe she is Jane Fonda selling workouts—but maybe the secret is a lot deeper. This is a strong woman who can live with a strong man. This is a weaving woman who is not threatened by anyone else's strength.

ע SHE DRESSES IN STRENGTH AND HONOR. This is a warrior woman who knows how to weave. SHE SMILES AT THE FUTURE. (Literally, at the "last day," the end of time.) As we have learned before (in Proem 3), a woman's faith is all future tense. Because she is strong, she knows the future is secure. This is her deepest strength; it is womb strength, the strength of a life-giver. Here is the deepest secret of *Eishet* <u>*Hayil*</u>. A man's strength is all "I." It comes from his *Midat ha-Din*. It is all about "don't cross that line." It is conquest and defense, acquisition and profound sense of self. It runs the matrix traced by the *Yetzer ha-Ra*—it is pure ego. Women can find that thread in the inner weave, and knowing how to trace its path is useful to them. Like a single gold thread inserted somewhere in the pattern, in can shine and stand out, and yet its major function is to reinforce a greater whole. The root of a woman's strength, however, is in her womb. For women, the vector of their faith starts in their womb and runs straight to the best possible future. Women find their deepest strength in saying "you" and in saying "we." We need to have strong "I," but that is not their grace note.

פ HER MOUTH OPENS WITH WISDOM, AND THE TORAH OF KINDNESS IS ON HER TONGUE. This we have known for a long time. *Eishet* <u>*Hayil*</u> has strength, but she is also gentle and kind and wise. She is a weaver of *midrash*. She lives Torah and weaves it into all she is. All can learn from her.

צ SHE IS THE ADVANCE GUARD FOR THE LAWS OF HER FAMILY; SHE NEVER EATS THE BREAD OF THE LAZY. In this verse *Eishet Hayil* is a *tzofeh*, a scout, a pioneer, an advance guard, protecting the *Halakhah* of her family. She is the boundary. In the previous verse she is woman. She is all *rahamin* and kindness. This is her Torah. In this verse she is woman, but woman with a spine. Here she honors her *midat ha-Din*. Even her bread works hard. She is real woman—strong and kind, feline, but with a backbone that will not be moved.

ק HER CHILDREN GET UP AND PRAISE HER—HER HUSBAND SAYS HAL-LELUJAH. No one is a prophet in their own city, but she is sincerely appreciated at home. What more could one ask?

ר MANY WOMEN ARE REAL TROUPERS, BUT YOU ARE THE BEST OF ALL. From you I have learned to respect all women. Women are strong and noble, but I think you're the top.

ש SOPHISTICATION IS A LIE AND BEAUTY IS EMPTY—BUT THE TRUE GIFT IS A WOMAN WHO HAS FOUND HER AWE OF GOD—SHE DESERVES HALLELUJAH. And the true inner secret, your deepest inner beauty, is the depth of your faith. I love you for your sense of the future. *Eishet Hayil* has *Yirah*. *Yirah* is fear. *Yirah* is awe. *Yirah* is faith. In other words, yes, you have your fear—a real, awesome awareness of the true risks and the odds. You know how hard it is, but you still have faith in the future. You have faith in the future, you smile toward the last day, even when you have no sense of how you will get there. That is your true strength. That is your beauty.

ת GIVE HER FROM THE FRUIT OF HER OWN HANDS—AND PRAISE HER IN PUBLIC BECAUSE OF HER WORKS. In the end, there is nothing we can say. *Eishet Hayil* is not dependent on our praise. She does not live through us, though she shares much with us. In the end *Eishet Hayil* is her own woman—she has done it her way.

Epilogue: The book of Job begins *Somewhere Over the Rainbow*. Once upon a time in the Land of Oz there lived a man named Job. Job was lionhearted and straight and God-fearing and stayed away from evil. Job cried deep into the night. The world was crazed and he was at his limit. He was afraid, scared to death of God, and that fear powered his faith in the future. Fearful, awesome, faith is real valor, hopeless, unvisioned faith that makes a goal-line stand without possibility—just because things must be better. Just because there must be a future. That is real strength. Carol, you've taught me to be in awe of my gentleness; now is the time for you to honor your strength. Every woman knows how to gird her loins—but you're the top.

7

Heartbeats and War Drums
or All Spirituality Isn't Sensitive

This proem has always been the "other title essay" of this book. It is woven around a set of original midrashim created in a fifth grade day school class that are then contrasted with a Talmudic text.

Surrounding the dialogue between the kids and the Talmud is a second confrontation. The trigger for this proem was a session on spirituality at a conference in England. That session bothered me greatly, because its truths seemed to reject a number of important personal prayer experiences. In *Annie Hall*, Woody Allen complains, "She said she had the wrong kind of orgasm. I've never had the wrong kind of orgasm. Every one of mine was right on." The English woman made me feel that I had been having the wrong kind of spiritual experience. This was something I needed to work through. This proem created the process for that reflection.

Both the kids' work and the Talmud text focus on "The Song of the Sea," the songs of praise that the Families of Israel sang after the miracle of redemption that took place at the Red Sea. The reason for the centrality of this passage is that while the men are doing their spiritual thing onstage, the Torah refers to the fact that the women grabbed their tambourines (timbrels) and did their spiritual thing. The Torah, therefore, suggests the possibility that men and women may have somewhat different spiritual needs and that there may be a multitude of different spiritual connections.

The premise echoes what seems to be happening in the Jewish world. As women have moved toward appropriate co-equal roles in Jewish life we've seen a de-emphasis of boundaries and a growing emphasis on the spiritual. It has been a battle between those who want to define Judaism as a central core of feelings and those who want to see Judaism bounded by rules and procedures (however strict or liberal). Based on what we have learned so far, these differences echo the **Midat ha-Rahamin** and the **Midat ha-Din.** The conclusion that would be too simple is to suggest that women are spiritual, while men are "legal."

Instead, this proem follows a path initiated by Carol Gilligan, who, in her break-through book, *In a Different Voice*, refused to accept the fact that women were lacking in ethical/legal judgment. Just as Carol Gilligan suggested that women have a different sense of judgment and justice, this essay suggests than men may have a different sense of spirituality.

Prologue: At the LIMMUD Conference in Oxford I attend a session on teaching children to pray. This is the trigger. After we introduce ourselves, Marcia Plumm, the rabbi leading the session, tells us that we are going to begin with personal moments of prayer. We are told that we can get in touch with the *Shehinah* any way we want, using a prayerbook or not using a prayerbook, standing, sitting, etc. She teaches us a *nigun* (a wordless Hasidic melody) explaining that it often helps her pray. Then we are set free with our task. There are no rules; there are no boundaries. It is all very soft, gentle, and kind—a whispered approach to the spiritual. I am put off. I don't know what to do. Unlike most of the crowd, who are now lying on their backs with their eyes closed, I pick up a siddur and head to the corner.

Lost for something to do, I fall back on a traditional path. I open up to the Psalms and start reading *Tehillim*. I am somewhat angry about the "goyish" nature of the non-structure, but I try to get into it. Surprisingly, a line strikes me. It is one of those lines I had always mouthed and not really considered: WHO MAKES THE BARREN WOMEN DWELL IN HER HOUSE AS A JOYFUL MOTHER OF CHILDREN (Psalms 113.9). That morning this verse stops me cold. It strikes my heart and I shiver. I had always read past that line, not thinking of barrenness as a real problem in the suburban world of good nutrition. But that morning I see a good friend's face. Like many good children of my age, she had delayed starting a family for a while. Now fibroids in her uterus are forcing an operation. She may well emerge sterile, having missed her shot at children. I feel a few tears drip from my heart to my stomach. I know that nothing is showing. I cry within and pray for her: WHO MAKES THE BARREN WOMEN DWELL IN HER HOUSE AS A JOYFUL MOTHER OF CHILDREN.

My meditation then goes deeper. I think of myself: divorced, forty, childless, no present steady girlfriend. I admit to myself (as I often do to my mother) that I am barren. Then I smile to think of Kent, Ben, Brett, Danny,

B.J., Ira, Roberta, Bennie, Mark, and many more: the children of many periods of my life. They are my former students and campers—the ones I've been privileged not just to teach or counsel, but to mentor and co-parent. They are the ones whose lives are still intertwined with mine. The words of the psalm renew themselves in a different way. I realize that in one sense I am a barren man with children. These words become for me now, not a petition, but an expression of my thanksgiving: WHO MAKES THE BARREN WOMEN DWELL IN HER HOUSE AS A JOYFUL MOTHER OF CHILDREN. In this prayer experience I have discovered two new insights into a long-lost phrase—I have uncovered a secret treasure that was long overlooked because it was hidden away in an obvious place. I am proud of how sensitive I've been and the wonderful things I will have to share once we come back together. I take my seat and have to sit for a long time while the others finish their spiritual experiences. I am impatient (and you already know how poorly I sit still). Like an ex-smoker, I am overbearing on the issue, and I can't wait to share my sensitive men-have-wombs-too prayer experience. I am made to wait a long time. I fidget. I try to keep quiet. Eventually the *nigun* is sung again, and the group members slowly withdraw from their trances and daydreams.

The rabbi doesn't want to talk about the content of our prayers. I am furious. She just wants to talk about the process. I am ready to burst, but I am wearing my sensitive man suit, so I calm myself. Eventually one of the women in the group hunts through her prayerbook, the *English Reform Prayer Book*, and reads us a passage about how it is a mother's responsibility to teach her children to pray because this is the only way they will have a moment of peace and calm in their life. At that moment I laugh to myself, fantasizing the image of my mother (and my father), who did their best to civilize me into the dignity and decorum needed to attend services, tying my hands, putting a piece of gaffer's tape over my mouth, and telling me, "We are doing this for your own good—otherwise you will never have a moment of peace and calm in your life." I struggle against the bonds.

I break into the conversation and politely suggest (because I'm running on my sensitive mode) that the passage is sexist, both because it suggests that only mothers can teach children to pray and because the model of prayer it implies may work for little girls but is far from the spiritual side of most nine-year-old boys. To make my point I share the contrasting images of the women's minyan at CAJE and the boys' minyan at the Akiva Academy. Those memories will form our proem texts, which will contrast with our Torah Text (as explicated by a wonderful group of kids).

Come and Hear:
If you want to know the truth about male and female spirituality, listen to this story. It is the wisdom of a fifth grade class at the Adat Ariel Day School.

Our Torah Text:
At the end of chapter 14 of Exodus we experience the big, big biblical f/x sequence—the splitting of the Red Sea. It culminates with this observation: AND (ALL) ISRAEL SAW THE GREAT HAND WHICH ADONAI WORKED ON THE EGYPTIANS; AND THE NATION WAS IN AWE OF ADONAI, AND THEY BELIEVED IN ADONAI, AND IN MOSES, GOD'S SERVANT. Like the crowd at Disney Land/World, the people gave the electrical parade a standing ovation. Chapter 15 continues the story, describing, in parallel scenes, the separate reactions of men and women to this event. It consists of two sequential close-ups. First we get the men's version: THEN MOSES AND THE SONS OF ISRAEL SANG THIS SONG TO ADONAI. THEY SAID, SAYING: "I WILL SING TO ADONAI BECAUSE HE SCORED TOTAL VICTORY. THE HORSE AND ITS RIDER HE HAS THROWN INTO THE SEA..." This then leads into a long song of praise, a description of God as a "Man of War" who utterly defeated and decimated the Egyptians. At the end of this chapter we find the parallel women's experience: AND MIRIAM THE PROPHETESS, AARON'S SISTER, TOOK IN HER HAND A DRUM, AND ALL THE WOMEN WENT OUT AFTER HER DRUMMING AND DANCING. AND MIRIAM ANSWERED THEM (masculine, meaning "the Sons of Israel"): "YOU (masculine plural) SING TO ADONAI BECAUSE HE SCORED TOTAL VICTORY. THE HORSE AND ITS RIDER HE HAS THROWN INTO THE SEA..." This biblical scene then fades to black.

Rabbinic Commentary:
One would expect Rashi and his crew to make a big deal out of the men singing, "I WILL SING TO ADONAI" and the women singing "YOU guys SING TO ADONAI." I thought there would be great wisdom revealed in explanations of why men were first-person praise and women were second-person praise. As I went over the passage my divining rod bent at the possibility of explaining why the men's song was singular and the women's song was plural. I expected a lot. But, when I opened up the commentaries and collections of midrash I got noth-

70

ing. Silence. Having been through all the official rabbinic answers in my quest to find the essence of "male" and "female" worship, I was awestruck by the tradition's silence on this passage. It was as if this passage, which cried out for comment, scared them. Or perhaps it was a scream that came from my reality, not theirs. Nowhere that I can find does the tradition comment on the difference between "**I WILL SING**" and "**YOU (GUYS) SING.**" Somewhere in the difference between the men's and women's songs should be the difference in their spiritual needs.

When the tradition was silent I did what I often do; I brought the problem into the classroom. I turned it over to some day school students with whom I was doing a "guest shot." I introduced the passage and gave them (because I am "pro-choice") the opportunity to invent one of two midrashim. One was our question, "**Why do the men sing one thing and the women sing another?**" The second was a question I borrowed from Rashi, who borrowed it from the *Mekhilta* (an ancient collection of midrashic sermons): "**Where did the women get the timbrels?**" (Because if most of us played the "What would you take from your house if you only had five minutes?" values clarification game, very few of us would have our tambourines on the list.) As usually happens, the kids added a third question, they wanted to know: "**What did the Egyptian horses do wrong, that they deserved to die along with the Egyptian soldiers in the Red Sea?**" None of the fifth graders wrote midrashim that answered my question. Still, they taught me my answer!

One group of three girls presented a well-worked, carefully rehearsed and re-edited collective story that answered the question: "**Where did they get the drums?**" These girls answered with a rehearsed performance, each reading her assigned part. They said: "**They didn't actually have drums with them. But it was such an emotional experience, and their hearts were beating so loudly, that their heartbeats sounded like drums. When they sang, they sang with their hearts.**" It was really a beautiful answer; it sent a shiver through me.

One of the boys stood up and said, "**Wrong! I wrote about why the horses had to die, but this is the right answer—I think they were Egyptian [war] drums that floated to the surface.**"[4] This boy's midrash

---

[4]This was an equally intriguing answer that matched a wonderful midrash (from *Pesikta d'Rav Kahana*) that taught that the Menorah which the Macabees fashioned in the Temple was made from eight iron spears left by the Syrians.

taught a powerful truth, too. Both the process and content of these interpretations reveal a lot. As I reflected on the "boy's" truth and the "girl's" truth, two opposite and powerful memories came to mind.

Our Proem Text: Three Memories:

Memory One: It was the second CAJE conference in Rochester, New York. Late in the week a women's minyan was organized. For obvious reasons, I never worshiped in that particular setting, but I did wind up with the job of processing the evaluation forms. One of those forms told the story of a mother who led services and chanted the *daven*ing while singing her newborn to sleep. It was liturgy as lullaby. I cried a single tear when I read the description and internalized the image. Since that time it has always stood as one of my paradigms of true spirituality.

Davar Aher: A Second Proem memory: A couple of years earlier I was a student teacher at Akiva-Schechter Academy on the south side of Chicago. The upper school was an "orthodox" day school that held a *minyan* every morning. The *minyan* was loud and often edged toward sheer chaos. There was talking and shouting. Rabbi Well, the school principal, had perfected the fine art of loudly projecting the words to selected Hebrew prayers in such a way that they effectively conveyed the message, "Solomon Kossoff, shut up and pray." Meanwhile, eleven-year-old Robert Stern (with his blonde hair halfway down his back) was usually dancing and bouncing in his black high-tops around the instant sanctuary (which was built in the multipurpose room every morning out of benches and portable room dividers). In the back, David and Kenny, the eighth graders, were usually sneaking in a conversation about the Cubs, while many of the other boys were doing the "*Sam Samansky Shuffle*." *Sam Samansky* were the secret magic words you mumbled at Akiva when you lost your place or couldn't read Hebrew fast enough to keep up. To fake it, so you looked like you were praying, you shukkled hard and did the *Sam Samansky* mantra. The *minyan* smelled like a locker room—sweaty adolescence—and looked like the requisite yard scene in all prison films. It was constant Brownian motion manifesting the calm found in Penn Station at rush hour. Yet it had a holiness all its own. When Ari Roth led services he sang like an angel, and his voice arced peacefully over all the chaos.

When Andy Shapiro studied *Mishnah Brakhot* and then tried to apply the law he had learned that "people in clothes with holes shouldn't lead services" to Ronnie's serving as *Saliah Tzibur* in his well-aged dungarees, the *Shehinah* was present. And at those moments when the energy came together into a powerful rendition of some hymn or prayer, the power of male voices in unity and competition—often in the unity of competition—made the earth shake. Even though my job as teacher was that of prison guard and groundskeeper, it was one of the great ongoing worship places in my life. I fully admit to having no knowledge of what my future wife and all the girls were doing beyond the *mekhitzah;* indeed they were far from my consciousness at that moment. I was busy jostling shoulders and talking to God.

DAVAR AHER: A Third Proem memory: A friend of mine, Les Bronstein, told me that his most successful innovation as a Hebrew school principal was introducing a daily service into his afternoon Hebrew school. It was coed, he used his guitar, and it was anything but orthodox, but it ran on boys' energy. The whole service was sung and usually done standing; it was filled with stories and "gospel" shouting and was loud and joyous—sort of a rock 'n' roll Hasidic thing. I never saw it in action—it, too, lives in my imagination only as a story.

When I came to teach Hebrew school again for the first time in ten years, I suggested to my principal the idea of our adding a daily service. She agreed. I was in for a few surprises. The services that emerged were more rooted in Prussian spirituality than in my visions of rock 'n' roll Hasidism. Boys were made to take off their baseball caps and replace them with *kippot* (because despite the *Halakhic* [Jewish legal] validity of their actions, it violated the spiritual aesthetic of this Reform congregation). The service quickly became a regular center of repression and punishment. Kent got himself in trouble when he taught the whole class to perform the national magic trick with their *kippot*[5]—personally, I thought the idea of *kippot* being a source of magic was great. Brett got sent out when he started dancing and saying "groovy" on one of the up-tempo tunes. In this universe, spirituality was exclusively quiet and calm and peaceful—and

---

[5]"The National Magic Trick" is the rhetorical creation of Penn and Teller, who once tried to get the whole country to learn how to make a handkerchief disappear in their respective cupped hands. Kent replaced the handkerchief with his white satin *kippah.*

oppressive to most of the twelve-year-olds whom I was obligated to try to Super Glue into their pews. The worst thing, by far, was *Shalom Rav*—the peace prayer. My kids loved the tune. They sang it loud and off tune and with a perverse but real joy. Every time we were not quiet and good during the *Amidah*, *Shalom Rav* was said rather than sung. And it resulted in a war. The class tried to recite it faster and faster, edging it back toward song; the principal, true to her convictions, aggressively slowed it more (like a good mother), bringing peace and calm back into their lives.

A Gender-Based Commentary: After the

session in England, I told the whole story—all the stories—to a friend, Debby Weissman, an Orthodox, feminist professor at the Hebrew University—and a brilliant thinker. In return, she told me one story that helps to make sense of this whole reflection. Debby explained, "**When I lived in New York I belonged to a wonderful Orthodox synagogue. Every year they used to have the best Purim s'udah. The men would get drunk. The rabbi would dance with a bottle like it was a Sefer Torah, and then he would deliver the best Purim Torah. His Purim Torah would be hysterical. And his Purim Torah would be profound and deep. Now I live in Jerusalem, and I belong to an amazing egalitarian Orthodox synagogue. It is a place with the mekhitzah down the middle, which we take down during the davar Torah. When we take the Torah out, a man carries it around to the women's side; a woman takes it from him and then carries it around the women's side, and hands it off to another man, who brings it around the men's side and then up to be read. In Jerusalem we don't have the same quality Purim s'udahs. They are too tame. I think, sometimes it is because families sit together."**

Once synagogues were men's spaces. They ran on masculine energy. They were places where boys could romp and play and edge into manhood without having to sit still a lot, be quiet, and lower their energy levels. The service was free-form, a balancing of private and public moments—a free-floating set of temporal, interpersonal, and physical boundaries. Each man had his own space, his own time, his own sphere, yet they linked and floated into a whole. Simply put, sometimes you sang together; sometimes you put your *tallit* over your head, stood in your corner, and turned within; sometimes you got up and talked to your neighbor; and sometimes you all sat and all listened to a presentation. The rules were complex and hidden (like the way a pack of wolves delegates authority and territory), but they worked well—and everyone understood his freedom and its limitations. Simply put, traditional "all men" minyanim were garage experiences, something the "boys" did when they were alone together. When the women joined in, when we invited the women in, we moved the service to the parlor and put on our "living room manners." Debby taught me that, had services started out as all-women's events, then added men into the process, the same kind of radical transformation would have been felt; they would have moved from the "kitchen" or "sewing circle" into the living room as well. It is the difference in *daven*ing with the plastic slipcovers on or off.

In the 1800s, when Reform Judaism came on the scene, women were added to the central sanctuary. I strongly suspect that once they were there, the women didn't impose change in the worship procedure on the men; rather, men changed the way they acted because women were now fully present. Dignity and decorum (Prussian spirituality) became the rule, partially because of their imitation of the Lutheran world around them, and partially because families now sat together. The synagogue was no longer male space, male process, male time—it became an extension of the home. The decorum changed the dynamic; you couldn't roam around anymore. The liturgical process changed, too—authority was more centralized and organized, and the dominant process now was the alternate oral reading of specific portions, rather than the overflowing private and public loops of chanting. The whole affect softened—freedom of external expression was slowly lost. While a man could still express himself inwardly (in heart, mind and stomach) any way he wanted—the individuality and camaraderie found in the oral dueling and dialogue of the previous worship form was cut way back.

THE BRAIDED TRUTH: *Daven*ing has moments that are like Robin Hood and Little John testing each other with quarter staffs on the logs. Men's voices confront each other over speed and dominance. There are little battles over who finishes first or who is being rushed. Melodies and pitches challenge each other. Harmonies often start, are interrupted, and then find a unity. But, like Little John and Robin's jousting match, the struggle ends in a deep comaraderie found in shared experience. In truth, the whole energy level dropped once the women were sitting next to the men and men fell back into their best parlor manners. (In fact, I believe that the Little John and Robin dynamic is a key metaphor for understanding many male friendships, and we will return to it over and over again in the work.)

Anyone who is sensitive to the Jewish tradition knows that women's connection to prayer is powerful and important. The *Amidah*, the central Jewish independent prayer experience, has as one of its key models Hannah's prayers.[6] The rabbis teach that when we say the Amidah we stand just like she did, lips moving without a sound being emitted, silently voicing—in great faith—our deepest desires, just as she did. Likewise, the women's movement has long felt and voiced a connection to *Ecclesiastes Rabbah*, Proem 23, a story where Rachel's prayers and words to God change God's heart, after Abraham, Isaac, Jacob, Moses, and Jeremiah have all failed to do so. Women's spirituality is powerful and awesome—and in finding my own path to prayer, getting in touch with my male-womb, accepting the mother-within-me, and using my feminine side are all important factors. I thank the women's movement for opening me more to those gifts. I love the times when my prayers sing a child to calm (especially my child within), yet at the same time I want to wear my baseball cap in services, race my neighbor to finish the Amidah, dance my *Sam Samansky* shuffle, bounce and dance in my high tops, and find my own independent, nonresponsively limited prayer space. There is a male side to my spiritual connection that also needs to be nurtured. It is often loud and aggressive, and that side brings us back to the Red Sea.

DAVAR A<u>H</u>ER: A second look at our TORAH VERSE:

Here, once again, is the problem—the text problem. The men, following Moses' lead, start the prayer. They sing the "God is a Man of War" victory hymn. I always imagine it with all of the affect of a post Rose Bowl victory brawl. It would make a great Budweiser commercial. The Torah description is: Then Moses and the Sons of Israel sang this song to Adonai. They said: "I will sing to Adonai because He scored total victory. The horse and its rider He has thrown into the sea...." At the end of the entire song we are then told of the women's involvement; they beat drums, dance,

---

[6]This text is explicated in Chapter 8, *The Mamas and the Papas*.

76

and sing: "YOU (MASCULINE PLURAL) SING TO ADONAI BECAUSE HE SCORED TOTAL VICTORY. THE HORSE AND ITS RIDER HE HAS THROWN INTO THE SEA...."

The Torah Problem: In order to find the lesson we are seeking in this text, we need to understand why the women's response is different than the men's. In the process, once we figure out why the women are different than the men, we'll understand how the men are different than the women, too. We need to answer three questions: (1) Did men and women sing at the same time (in different places) or one after the other? (2) Why did the men and the women sing different things? And what do these differences represent? (3) Considering all these differences, the bottom line is: what can the Torah teach us about men's and women's spiritual sides?

Rabbinic Commentary: Even though Rashi won't directly answer our questions, we start with him, because that is what Jews do. He goes to work on the women's verse: AND MIRIAM THE PROPHET-ESS, AARON'S SISTER, TOOK IN HER HAND A DRUM, AND ALL THE WOMEN WENT OUT AFTER HER DRUMMING AND DANCING. AND MIRIAM ANSWERED THEM. Rashi starts by glossing a Talmudic passage that explains what the men did (*Sotah* 30b): **Moses said the Song to the Men, He said it and they answered after him.** Then Rashi adds his own insight about the women: **And Miriam said the Song to the women and they answered after her.**[7] So far, Rashi has taught us a truth which is not so obvious today—that men and women are different. But when it comes to spirituality, we still don't understand that difference. To understand more, we need to check out Rashi's source.

So let's go TALMUD DIVING: The *Sotah* text from the Talmud tells us: **Rabbi Akiva taught: "In the hour that Israel went up from the Sea they wanted to say a Song of praise"**—*which one of three ways* **did they sing this song?**

[1] Did Moses relate to the Men of Israel like a *man* leading *men* (like Gladys Knight and the Pips)?

[2] like a *boy* leading *men* (like a songleader teaching a new song)?

---

[7] In his rendition of the Rashi, Silbermann completes Rashi's meaning with the words **and they answered after her,** based on a long grammatical proof. Rashi's (as understood by Silbermann) comment begs lots of questions about the relationship of the men's prayer to the women's prayer, but it does teach us one thing—two distinct religious experiences were going on.

[3] or like a *teacher* in relationship with his *students* (like a whole congregation of Elvis impersonsators)?

The Talmud then tries on each of the three answers for size.

[1] THE GLADYS KNIGHT AND THE PIPS MODEL:

Akiva presents the first possibility—he suggests that the dynamic of the Song of Sea is like a *man* leading *men*. In our terms, it is like the Pips doing "Georgia" and "movin' on" in response to Gladys' "He is leaving on a midnight train to Georgia." **"In my opinion,"** Akiva says, **"it is like a man who publicly leads the congregation in Hallel and then the men answer after him using the opening words of the chapter as a chorus line. It worked this way. Moses said: 'I WILL SING TO ADONAI' and they responded 'I WILL SING TO ADONAI' and Moses said: 'BECAUSE HE SCORED TOTAL VICTORY' and they sang the chorus: 'I WILL SING TO ADONAI.'"**

The model here is Gladys Knight and the Pips. Moses has a creative religious experience, and the men of Israel do the "Movin' On," "Georgia," and "I gotta go…." do-wop bits. They experience their prayer through his charisma and artistry, supporting his work on their vocal platform. In this model, Moses is exempting the men from their obligation to thank God, and they are getting credit for his prayer by essentially answering "Amen." If we follow this lesson, we learn that we men need great leaders in order to be spiritual. (But that great leaders need us, too.) This is the Hasidic rebbe thing.

[2] LIKE A SONGLEADER TEACHING A GROUP A NEW SONG:

Songleaders do this thing where they sing one line and then you sing that line back to them. Antiphonal singing is call and response. Some gospel music works that way, too, though it tends toward both choruses and improvisations. Rabbi Eliezer is next. Rabbi Eliezer suggests the next model: he thinks it is a call-and-response, songleader kind of thing. Rabbi Eliezer is introduced as the son of Rabbi Yosi from the Galilee (at some point we'll have to talk about the power of sons carrying both their father's name and their father's Torah). He argues that Moses is like a *boy* leading *men*—or like a songleader teaching a new song. **Rabbi Eliezer, the son of Rabbi Yosi from the Galilee, said, "In my opinion is it like a boy who leads the congregation in Hallel and all the men repeat all that he says after him. It worked this way. Moses said: 'I WILL SING TO ADONAI' and they responded 'I WILL SING TO ADONAI' and Moses said: 'BECAUSE HE SCORED TOTAL VICTORY' and they sang: 'BECAUSE HE SCORED TOTAL VICTORY.'"**

Rabbi Eliezer is defining a dynamic, not impugning Moses' maturity. In other words, he is not calling Moses a *boy*, but rather suggesting the process echoes a congregation that is not led by a controlling party. This takes a little explanation. According to Jewish law, a boy can't exempt a man from a *mitzvah*. Therefore, while a boy can lead the singing of *Hallel*, he can't "make" *Hallel*—his *Hallel* doesn't count. His *Hallel* is an H.I.T., a *Hallel*-in-Training. This means that when a boy leads, when a boy is the public voice, every man in the congregation must still make *Hallel* for himself. Every man must fulfill his own obligation; the leader can't take his place. When a boy leads, you can't just say "Amen"—you must take responsibility for yourself. Rabbi Eliezer sees Moses as a coordinator or facilitator of prayer, the songleader—not the performer, the metronome for spiritual process. In the end, each man is on his own—they are each alone, standing together in their spirituality, but each needing to take responsibility for himself. It feels a lot like *Hallel* in the Klondike, everyone living in his own tent, working his own spiritual claim, but still singing together in the tavern. It is being independent, but not alone.

[3] LIKE A WHOLE CONGREGATION OF ELVIS IMPERSONATORS:

In *Honeymoon in Las Vegas* we are presented with the surrealist vision of a convention of Elvis impersonators. Elvis impersonators have the same source, but they are no chorus. Each one does his own impersonation of the King in his own way. The source is common, but the repetition is unique and personal. Rabbi Nehemiah is the third up. He formulates a completely different model. Both Akiva and Eliezer speak of the *Hallel*; Nehemiah switches the focus to the *Shema*. **Rabbi Nehemiah said, "In my opinion Moses and the guys said it like a scribe leading the *Shema* in the syna-**

gogue. In other words, it is like a whole convention of Elvis imperson-ators, each doing his version of Elvis' Shema at the same time. **The scribe/teacher begins the song and the congregation continues the process."**[8]

This takes a short technical explanation. In those days, light years before Guttenberg, prayer was an oral experience. At best, there were just one or two prayerbooks per congregation. Most prayers were improvised. The *Sheliah Tzibur* (the "community representative"—not "boss") said the open-ing words loudly, and everyone improvised his own variations. Then, when time was up, he would sing the closing words and everyone would join in. The *Shema* didn't work that way, though. The *Shema* was important enough for everyone to know it by heart. When it came to the *Shema*, the *Sheliah Tzibur* would start, and the whole crew would do the same words and routine at the same time. It was well-balanced unity and diversity. *Hallel* didn't follow this process because people didn't know it well enough— it was said only a few times a year. It took more formal organization. Likewise, the *Shema* was different because it was said twice publicly every day and had to be precise, because it was Torah. A *Sofer*[9] leading the *Shema* begins and authenticates the text—it has to be done right, but because it is well known, and because it is an obligation, every man says it with him. You can't say "Amen" to the *Shema;* you have to say it yourself, you have to fulfill your own obligation. But a Torah expert, a teacher, can set the pace and make sure you do it precisely. First Elvis, then the imper-sonators.

Review: The Red Sea experience, the song that burst forth as a spiritual response to the freedom and the miracles, is the primal *minyan*

---

[8]The Sotah passage continues with this explanation of the derivation of these opinions. **Where do these different models come from? They come from the verses "'THEN MOSES AND THE SONS OF ISRAEL SANG THIS SONG TO ADONAI. THEY SAID, SAYING: 'I WILL SING ADONAI BECAUSE HE SCORED TOTAL VICTORY. THE HORSE AND ITS RIDER HE HAS THROWN INTO THE SEA...'" Rabbi Akiva believed that the key is the word "say-ing,"**explaining that this teaches that after every verse they said, "I WILL SING ADONAI." This is what they were "SAYING." Rabbi Eleazar, the son of Rabbi Yosi from the Galilee, also saw "SAYING" as the key, but he explained that they were to be "SAYING" everything that Moses said. Rabbi Nehemiah saw the key in the double verb, "THEY SAID, SAYING," explaining that "THEY SAID" meant that they "SAID" it all together. "SAYING" meant that they were "SAYING" it following Moses' "lead."

[9]Based on a number of other Talmudic settings, Rashi renders *Sofer* as a teacher of young children. I understand Rashi's reasoning but sense that the meaning here is different, closer to the primal mean-ing of *Sofer* and the context.

experience. The Gemara has an inquiring mind; it wants to find the essence of the process. In exploring this biblical moment, they are looking for the essence of the Jewish people's spiritual connection. Its first question, "How did the men pray?" is really asking, "How can we find our true process of prayer via their experience?" Three models are suggested: praying like **THE PIPS** (*men* responding to [rather than echoing] the spiritual energy of a charismatic leader); praying like **MEN LEARNING A NEW SONG FROM A SONGLEADER** (echoing precisely the words, notes, intonations, and patterns first vocalized by the leader—but not necessarily "drafting" his spirituality; this is like a congregation led by a *boy*—each man has to do the whole thing for himself, but they all do it together); and praying like a **CONGREGATION OF ELVIS IMPERSONATORS**, where each man recreates the original performance with his own voice, with his own spiritual snapshot of what the inner Elvis was really like (after all, Elvis impersonating is a way of life, not just a fashion statement).

In the Talmud, it is suggested that on Mount Sinai first God said a piece of Torah, then Moses said the piece of Torah after him. Finally, the two of them said it together. (And then implied, but not stated, in the Torah is that Moses then went on to teach his rendition of God's Torah to the Jewish people.) I think that the men of Israel did the Song of the Sea, and we need to pray as Moses learned Torah. First God says it to us, and we listen. This is the prayer of **GLADYS KNIGHT AND THE PIPS**, where the words, message, and moment are awesome, and we can do no more than a few "movin' ons." This is the magic of meeting God in Les Bronstein's rock 'n' roll minyan. Then we say it together, one after the other. We say the Song the way that Moses first learned and later taught it, **ECHOING THE SUPREME SONGLEADER**, one call and response at a time. This was the magic of listening to Ari Roth's voice arc above the *Sam Samanskys*. Finally, we come to say it on our own, doing our own best **INDEPENDENT RENDITION OF THE KING**. This is what I do every time I don the magic yarmulke Kent gave me.

And Now Back to the Women... The passage in *Sotah* we've been considering continues this way: **Rabbi Yosi of Galilee taught: when all of Israel went up from the Sea, they wanted to say a Song of praise—how did they say the song? Listen to this one, it**

is supremely cool. The baby sat on its mother's knee, and the newborn sucked at its mother's breast (take this two ways, literally and mythically). When they perceived the *Shehinah*, the baby raised its head, and the newborn let go of the breast, and they said: "THIS IS MY GOD AND I WILL PRAISE HIM." When we take this passage literally, we learn that women's God connections are so deep, they can bring their babies to the Red Sea just by singing them songs on their knees, and just by nursing. When we take the passage mythically we realize that experiencing God at the Red Sea is so awesome that when it happens to us, we are as unable to verbalize a response as would be an infant. When we come directly into the wake of God's works we are spiritual infants.

To explain the depth of women's spiritual connection, we need to go back to the Torah with Rashi's help. Listen to his whole reading of the women's verse. AND MIRIAM THE PROPHETESS: **How do we know that Miriam was a prophetess?** Easy, because the Torah clues us with the next words, AARON'S SISTER. That unnecessary description (why did the Torah say that about her at this moment?) promts us to look at *Sotah* 12b, where we learn: **"When she was only AARON'S SISTER before Moses was born, she said, 'In the future my mother will give birth to a son who will deliver Israel.'"** In other words, when she was just AARON'S SISTER, before Moses was a glimmer in his father's eye, she made her first prophecy. And now back to the action: TOOK IN HER HAND A DRUM, AND ALL THE WOMEN WENT OUT AFTER HER DRUMMING AND DANCING. Here comes one of our favorite questions. **Where did the drums come from?** Rashi doesn't tell us about heartbeats or war drums; he talks about the womb: **The righteous women in that generation were confident that God would perform miracles for them, and for that reason they had brought the drums out of Egypt with them in faithful anticipation.** AND MIRIAM ANSWERED THEM: "YOU SING TO ADONAI BECAUSE HE SCORED TOTAL VICTORY. THE HORSE AND ITS RIDER HE HAS THROWN INTO THE SEA." These explanations reveal something deeper. Miriam is a prophetess because she has deep connections to the womb—to life that will be born. The women brought drums—because they had faith in future miracles. And back in *Sotah*, the women were supporting their babies, the Jewish people's future, in their spiritual expressions. In other words, for the rabbis (no subjugation intended), women's spirituality comes from the mommy place, from the instincts it takes to find the courage to be a mother. We men have it harder. Our spiritual skins are thicker and more skeptical.

Davar Aḥer: **My Midrash—My Truth:** While the men were celebrating with their war chant, the women could recognize the power and importance of that expression, but they needed to do something else. They could beat the drum and dance, but they couldn't sing the same song. The men said, "*I WILL SING* ADONAI BECAUSE HE SCORED TOTAL VICTORY. THE HORSE AND ITS RIDER HE HAS THROWN INTO THE SEA." Men could root themselves (and really get off) on the use of power and the imposition of Divine Justice. The women took out their drums; their faith was deep, but it was different. I think they saw something else. I think they realized that their children were now safe. They knew that their children would grow and prosper. They played their drums and, I suspect, danced a dance to their children's future, while the men sang of war—the women's only words were: "*YOU* (masculine plural) *SING* TO ADONAI BECAUSE HE SCORED TOTAL VICTORY. THE HORSE AND ITS RIDER HE HAS THROWN INTO THE SEA." Inside they were singing different songs.

When the men of Israel witnessed the miracles at the sea they were really impressed with God's power. God was their Hero. God was better than John Wayne, Clint Eastwood, Charles Bronson, Steven Segal, Sylvester Stallone, Arnold Schwarzenegger, Jean-Claude Van Damme, Bruce Lee, Chuck Norris, and all the rest. Every man in Israel wanted to be like God and destroy Israel's enemies, defend hearth and home and country, and find the power within. With newfound pride and confidence, with their manhood restored by God's example, the former slaves sang their war hymn. For them it was praise of God's might and praise of their own potential. The King of the Universe had renewed His image, and every Jewish man shared in that sense of potency.

The women objected. Where the men saw God's glory in the drowning horses and dying Egyptians, *midah k'neged midah*—well-measured equal justice for all the Jewish babies that had been killed in the Nile—the women saw just death and horror. They empathized with the lives that were lost— their wombs cried out. They appealed to God and said, "Stop the men from singing—there is too much horror here for a celebration." God responded. God always responds—just not always according to our expec-

83

tations. That is God's way. Midrashic God stopped the angels from singing, saying, "How can you rejoice while my legions are dying?" But God allowed the men of Israel to continue; their spirit needed to celebrate this victory. The women understood, picked up their drums, and accompanied the men's prayer, even though it was one they couldn't say themselves. While the men found their own ability to act and control their future in God's example of the Just Warrior, the women danced different hopes to the same drummer—their dance was a lullaby of faith. God had also affirmed their faith—their role as givers and sanctifiers of life.

The Conclusion, A Braided Truth: When

we were younger and full of naïve beliefs about how easy it was to change the world, we listened to the mothers and took all the toy guns away. I was a little bit sad, because playing army had taught me much of the world and contained some of my best childhood moments. I learned leadership and strategy, mastered the way trees grow, and came to understand both loyalty and friendship in my days of playing soldier—but I had now seen the horrors of real war on TV and in *U.S. News and World Report*—and so I quelled my boyish memories, my Tom Sawyer moments, and agreed to throw all the toy weapons on the pyre. It was the peace-loving, non-sexist, politically correct thing to do. Just about everyone I knew did it, too. Instead of guns we gave the boys dolls to play with—"Let them learn to nurture," we all said. The mistake was the word "instead." Just about every parent who ever deprived a son of toy weapons knows that the boys fabricated them from clay, from rulers, from sticks, from soap, from fingers—from everywhere; that is part of the boy's spirit. One can just about not teach a boy not to fight—the key comes in balancing and limiting the conflicts, not in trying to hide them deep inside the stomach. But one can also teach a boy to nurture. Even the best backyard warriors have found some freedom and joy in the times they've played with dolls. We can't take the guns away—that is castration—but we can "also" give them dolls to play with. The same is true of boys' spiritual connections.

Read Rashi on our passage once more, and you'll notice there is no *mekhitzah* and no temporal separation.[10] Moses said the Song to the men;

---

[10]This follows my reading of Rashi as interpreted by Silbermann. Cassutto goes the other way. He believes that the women are, indeed, just the spear carriers and the backup chorus.

he said it and they answered after him. And Miriam said the Song to the women and they answered after her. Men and women are standing together, interwoven, but responding differently to the same event. We're sophisticated enough to know that those with a "Y" chromosome aren't totally on one side while those without one are on the other—emotions are not bounded by a *mekhitza* either. Rather, in language we have already come to understand, every Jew's *Yetzer ha-Tov* echoed God's *Midat ha-Rahamin* and had pity on the lives wasted in a foolish war, while the *Yetzer ha-Ra* echoed God's *Midat ha-Din* and had great joy in celebrating the just punishment of evil oppressors. Men and women are different blends of male and female. Men also felt the loss of life—women, too, celebrated God's conquests—but by and large, that wasn't their dominant feeling.

When I talked about this text with Rabbi Richard Israel, who is, after years in Hillel, spending the year directing an elementary day school, he said just this: "When a boy hurts his knee he always comes to the office crying. When a girl hurts her knee, she also comes to the office crying. The difference is, the little girl is crying, but there is always someone with her." Boys and girls cry differently. They tend to cry out differently, too. (Think Hannah!)

I am proud of my soft womblike meditations because they enrich my life. I am stronger now for having seem myself as **the barren woman** whom God has allowed to **dwell in her house as a joyful mother of children**, but sometimes I need to wear a baseball cap. My spiritual connection is most often best voiced in the rock 'n' roll Hasidim of locker-room victory cheers. The Jewish people and I lose if all those moments are taken away from me. I need to joust with Little John and I need to sing my war hymns to complete God's image within me. Sometimes I don the magic *kippah*, swirl my *tallit* like a cape and, with a trembling lip, sing a medley of "God is a Man of War" and "Love Me Tender."

Epilogue: A Reprise: A couple of weeks later, hot off my Adat Ariel success (and because I had already done the drawings), I took the Make Miriam's Midrash lesson to a family session I was doing as a scholar-in-residence in Des Moines. There, working in groups of families, we created various "new midrashim." This one stood out. It is a wonderful echo (literally) of the famous midrash where God chastises the angels for

The Mamas and The Papas
Beyond a Politically Correct Gender-Balanced Liturgy

At the moment, the Jewish women's movement and non-movement has centered its challenges to the liturgy of the Y-chromosome on the first blessing of the *Amidah*. It is a wonderful choice. Most Jewish worship is public. People are singing and chanting against each other. To apply Deborah Tannen's jargon, it is "**report talk**"—a lot of public praise, a lot of Jewish history. In the heart of the service, in the part of the service that centers in the heart, the practice changes. The Amidah's goal is what Deborah Tannen would call "**rapport talk**." Here, in an extended private and personal prayer, people are supposed to "ask" rather then "tell"; people are supposed to admit "vulnerability" rather than pose and posture as the chosen.

Traditionally, Jewish men pull their *tallitot* over their heads, covering their faces during the Amidah. The official texts state that it is done to create "blinders" to enable "**Kavanah**." I believe that it is also to make this moment like being in a movie theatre, a place where men can cry (without being seen). The matrix of the *Amidah* is in many ways the matrix of tears, and not surprisingly, when the rabbis needed to learn how to cry—how to admit their needs, weaknesses, and vulnerabilities—they turned, not to their fathers, but to their mothers. No wonder women want to publicly add the faces that have always loomed large in the privacy of the *tallit*. Such is the public discussion today—whether (and then how) to add Sarah, Rebeccah, Rachel, and Leah to the gallery that has always held portraits of Abraham, Isaac and Jacob. And the very argument over this text is a battle between *kevah* and *kavanah*—the long-term and well-proven pattern of survival versus the immediate outpouring of great need.

This proem had been sitting in my brain for awhile, but I put off writing it for over a year because it wasn't a big intellectual challenge; it was really just going to be a one-sentence insight—a lot of texts and a few well-placed caveats. For those of you who want the one-line version: "Sarah, Rebeccah, Leah, and Rachel should be added to the first *brakhah* in the Amidah, not so women can get their due, but because all Jews, male and female, need their example of praying from the vulnerability of the Midat ha-Rahamin in order to fully daven the Amidah." Then some of my female and male students dragged it out of me. We were studying some "male gemara" that teaches the rules for Jewish worship. My female students (circa sixteen-years-old) were offended that prayer, which is a matter of the heart, was regulated and "judged." To respond to their concerns, we studied the story of Hannah and the Talmud passage it generated.

(Then, as a second way of telling the same truth, we'll look at a fragment of Lamentations Rabbah. All of this will teach us the need to balance our **Midat ha-Din** (our rule-making capacity) with our **Midat ha-Rahamin** (the source of our tears).

Pre-Text: All women become like their mothers. That is their tragedy. No man does. That is his. (Oscar Wilde, *The Importance of Being Earnest*.)

The Torah Text: ADONAI SPOKE TO MOSES SAYING, "COMMAND AARON AND HIS SONS (THE PRIESTS) AND SAY TO THEM, "THIS IS THE TORAH OF THE BURNT SACRIFICES" (Leviticus 6.9).

The Proem Verse: NOW HANNAH, SHE SPOKE IN HER HEART (1 Samuel 1.13).

Commentary: Jewish worship grows out of two places at the same time. On one hand it is all *keva*, rules, limits, and boundaries. It is rooted in that "positive-time-bound" place that is the core of all that is the Judaism of discipline. To state the obvious, these are male, masculine, *Midat ha-Din* kinds of things. This is the side that comes from "COMMAND AARON AND HIS SONS (THE PRIESTS) AND SAY TO THEM, "THIS IS THE TORAH OF THE BURNT SACRIFICES," because from the Torah of Sacrifice grew its replacement—the rules that bound how we now pray.

The other side of Jewish worship grows out of the heart rather than the wristwatch. Its roots are in "HANNAH, SHE SPOKE IN HER HEART." Rabbinically, we call it *kavanah*. *Kavanah* is translated as "intention," but it really means "aiming." It is a single word used to access a phrase—*Ki-vein et libo*—which means to "aim one's heart." In the blend that is Jewish worship, half of it is rooted in the fire, blood, rules, and regiment—all the majesty of the altar. The other part comes from quieter moments, and to be honest, it comes from the tear glands. Tears of joy. Tears of profound, unmitigated pain and fear. One part blood. One part tears. In the same way, Jewish prayer is both public and private. It is both about "public speaking" and about "intimate conversation." It is both "pillow talk with God" and "public anthems and great spectacle."

When the rabbis asked the question, "Should Jewish worship be *Kevah* or *Kavanah?*" there was only one possible answer—"Yes." Per usual, they want it both ways. But the crisis that precipitated this essay, stemmed from the truth that men wrote down the merged ("balanced") version. They saw worship the way I do, as a person wearing the armor and padding of rules and routine, protected and simultaneously hidden among a crowd. In this larger frame, the worshiper is now able to admit the inner longings of "his" heart. Apparently, *kevah* is on the outside, *kavanah* on the inside. And the pattern is clearly: first *kevah*, then *kavanah*. It is a discipline-to-insight, not insight-to-discipline, kind of mantra. Slowly I have come to realize that this articulated Jewish pattern I had learned as a child is not the only possible pattern the tradition supports. There is at least one other possibility—its opposite. The other conception of Jewish worship is directed at those who wear their *kavanah* on their sleeves.

The Prologue: After long procrastination on this proem, I decided I had to start writing because "my girls" needed it. (Yes, "my girls" is paternalistic, but I cherish the warmth it implies. I also call my male students "my boys.") I was teaching my juniors and seniors at the Los Angeles Hebrew High School today, a day when all of the boys, except for Jon, were absent, and when almost all of the girls were there. We were studying *brakhot*, a Gemara about places where miracles have occurred at which it is now "a mitzvah" to say a *brakhah*. The "young women" were having a hard time with the passage.

Jesse asked, "Like—on whose authority do we have to say these blessings?" I answered her question. I gave a restatement of the "legal" procession of *Torah she-b'Al Peh* (oral law) as it grew from Torah into Talmud. I explained the difference between "Orthodox Halakhah," "Conservative Halakhah," and "Reform Halakhah." I talked about "authority" and "law committees." I had done what I thought was a good five minutes on Jewish law as we face it today. When I was all done, she wasn't satisfied. She looked like the proverbial kid who wanted the answer "Cleveland" and not "the birds and the bees" to the question, "Where do I come from?" Jesse gave me a big smile and said, "In other words, we can do what we want?"

A little voice inside me wanted to become a big voice that yelled, "What?" at being so completely *not* comprehended. But before I could even take my big swallow of exasperation air, Michel (pronounced "Michelle") asked, "Why do we have to have rules for prayers? You should just say a *brakhah* when you feel like it." The weird part of it for me was that this statement was said with love, not anger; commitment, not rebellion. I am used to kids rebelling against prayer. I am used to kids challenging the authority of the tradition in order to not be made to pray, but that wasn't this discussion. My reflex is to jump into debate mode and go on the attack. But I didn't. I sensed that wasn't what was going on. I had taught a lot of good lessons that way—opening up the Jewish tradition by defending its honor. But that wasn't to be today's lesson—it felt off-target. Slowly I realized that in a lot of ways, I had been here before. They were telling me, "I want a Judaism of *connection*, not a Judaism of *commandment*." It wasn't just the old *keva* (structure) verses *kavanah* (spontaneous intention) debate. That debate is part of every course on the siddur—even the rabbis do it big time. This wasn't that debate; it was the second cousin of that debate. What it centered in— was a deeper sense of what it means to be a Jewess.[11]

Having learned from experience, I wasn't only going to try to defend the traditional Jewish attitude of "rules" for when we should be "spontaneously Jewish." I decided, rather than confront the "girls" on their rejection of authority, I was going to (a) affirm their spiritual connection, and (b) try to show why a (male) tradition also found spirituality in a religion

---

[11]According to Jesse, when I brought the first draft of this essay to class, I misunderstood her. Her question wasn't questioning absolute authority, but the authority of whoever made the "bad" choices of the particular miracles listed in our Barita. In other words, she had meant, "I know it was a rabbi, but if a rabbi teaches a bad lesson, do I have to learn from it?" I know she feels that the situation is different, but I still understand that the core issue is the same: Does "authority" (*keva*) take precedence over "meaning" (*kavanah*)?

of boundaries and obligations. Theirs wasn't a rejection, it was honestly a communication gap. And in order to ask these future Jewish leaders to hear the wisdom of the Torah of *Midat ha-Din* on worship, I also had to articulate the way the *Midat ha-Rahamin* wants to pray. It was time to write this essay. I needed to relearn this material, I needed to learn from them, in order to teach them.

A Fantasy Talmudic Sugia
FROM THE UNWRITTEN SEDER OF NASHIM II: THE LIBERATION[12]

A Mishnah: The House of Hillel and the House of Shammai (both houses of men) both used to say: "GOD OF ABRAHAM, GOD OF ISAAC, AND GOD OF JACOB."

After the coming of the liberation, some of The House of Women said that one should say: "GOD OF OF ABRAHAM AND SARAH, GOD OF ISAAC AND REBECCA, GOD OF JACOB, RACHEL AND LEAH."

While others said, "That subjugates women to their husbands," so they said: "GOD OF ABRAHAM AND GOD OF SARAH, GOD OF ISAAC AND GOD OF REBECCA, (AND) GOD OF JACOB, GOD OF RACHEL, AND GOD OF LEAH."[13]

---

[12]I hate to explain a joke, but sometimes it is necessary. In the real Talmud, there is a *seder* (order) called *Nashim* which means "women." An order is a cluster of "divisions." "Women" make up one sixth of the Talmud. This tractate comes from the not-yet-written sequel to *Seder Nashim*.

[13]Consider this *Tosefta Nouveau*. (F.Y.I. *Tosefta* means "addition." It is a collection of rabbinic material that parallels the Mishnah, holding extra chunks of preserved material from the rabbis who "taught" the stuff that became the Mishnah but didn't make it into the Mishnaic collection. You can figure out *Nouveau* on your own.) When my class studied my "Sugia" and got to this point,

Michel said: "Why do we have to use any gender language for God? When I was a kid they always used to call God He. I always saw 'Him' as a 'Man'—an old man with a beard. It took me forever to get that God out of my head."

Traci then said: "It is sort of like pink elephants. Once they tell you not to think of pink elephants, then it is almost impossible to think of anything else."

Josh, running on a different sync-track, next said: "It is just as sexist to call God 'She' as 'He.'" Then he added, "Maybe it should be 'He' one time and 'She' the next."

I said, "I do intentionally call God 'She' every time one of you calls God 'He.' I do that to shake up your thinking. But when I am doing my own writing and thinking, I carefully choose masculine and feminine God language to fit the relationship I am describing. I don't want God to be an 'It.'"

Akiko then said, with her own syncro-mesh engaged, "It is like Voltaire. If God didn't exist, people would need to invent God."

Then we got back to the text.

91

While still others said, "That still subjugates women to their role as men's companions," and so they came to say, "GOD OF ABRAHAM, GOD OF ISAAC, AND GOD OF JACOB. GOD OF SARAH, GOD OF REBECCA, GOD OF LEAH AND GOD OF RACHEL."

And Gail Dorph said, "I like the idea that women have their own spirituality and aren't lumped with the men." While others said, "I don't want the mothers stuck behind a *mehitzah*" (screened into a women's section).

Dr. Sidney Freedman taught: "Leah should precede Rachel. Not only was she the firstborn, but she was also the mother of the tribe of the Jews, the mother of most of us."

Then Nancy Adel added: "What about Zilpah and Bilhah (the two handmaidens of Rachel and Leah who also mated with Jacob and bore some of the tribes of Israel)? Shouldn't they be included?

The Gemara now discusses this text:

Rabbi 1: Why do we have to change the *siddur?* Why can't we just stick with the traditional text?

Man 1: We have to change it so our wives will still sleep with us—and not "beat us up" over 3,000 years of male domination. A few additional words will alleviate a lot of aggravation.

Woman 1: We have to change it so that girls can have role models to identify with. When I was growing up as a girl, I thought that Jewish women didn't really belong in the synagogue. I almost left the religion. I couldn't find myself anywhere in the prayerbook except for that obscene blessing about "not being a woman."

Mar Joel: We have to change the text, because I (as a Jewish man) personally need the stories and examples of the matriarchs in order to learn how to make myself vulnerable enough to really enter the *Amidah*.

Gemara: How so?

Mar Joel: Because we are taught (in the Talmud),

"From the day that God created His world there was no man who called the Holy One *Tzeva-ot* until Hannah came and called God, *Tzeva-ot*" (Brakhot 30b),

and it says in the Midrash,

92

"Immediately, the mercy of The Holy-One-Who-Is-to-Be-Blessed was stirred. God said: 'For your sake Rachel, I will restore Israel to their place'" (Lamentations 23.1).

Commentary: This pseudo-Rabbinic text grows out of two real texts. The first one comes from the Talmud, *Brakhot 30b*, where, among about a dozen other theoretical origins for the practices of the *Amidah*, the rabbis imprint our present ritual form on the story of Ḥannah. Before we can read the Talmudic interpretation, here is the biblical "original" (as mutated via a translation by your "male" author). The second one, *Lamentations Rabbah Proem 23*, we will come to latter.

The Torah Text: 1 SAMUEL 1.9-19: (Ḥannah arose. You never know where to begin a biblical translation; you never know the beginning of the story you should study. Sometimes I think every passage really has to begin at *Bereshit* in order to make sense. I started my excerpting of the text here; I left out the previous verses about the family situation and Ḥannah's barrenness. So let's do the flashback that Jesse called for and honor her lesson. There was a certain man from Ramat Ha-Tzophim in the hill country of Ephraim. His name was Elkanah the son of Jeroham, son of Elihu, son of Tohu, son of Zuph, an Ephraimite. He had two wives; the name of the one was Ḥannah, and the name of the other Peninnah. And Peninnah had children, but Ḥannah had no children. Now this man used to go up every year from his city to worship and to sacrifice to Adonai Tzevaot at Shiloh, where the two sons of Eli, Hophni and Phinehas, were Adonai's priests. On the day when Elkanah sacrificed, he would give portions to Peninnah his wife and to all her sons and daughters; and, although he loved Ḥannah, he would give Ḥannah only one portion, because Adonai had closed her womb. Her rival used to provoke her miserably, and irritate her, just because Adonai had closed her womb. So it went every year; as often as she went up to Adonai's house, she used to get her riled up. Therefore Ḥannah wept and would not eat. And Elkanah, her husband, said to her, "Ḥannah, why do you weep? And why do you not eat? And why is your heart sad? You are more important to me than ten sons." Just like a man, I wanted to cut to the "rule making part." Like women, my girls wanted the whole story and the whole relationship. They were right. I had left out all the menstrual periods that brought on tears. I left out all the times that they watched the calendar and the thermometer. I left out the actual biblical statement where Elkanah, her husband, says,

93

presenting a wonderful empathic gift (unaccepted), that "YOU ARE MORE IMPOR-
TANT TO ME THAN TEN SONS." I though it was unimportant until Jesse wanted
to blame Elkanah, to make sons a patriarchal demand, not a shared desire.

So now we return to the story: HANNAH AROSE AFTER SHE HAD EATEN AT SHILOH,
where they had gone to celebrate the holiday. AND AFTER SHE HAD DRUNK—
remember, even though she will deny it later, the fact that the Torah witnesses her drinking. Later, this detail will be important to Eli's defense
effort. And, in fact, at this moment the text takes a a quick cut to introduce Eli. ELI, THE PRIEST, WAS SITTING IN A CHAIR BESIDE THE DOORPOST OF ADONAI'S
SANCTUARY. This story will be a woman's bitter heart versus a priest's rigid
enforcement of the law. But never forget that all priests are the descen-
dents of Aaron, and when it works best, their law shares his compassion.
There will be no bad guys in this story, only misunderstandings.We cut
back to Hannah. SHE WAS BITTER OF SOUL, and we know why—because she,
like every other matriarch, was barren. AND SHE PRAYED TO ADONAI, but not
just prayed, AND CRIED AND CRIED. And she didn't just cry, either; she took
action, SHE VOWED A VOW AND SAID: "ADONAI TZE-VAOT. IF YOU SEE THE SUFFERING
OF YOUR SERVANT (most translations call her a maidservant, but even though
the Hebrew noun can mean only "a woman servant," womanservant/maid-
servant conjures up Hazel for me. I see the black dress and the white apron.
It doesn't work, because here, in the tradition of Isaiah's "SUFFERING SER-
VANT," servant here should be an honorific. All Israelites work for God, so
let's call her a woman God-worker. Seeing her as a God-worker feels better—more true—than does seeing her as part of the cast of *Upstairs
Downstairs)*.

IF YOU REMEMBER ME AND DO NOT FORGET YOUR SERVANT (Can God forget?),
IF YOU GIVE YOUR SERVANT A MALE CHILD, THEN I WILL GIVE HIM TO ADONAI. Stop
the music! Stop the music! This offer is the whole ball of wax. Everything
spins on the fact that I can't understand this offer. She says, "Give me a
kid, and I will give him to you. I don't have to be with him, I just have to
know I had him." It is really spiritual. It is deeply woman (I think!). I just
don't understand it, and this passage is a hymn of praise to this wonderful
mystery that is beyond my selfish, male, possessive, rational comprehension. FOR ALL THE DAYS OF HIS LIFE—AND NO RAZOR WILL EVER TOUCH HIS HEAD.
Yes, this is like Samson. It is a Nazarite vow. It is as if Hannah went to her
local post office and filled out her 1040 Vow Her-Son-to-God form. AS SHE

CONTINUED TO PRAY BEFORE *ADONAI*, ELI WATCHED HER MOUTH.[14] Remember Eli; here comes the confrontation. The confontation is the connection to the *Amidah* and to all of Jewish worship.

AND HANNAH WAS SPEAKING ONLY IN HER HEART, JUST HER LIPS MOVED; BUT HER VOICE COULD NOT BE HEARD. Our question, the Talmud's question, is: can you learn to pray like Hannah? Can you find your Hannah place? Can you reach the bitterness in your soul, the place where Eli sits at the door and watches? ELI THOUGHT THAT SHE WAS DRUNK. Remember, she had been drinking. Everyone (except the working priests) had been drinking. That night Shilo was a party town. Think of it as spring break. ELI SAID TO HER, "HOW LONG WILL YOU BE A DRUNKEN FOOL? LOSE THE WINE!" Listen, I know a really good Twelve-Step program. HANNAH ANSWERED AND SAID, "NO! MY MASTER, I AM JUST A WOMAN WITH A HARDENED SPIRIT." Here is the Torah of *The Joy Luck Club*, of *The Piano*, of *Possessing the Secret of Joy*, and even of *Wuthering Heights*—bitterness, a woman's hardening, gives a lot of spiritual energy. Hannah was a Brontë kind of woman. "WINE NOR HARD LIQUOR I HAVE NOT DRUNK: I WAS ONLY POURING OUT MY SOUL TO *ADONAI*. DO NOT THINK YOUR SERVANT IS A WOMAN OF *B'LI-YA-AL*!" *B'li Ya'al* is a mystery. We'll work on it in the Gemara.

"IT IS BECAUSE OF THE LARGENESS OF MY ANGUISH AND MY ANGER THAT I HAVE SPOKEN THIS LONG." In my worst misogyny I see this as a "My anguish is bigger

---

[14]More of *Tosefta Nouveau*. (Or, my class does *Mikraot Gedolot*). This is the way my class discusses this passage from the Torah in preparation of studying the Gemara:

Michel: "Do you want to know how this story reflects man versus woman? When Hannah is in a sense praying to God, and her lips are moving and she is having this spiritual moment, all Eli can see in her is being drunk. He can't see the spiritual, he can't feel that. That's the whole point. He looks for this literally—how it seems—kind of understanding, while she is in this spiritual other world—other thing, that he can't understand."

Traci: "Women tend to let their feelings out more, they tend to be freer—they tend to express their feelings. Men tend to like to keep their feelings inside. Like it is okay for a woman to cry, and like maybe you're not a real man if you start crying. *It felt like she was about to say that Eli was sort of telling Hannah. 'Stop crying, grow up and be a man!'*"

Michel: "I have a question. Do you think that men are capable of in any way gaining this spirituality that women have? Maybe men aren't quite there yet, but it is slowly changing. Now, it is still okay (for a man) to cry, but there is still that stereotype out there. But it is a little bit more accepted."

Me: "Do you think women can be lawyers? Of course they can. Even though you might think of judging and arguing and fighting over small points as a man's thing, women can be very good at it. That is something we have now learned! If we think women are capable of rooting themselves in the judging place, then men are certainly capable of rooting themselves in the feeling place."

Akiko: "But you can think of being a lawyer as being both components. Though a man could be a really good lawyer 'cause he could think of the little logistics of everything, but a woman can go and do the job to the same quality in a different way, her strengths."

than your anguish" kind of thing. Woman aren't big on carrying a big stick. I can make fun of it. But I know the message here is deep anyway. ELI ANSWERED AND SAID: "GO IN PEACE." He was cool. He was doing the best he could. He gives his best wishes: "AND MAY THE GOD OF ISRAEL GIVE YOU YOUR 'ASKING' THAT YOU ASKED OF GOD!" AND SHE SAID, "Thanks, sorry I went off on you, too; I appreciate it. LET YOUR SERVANT FIND FAVOR IN YOUR EYES!" THE WOMAN WENT HER WAY. Cross-dissolve. SHE ATE, AND THAT FACE WAS NO LONGER HERS. Can you see the smile? THEY GOT UP EARLY IN THE MORNING AND WORSHIPED BEFORE *ADONAI*—forgiving God, too, or at least needing the relationship too much to stay bitter. AND THEY WENT TO THEIR HOME IN RAMAH. Cross-dissolve. THEN ELKANAH KNEW HANNAH, HIS WIFE, AND *ADONAI* REMEMBERED HER. Fade to black. Big smile.

A Gender-Based Commentary: The outline of

this story is simple. A priest who is following "the rules" doesn't recognize the spiritual connection of a "woman deep in 'spiritual bitterness,'" but when confronted with her truth, he experiences a sense of "radical appreciation."

In other words, the two deep keys to this story are: (1) the irony that Hannah's "spiritual bitterness" makes for sincere prayer, and that (2) while Samuel is following the post–Nadav and Avihu[15] ruling of that the Tabernacle is a Booze-Free Zone, he does come to recognize the profound depth of Hannah's prayer.

This, however, is what freaks me out about this story—it is the part that is beyond my comprehension. On one hand, Hannah is obsessed with having a child. On the other hand, she offers to immediately give up the child for which she is praying. I just don't get it. I just don't understand the birthing without the having. Maybe I am too selfish. I know I am too much a man to understand the non-logic, the pure emotion of the statement. And I surely have learned enough about women to know that to reduce it to my logic makes no sense for them. Oscar Wilde puts it this way (in the voice of one of the women in one of his plays): **"Man, poor, awkward, reliable, necessary man belongs to a sex that has been rational for millions and millions of years. He can't help himself. It is in his**

---

[15]Nadav and Avihu were two sons of Aaron who worked as priests in the Tabernacle. Once, without permission, they sneaked into the Tabernacle and did their own worship thing. They were found dead, burned to death. The next day Moses gave the priests a new set of instructions that included, "Don't drink and sacrifice." Rashi explains that this was a reaction to Nadav and Avihu's drinking on the job. From there the Mishnah expands a ruling about no "drinking and praying."

race. The History of Woman is very different. We women have always been picturesque protests against the mere existence of common sense. We saw its dangers from the first." (Oscar Wilde, *A Woman of No Importance*, Act Two.) I'll accept this faithful dislogic as a great, wondrous mystery, the reason, that I, like the Rabbis, must study Hannah.[16]

---

[16]Our *Tosefta Nouveau* continues, essentially (but not completely) dealing with the question: Why was Hannah bothering to ask for a son if she was willing to give him up?

ELI SAID TO HER, "HOW LONG WILL YOU BE A DRUNKEN FOOL?"

Michel: I have a question. Isn't his assuming that she is drunk kind of unlawful in the sense that he is causing her public embarrassment? Why isn't he condemned for it?

Me: Good question. You've anticipated the Gemara.

SHE VOWED A VOW AND SAID ... "IF YOU GIVE YOUR SERVANT A MALE CHILD, THEN I WILL GIVE HIM TO *ADONAI* FOR ALL THE DAYS OF HIS LIFE."

Rachel: Hannah wasn't really giving the child up, because she could always still love him.

Me: She's gonna love him, but she ain't gonna have him.

Micah: She wasn't going to sacrifice him. She was giving him to God's service, but it wasn't like what Abraham was willing to do with Isaac. She is just going to dedicate him.

Rachel: I think maybe it's nature. Women have an endless desire to reproduce. It is like nature in the sense that animals, including people, have the desire to reproduce, to keep life going, even if it is an unconscious thing.

Michel: In the Jewish religion, you have like one child and you are continuing a whole race. It is like if you kill a life, you kill a generation. Maybe her big issue was survival. It doesn't matter if you have that baby in your physical possession. You still know that you took part in creating this.

Akiko: Samuel grew up to be a famous Jewish leader and even anointed two kings. That's pretty good. He was worth having.

ELI ANSWERED AND SAID: "GO IN PEACE AND MAY THE GOD OF ISRAEL GIVE YOU YOUR 'ASKING' THAT YOU ASKED OF GOD."

Akiko: When Eli finally understands and tells her he hopes her prayers come true, it is such a guy thing to say.

Me: What was he supposed to say? "I feel your pain"?

Akiko: That was such a guy thing to say. It's like, "Oh, my God, I made a mistake," but he can't admit that he made a mistake, so he just says something nice.

Michel: He acted like by saying that he made everything okay. He never apologized, he never acknowledged that he messed up.

Micah: But what if he really meant it?

Traci: Here we have Micah, sensitive but supportive…

Akiko: After he realizes that she's not drunk, he comes to his own thing where he is understanding, but before he gets to be understanding he is a stupid idiot.

HANNAH ANSWERED…"IT IS BECAUSE OF THE LARGENESS OF MY ANGUISH AND MY ANGER THAT I HAVE SPOKEN THIS LONG."

Akiko: But why was she crying? Does she really want a baby?

Traci: If I had a baby, it would be so hard to give the baby up. (CONTINUED ON NEXT PAGE)

Let's go TALMUD diving: In the rabbis' discussion of how Hannah is the model for the Amidah, we understand a lot more about her spirituality. So let's turn to **Brakhot 30b**.

Mishnah: One should only stand up to say the Tefillah in a "heavy" frame of mind. The Hasidim used to wait an hour before praying, so that they might aim their hearts toward their Father in heaven. EVEN if the king greets a person [while praying][17] one should not answer; EVEN if a snake is wound round one's heel one should not interrupt one's prayers.

Commentary: Our Mishnah never mentions Hannah, but it defines the conditions necessary for her entrance in the Gemara. We learn two things. First, that *KAVANAH* is a necessary part of the Amidah. Second, that the Amidah also has a rigid *KEVA* (form) that should not be interrupted. The puzzle of this Mishnah—the snake and the king question—is: "Is the *KEVA* (the *Katta*) so important that it may not be broken even when *KAVANAH* fails, or is the *KAVANAH* supposed to be so intense that one no longer notices the *KEVA* (or challenges to it)? The stories told later in the Gemara, with their two punchlines—**"For Jewish kings do not interrupt (because they will understand), but for non–Jewish kings, do interrupt,"** and **"If it is a snake, do not interrupt, but if it is a scorpion,**

Akiko: I don't think that she wanted a baby for the reasons that we want a baby for—like "Oh, like I can have a cute little puppy dog and have cute little babies." Does she want to have a baby so she can have a wonderful prophet and say, "That's my son the prophet," or for the joy of having a baby? Does she want the baby to grow up with her [*and she is just saying the other because she thinks that is the only way God will give her anything*]?

Traci: Or does she want the baby just so she can give something wonderful to God?

Michel: It doesn't say she wants a baby and then will give the baby up. Maybe what it really says is that she wants a baby so that she can give the baby up. The point of having the baby is so that she can dedicate it to God.

Me: I think she wants a baby so badly that she is even willing to give the baby up.

Rachel: I like Michel's idea that she wants the baby in order to give God a gift. If she has a baby she can give something to the world, she can give something to God.

Michel: Couldn't her husband have a baby with another woman if she didn't birth one? The whole point is, maybe, that she didn't want her husband to have sex with another woman. *Maybe that is why her spirit was so bitter.* If she had a baby, it would make her a useful wife (not that she isn't useful in other ways).

[17]*Tosefta Nouveau* continues.

Akiko: What is "honest depression?" Could I be like falsely depressed?

Rachel: You could act depressed because you wanted attention.

deal with it at once!" —suggest that retaining the *KEVA* is an act of conscious will, not of the depth of the meditation. But that is not our central story. The Gemara is going to ask, (1) where do we learn the import of *KAVANAH,* and (2) where do we learn the *KEVA* used to achieve it? (After all, men are having the discussion.) Here, however, is where Ḥannah enters the Gemara.

Rabbi 1: Where in the Torah do we learn these laws in our Mishnah?

R. Eleazar: The Torah teaches them to us via the example of Ḥannah (1 Samuel 1.10), where it says about her:

Torah: AND SHE WAS BITTER OF SOUL.

Rabbi 1: But how can you learn from this? Why would "bitterness of the soul" be a good model for the right *KAVANAH* for learning how to really pray the *AMIDAH*?

Rabbi 2: Perhaps Ḥannah was different because she was exceptionally bitter at heart!

Commentary: At first the rabbis object to using the example of Ḥannah, not because she is a woman, but because of the bitterness of her prayer. It is as if they think that the proper *KAVANAH* for the *Amidah* should be all "sweetness and light." Then they give an amazing response: "Deep, soulful bitterness, and honest depression," may be just the right way to pray the *Amidah*. They are shocked at that lesson that bursts from their hearts (which makes no sense to their minds), so they check it out. They check it out by looking at the example of King David, who was a prayer expert—having written all those psalms—and the rabbis figure out that he was deep into bitterness, too. Eventually, after a lot of reflection on bitterness, the rabbis pick up the Gemara here, reflecting on the example of Ḥannah.

R. Hamnuna: **Let's count the laws that can be learned from these verses about Ḥannah's prayer!**

Torah: AND ḤANNAH WAS SPEAKING ONLY IN HER HEART ...

R. Hamnuna: **From this we learn that one who prays must aim the heart.** And really work up their *KAVANAH*.

Torah: JUST HER LIPS MOVED ...

R. Hamnuna:	**From this we learn that one who prays must mouth the words distinctly with the lips.**
Torah:	BUT HER VOICE COULD NOT BE HEARD.
R. Hamnuna:	**From this we learn that it is forbidden to raise one's voice in the** *Amidah.*

Commentary: These first three "lessons" connect the KEVA

and the *KAVANAH* of *Amidah*. They suggest that "**heart-pointing**" and "**mouthing but not uttering**" are interrelated, and both are learned from Hannah. The next part of this text is different. We leave spirituality (and the world of the *Midat ha-Rahamin*) and move over to "laws of interpersonal relationships." Here the *Midat ha-Din* takes over. Here the male rabbis perceive (wonderfully) that not only did Hannah have a spiritual connection, but she knew how to take care of herself. It is a three-dimensional portrait.

Torah:	ELI THOUGHT THAT SHE WAS DRUNK ...
R. Hamnuna:	**From this we learn that a drunken person is forbidden to say the** *Amidah*.
Torah:	ELI SAID TO HER, "HOW LONG WILL YOU BE A DRUNKEN FOOL?"
R. Eleazar:	**From this we learn that one who sees a neighbor doing something unseemly must reprove the neighbor.** In other words, not minding your own business can be a holy thing.
Torah:	HANNAH ANSWERED AND SAID: "NO! MY MASTER."
Narrator:	There are two ways to understand this comment. **Ulla (or, as some say, R. Jose b. Hanina),** came up with theory A and **said:**
Ulla (or Jose):	**She was** in essence **saying** to him:
Hannah (A):	**You are no "master" in this matter. The holy spirit does not rest on you; that is obvious if you suspect me of this thing.** What kind of holy jerk are you, if you don't know the difference between DUI and spiritual perfection?
Ulla:	**Or others explain** in theory B **that she** was in essence **saying** to him:
Hannah (B):	**You are no master,**

Ulla:	meaning:
Hannah (B):	**The *Shehinah* and the holy spirit is not with you in that you take the harsher and not the more lenient view of my conduct.** It did look like I was drunk. It was one possibility, but if you know spirit, then you should know *KAVANAH*. If you do know about *KAVANAH* and didn't even consider that I could be deep in prayer, than you aren't too spiritual yourself. **Do you not know that I** AM JUST A WOMAN WITH A HARDENED SPIRIT? WINE NOR HARD LIQUOR I HAVE NOT DRUNK.
R. Eleazar:	**From this we learn that one who is suspected wrongfully must clear him/herself.**

Commentary:

I love this passage, because the rabbis use Hannah to establish "rules" for feelings. Here, in an assertive way, she puts Eli in his place for his "judgmental" attitudes (it is all "heart" vs. "priest"), yet the "feelings" are codified and made back into a set of "rules" for balancing "feelings" and judgments. The Gemara continues (with some text I've edited for the sake of brevity) to explore some "rules" for relationships and then hits this high point.

Torah:	SHE VOWED A VOW AND SAID: *"ADONAI TZEVA'OT."*
R. Eleazar:	**From the day that God created "His" world there was no "man" called the Holy One, *"TZEVA'OT"* [Troops], until Hannah came and called God *TZEVA'OT*.** In other words, she was a unique soul, a champion God-connector. Let's listen in on her inner (midrashic) monologue and learn the way a world's champion *Amidahite* does it. **Said Hannah before the Holy One,**
Hannah:	**Ruler of the Cosmos, of all the hosts and hosts, that You have created in Your world, is it so hard in Your eyes to give me one son?** Come on, you are a Miracle Worker.
Torah:	These were her bitter inner thoughts while her lips formed the words. IF YOU SEE THE SUFFERING OF YOUR SERVANT.
R. Eleazar:	When that didn't work, **Hannah said** with an inner voice **before the Holy One,**

Hannah (B):	**Ruler of the Cosmos, if You will look, it is well,** and I can abandon my bitterness and give up on the endless prayer regime; **and if You will not look,** then I will use plan B— **I will go and shut myself up with someone else and let my husband Elkanah find out,** and this will look like adultery, like **I was alone with someone else, so they will** go into adultery checkout mode, looking to off me for doing the scarlet A. In order to prove their case they will do the biblical lie detector thing by **making me drink the *Sotah* water of the suspected wife.** Once they are into following your laws, then I've got you. Catch-22: **You cannot falsify Your Torah, which says (Numbers 5.28):**
Torah:	If she is innocent SHE SHALL BE CLEARED AND SHALL CONCEIVE SEED.

Commentary:
There is a long rabbinic tradition of men confronting God via prayer. Abraham does it over Sodom. Moses has his moments of changing God's mind (over the punishment of the Jewish people.) Honi, the Circle Maker, is the rabbinic expression of this behavior. And Levi Yitzhak of Berdichev has his famous trial of God, which was mutated into Peretz's story of Beryl the Tailor. But challenging God's justice, attacking God's boundary, standing *Midat ha-Din* to *Midat ha-Din* with God, seems to be a "male thing." We tend to believe that only men know how to challenge. But here the Talmud tells a different story. Here is a moment where Hannah becomes Moses. Here she uses the law to outsmart God. Having made her plea on the basis of emotion first, playing by her heart, the rabbis also voice her "plea" by some very clever "lawyering." In the Torah, and expanded in the Talmud, is a law known as *Sotah*, which is a drink given to a woman to check out her fidelity. It is particularly problematic to feminists (including your author) because it emphasizes a sexual double standard that defines adultery only as an act involving a wife, not a husband. Here, Hannah throws this law back in God's face and uses it to back God into a corner in which she says, "Either you 'choose' to give me a son, or 'I will make you' give me a child by setting you up to 'be a liar.'" Hannah may cry. She may be dominated by a matrix of emotion. But she is no wimp! The Gemara then works hard to close her "trap" door and explain why other women couldn't use this same Catch-22 against God.

102

Eventually the text picks up the theme of Hannah's "bitter soul" again. The bottom line, I think, is that Hannah knows how to "fight" for what she wants; she fights not like a man, not like a girl, but like a woman.

Torah: NOW HANNAH, SHE SPOKE IN HER HEART.

Narrator: R. Eleazar said in the name of R. Jose b. Zimra:

Rabbi Eleazar: She spoke concerning her heart. She said to God again with the inner bitter voice:

Hannah: Ruler of the Cosmos, among all the things that You have created in a woman, You have not created one thing without a purpose. Eyes were created to see, ears to hear, a nose to smell, a mouth to speak, hands to do work, legs to walk with, breasts to give suck. These breasts that You have put on my heart, are they not to give suck? Give me a son, so that I may suckle with them.

R. Eleazar also said: Hannah spoke insolently toward heaven as it says,

Torah: AND HANNAH PRAYED UNTO THE LORD.

Commentary: And with this final statement this piece of the Gemara's discussion of Hannah and *KAVANAH* for prayer begins to draw to a close. The Gemara makes Hannah parallel to Elijah, who also spoke insolently.

Conclusion: The final understandings I draw from these texts is that Hannah is a role model for the *Amidah* (as a woman) because the depth of "bitterness of the soul" is the core *KAVANAH* for the *Amidah*— and that ability to voice one's deepest and most sincere needs is something that definitely is related to the matrix of the *Midat ha-Rahamin*. Hannah may argue *Halakhah* with God, may use threats and make power moves; she may pray brilliantly out of her bitter soul, but her womb is her bottom line. It is the source of her emotional power. Women can tap into other places. Men, too, can find strength in their wombfulness, but women have an easier time making this connection. That is why the examples of David and Elijah, men who are also bitter of spirit, are important. The womb does lead to a spiritual path.

The example of Ḥannah is important to anyone who wants to use the *Amidah* to get to the heart of their souls. We need to find her ability to tap into the depth of our emotional and spiritual longing without being immobilized by it. That is the secret of Ḥannah, that is her womb power—to be totally in touch with the vulnerability of her longing, yet still have the strength and focus to act effectively. She is a real Lady of Valor.

Davar Aḥer: Lamentations R. Proem 14: When I want to *daven* the *Amidah*, the other place I go for inspiration is the story of Rachel as found in Lamentations Rabbah. Here are excerpts from that passage.

This is the scene: God, knowing that the Temple and Jerusalem must be destroyed, that Babylonia must conquer Israel—or else "His" judgments will have no meaning—struggles with Her emotional reaction to the defeat of Her children.

Narrator: **When the enemies entered the Temple and burnt it, God said,**

*K-B-H: **"I no longer have a dwelling-place in this Land. I will withdraw my *Shekhinah* from it and go back up to my former dwelling-place.**

Narrator: **At that moment The Holy-One-Who-Is-To-Be-Blessed cried and said:**

K-B-H: **"Woe is me! What have I done? I made my *Shekhinah* dwell down on earth for Israel's sake—but now that they have sinned, I have returned to the place where I used to dwell. Now I will be laughed at by nations—people will think of Me as a joke."**

Narrator: **At that moment Metatron, the Angel who was Israel's advocate in Heaven, came and bowed before The Holy-One-Who-Is-To-Be-Blessed. He said,**

Metaron: **"Master of the Universe, let me do the weeping, do not weep Yourself.**

Narrator: **God answered him,**

K-B-H: **"If you let Me do the weeping, I will go to a place where no one else has permission to enter, and I will weep in secret.**

---

* K-B-H refers to God: *Kadosh-Barukh-Hu.*

Commentary: This opening scene reveals a deep secret: God cries. God loses control of Her emotions. While God's public image may be that of an omnipotent King—the Ultimate Judge—in private, God cries like any Mother over the hardships Her children have brought on themselves. While God the King can say, "This is going to hurt me more," God, the Mother of Israel, sobs out of control. The use of the *Shekhinah* here only underlines the intimate, "Feminine" side of the Holy One.

Meanwhile, God sends for Moses, Abraham, Isaac, Jacob, and Jeremiah for comforting. A crying God got the boys together. It was a guy kind of thing. Probably it was a wake.

Narrator: **Moses cried aloud and wept until he caught up with Abraham, Isaac, and Jacob. They all immediately ripped their clothes, placed their hands upon their heads, and cried out, weeping until they reached the Temple gates. The Holy One saw them and called to them. Together they went weeping from gate to gate like men whose dead one is lying before him. The Holy One was weeping.** Then God delivers his ultimate line—it is a deep emotional echo of the Scottish play.

K-B-H: **"Woe to the King Who succeeded in His youth, but failed in His old age!"**

Commentary: Now hear this. Men can cry, too. Men can feel pain. But, as we shall see later in the piece, men usually rationalize their crying out of their own pain and loss. In this scene, the Patriarchs and God "cry in their beers," but God is crying for Himself, not for Her children, not yet. That is not to say that men don't have those needs and experiences; it is to say that it tends not to be their public faces.

The game that follows is simple. God, angry at Israel, declares (out of His hurt) that Israel will be in exile (have to stay in his room) until the Messiah comes— literally. God wants to be talked out of this position, but God needs to get past His pain, to allow Her love and empathy to take over. Each of the Patriarchs takes his shot at moving God out of His anger.

In the Midrash, Abraham is being Abraham. Abraham has always been a jail-house lawyer, outsmarting God with God's own words. That is the essence of his big Sodom scene, "SHALL NOT THE JUDGE OF THE EARTH DO JUSTLY." Abraham always plays "My **Midat ha-Din** is bigger than your **Midat ha-Din**. This is the essence of his intervention in this crisis, too.

Isaac, Jacob, and Moses try guilt. They each say, "We had a deal." They each say, "Listen, if you do this, all my self-sacrifice has no meaning." It may seem they are trying to tap into their "feminine sides" and share their emotions. It may seem female, or simply soft male, but the key is that they didn't put their Midat ha-Rahamin into it.

Narrator: **Then Moses said to Jeremiah:**

Moses: **Walk before me, so that I can go and bring them back into the Land—no one will dare touch them with us in the lead.** If God won't do anything, we'll do it ourselves.

Narrator: **Jeremiah replied** in a voice that sounded like Ed Begley, Jr.:

Jeremiah: **I can't walk along that road. Because I come from a priestly family, I am prohibited from contact with dead bodies.**

Narrator: **He said to him:**

Moses: You wimp! Come on, be a man. **Let's go anyway.** James Dean said, "That's the kind of Moses I want to play."

Narrator: **Immediately Moses went, with Jeremiah in the lead, and they came to the banks of the rivers of Babylon. When the exiles saw Moses, they said to one another:**

Exiles: **The son of Amram has come from his grave to redeem us from the hand of our enemies.**

Narrator: **Then a *Bat Kol*, a heavenly voice, echoed:**

Bat Kol: **This is My decree, that Israel should be in exile.**

Narrator: **Moses immediately told them:**

Moses: **My children, it is not possible to bring you back now, since this is a Heavenly decree—but the All-Powerful-One will soon cause you to return.**

Commentary: This time it is Moses acting as pure Moses. Here he is, indeed, the union organizer of Pyramid Workers Local 238. Here he is taking the Torah in his own hands. Moses knocks the chip off God's shoulder, does it with style, but still loses. The passage continues with Moses going through a whole other series of confrontations, but for our purposes, this is sufficient.

Then, in the text, Rachel makes a surprise, unannounced entrance at the last minute. In this story she is the cavalry.

Rachel: **Master of the World, You know that Your servant Jacob loved me very much and worked for my father for me for seven years. When those seven years were completed and the time for our marriage had come, my father planned to secretly substitute my sister for me. It was very hard for me, because I knew the plot, and I told my future husband. I gave him a sign, a way to tell the difference between me and my sister, so that my father could not make the exchange. After that, I changed my own mind; I held back my own desire and had empathy for my sister—that she should not be publicly shamed. On the night they switched my sister for me, I taught her all the signs that I had worked out with my husband, so that he would think that she was Rachel. More than that, I went beneath the bed upon which he lay with my sister— and when they spoke to one another she remained silent, and I spoke all the replies—so that he would not recognize my sister's voice.**

             I did her a kindness and was not jealous of her, and I did not expose her to shame. I am only a creature of flesh and blood, made out of dust and ashes—if I could get over being jealous of my rival, then You, The Ruler-Who-Lives-Forever, the One-Who-Is-Merciful, should be able to get over Your jealousy of idolatry (which isn't even a real competitor), and stop the exile of my children and end their slaughter by the sword, and prevent their enemies from doing with them as they wish.

Narrator: **Immediately the mercy of The Holy-One-Who-Is-to-Be-Blessed was stirred. God said:**

K-B-H: For your sake, Rachel, I will restore Israel to their place.

Commentary: Rachel saves the day. She does it by "breaking God's heart," and she breaks God's heart by tapping into her own *Midat*

107

ha-Rahamin and God's. Rather than confront God, rather than demand, rather than center the argument in her own pain, Rachel tells God, "I know just how you feel. It is hard to be rejected." Then, having acknowledged the feelings, Rachel can move God in the direction God really wants to go. That is the power of *Midat ha-Rahamin*.

Epilogue: This week at my minyan it got really crowded under

my *tallit*. When I throw it all the way over my head, I am like "boy Joel" who used to like to go under the covers both to hide and to fantasize, but who also got hot and stuffy and eventually had to come up for air. Today, under my *tallit*, Abraham, Isaac, and Jacob were there. So were Sarah, Rebecca, Rachel, and Leah. So was Hannah. So were Jesse and Michel. I now wish my mother had been there, too, but my father was also missing from today's *daven*ing. My *tallit* creates a virtual-reality siddur where I can, coached by my role models, work out my inner workings of the Jewish tradition. I cried some today—my Hannahness was coming through loud and strong. Afterward, I came up for air.

At my minyan, every Shabbat is a kind of mini-Simhat Torah, where the kids parade around with the scroll. Because we are a toddler universe, most of the kids are carried like a Torah scroll by their parents, behind whoever is carrying the actual Torah scroll. Today, I wanted to take the edge of my *tallit* and kiss the kids, too, just like a Torah. I held back. I wasn't that Hannah. I remember the now-circulating complaint of the woman rabbi who called it "sexual harassment" when a congregant told her he would rather kiss her than the Torah. I didn't need to complete the action—the fantasy was enough. Hannah and Rachel stood next to me, each taking an arm, each saying, "I understand your loneliness." "I understand what it is to always be looking for your place."

To solve the problem of the Mamas and the Papas is easy—we actually only need to talk about it in the right arena. It isn't a question of the politics; it is the need to counterbalance the priest in all of us. Sometimes being drunk isn't having had something to drink.

9
Weld
Neil Young Teaches the Torah of Male Bonding

Loneliness, alienation, and exile are all the same word. The sense of incompleteness is a constant spiritual issue. This book began with ADAM, the first earthling feeling alone, having no matching connection, and God tearing ADAM into MAN and WOMAN so they could fit themselves back together—and return to the original lonely state of their former union—unless we believe that the end of the loneliness, the Divine Connection, comes in the work and with the connection.

The last four sections of this book, three proems and a poem, move gender out of the spotlight and back into the chorus. Now, in the third act, the dual issues of loneliness and completion (**galut** and **shalom**) take center stage.

I would have dropped this essay (or at least moved it to the geniza) when I finally edited this book, but it is Carol's favorite essay. Therefore, because she likes it so much, I reread it, and realized that it is, indeed, the turning point in this work. It is the necessary movement away from anger and defense, from dwelling in darkness. It begins the movement toward the light.

This proem is designed to "weld" two of my most important boyhood texts back into a place in my newly reevolved manhood. One, our **Torah Text**, The Village Smith, is a fragment of "public" New England poetry memorized by all; the other, our **Proem Verse,** is a fragment of Jewish mystical teaching, taught to me long ago by Shlomo Carlebach, back when I went to college. The two are drawn together and then placed over a poem out of Robert Louis Stevenson's *A Child's Garden of Verses*. It is my favorite poem in my favorite book that my mother used to read me.

eld" is the name of an album by Neil Young. I somehow know that there is connection between it and this meditation. "Weld" is a study in distortion, feedback, and experimental guitar playing—there are no songs.

It is the bits that Neil played on solo guitar, with extensive electronic effects, before and after the songs on his last tour. It is "metal" cum "grunge" musical fore- and after-play. I saw one of the concerts it came from. I read the reviews of the album. I've never heard it, though. It's not something I would buy or listen to twice. But the idea of "Weld," the reality of "Weld," made sense out of this real-life happening.

Torah Text: The smith, a mighty man is he, with strong and sinewy arms...remember that old chestnut? Road stories are an old religious pursuit. Remember Dean Moriarty? Remember Jason? Remember Abraham? Remember Moses?

This is the story of a true mythic journey. I ended Passover this year in a pool in Palm Springs. With my friends Mark and Harriet, I fled to the desert to get sun and live the last few hours of matzah time. We worked on tans and talked of addiction and Judaism, Twelve Steps and spiritual pursuits. There were many stories shared. There were the right moments of silence. I strove to become a bronzed god; in the end I glowed pink. The holiday ended, and I took the Greyhound bus for home, Mark and Harriet stayed on, but I had teaching to do. Greyhound buses are always epic adventures. Remember Paul Simon—*Counting the cars on the New Jersey Turnpike*....

Proem Verse: When God showed Moses the first Torah it was written in white fire and black fire (*Tanhuma*, *Bereshit* 1).

When I got to the Greyhound bus station it was a working-class melodrama in action. A teenage boy fought with the bus officials over a ticket that had been wired to him. He looked tired and exasperated. I fantasized a runaway getting a ticket home—it could have been anything. The video machine cycled an endless musical riff that sounded like half the chord changes in "*So You Want to Be a Rock 'n' Roll Star.*" The paint was ten or fifteen years past faded. A woman came in with a boyfriend with a black eye. The boyfriend had the black eye. They tried to cash in a money order to buy a one-way ticket for her to North Carolina. Neither looked happy. It was too late in the day to buy the ticket. The money order was the wrong kind of money order. The agent expressed lots of regrets. I felt my own regrets. The scene felt tragic. It went on and on; the bus was almost fifteen minutes late. There were a dozen stories in the desolate desert city.

The ride from Palm Springs to Riverside was uneventful. I was halfway home. The first half of my journey I rode with an Hispanic man who sweated all over me, sleeping in his red tank top. I worked hard to seem relaxed. At Riverside, *down by the riverside*, I changed my seat. I went for room to spread out. It was to no avail; the bus refilled. A guy came on wearing major muscles and tattoos. He asked if the seat next to me was open. I bade him welcome. He sat and said, "I drove for forty minutes at eighty-five miles a hour to make the bus in time." I told him to take a couple of deep breaths and relax. He did it. I used my airplane manners and asked him what he did. He said he was a welder. I loved it. I saw the mask—the torch—the sparks. I was ten years old watching the welder. I was in love. It was all heat and light and adventure. I was an auto-age boy watching Walt Whitman's modern smith. Paul, the welder, showed off his strong and sinewy arms, tattoos to boot. He reached into his pouch and showed me pictures of his welding. It was nautical work, fixing old ships and making them whole again. Then he paused and confessed, "I've just been in jail for three months, and now I am headed home." I told him once more to take a couple of deep breaths and then relax. He did. At that moment the two of us welded a bond.

When I was a boy my mother read to me from Robert Louis Stevenson's *A Child's Garden of Verses*. My favorite poem was *The Lamplight*.

> MY TEA IS NEARLY READY AND THE SUN HAS LEFT THE SKY;
> IT'S TIME TO TAKE THE WINDOW AND TO SEE LEERIE GOING BY;
> FOR EVERY NIGHT AT TEA TIME AND BEFORE YOU TAKE YOUR SEAT,
> WITH LANTERN AND WITH LADDER HE COMES POSTING UP THE STREET.
>
> NOW TOM WOULD BE A DRIVER AND MARIA GO TO SEA,
> AND MY PAPA'S A BANKER AND RICH AS HE CAN BE;
> BUT, I, WHEN I AM STRONGER AND CAN CHOOSE WHAT I'M TO DO,
> O LEERIE, I'LL GO ROUND AT NIGHT AND LIGHT THE LAMPS WITH YOU!
>
> FOR WE ARE VERY LUCKY, WITH A LAMP BEFORE THE DOOR,
> AND LEERIE STOPS TO LIGHT IT AS HE LIGHTS SO MANY MORE;
> AND O! BEFORE YOU HURRY BY WITH LADDER AND WITH LIGHT,
> O LEERIE, SEE A LITTLE CHILD AND NOD TO HIM TO-NIGHT!

I loved that poem. Since I was five or six I've wanted to be a lamp-lighter. When I was sixteen I tried to turn it into a rock tune; at that I failed. I still liked my new chorus line: "*Lamplighters can't really light the world—but then they do.*" The poem has stayed with me. I am the same middle-class boy looking out the window and coveting a working-class gig. I love the heat and light and adventure. Part of me is deeply envious of the welder.

At that moment I had an instant understanding. It was a spark of epiphany. For women it is weaving. In their literature they talk about weaving and embroidery as a spiritual process. They are both acts of actual meditation and metaphors for the spiritual process. I talked to Paul, shared my boyhood dreams of welding. I realized that all men are welders. Welding is our metaphor. Welding is our meditation.

I realized that a welder was James Cagney in *White Heat*—sitting on the explosion, **"Top of the world, Ma."** A welder has compressed fire in his tanks and has the skill to let it out in one steady stream—a rage of sparks rather than an inferno. I realized that the Rocketeer and his father Rocket Man were nothing more than flying welders, tanks on their backs, flying to their dreams, fire shooting out of their tushes in a steady stream, a mask to shield their empathy. Moses, too, is a welder, the sensitivity of his caring hidden behind the veil—the visual image of power—welding his molten words into stone and hearts. Welding is making the abstract—plastic. And welding takes fire, heat, and a mask.

Paul and I talked shoulder to shoulder. We did politics and personal drug tales. I had smoked a little pot and taken a few pills to finish papers and then quit because I didn't like the writing I had done. He said, **"One day I realized that there was this needle in my arm, and that wasn't me."** We were welded and welding.

He was the ex-con, I was the Sunday school teacher, professor—two men on a Greyhound bus. The conversation was easy. After we finished with rap music, the wilderness, his childhood dream of playing an accordion, and my hatred of "Lady of Spain," we got to Bush, the recession, and homelessness. I told downtown L.A. stories about how desperate the spare change seekers had gotten.

He then said, **"A few years ago I was living with my sister-in-law in an apartment in New Mexico. Actually, it was a shack that a strong wind** could blow down. But I used to go to this food pantry and get stuff, really it was just sandwich stuff, but we used to go out feeding the homeless." Then there was a spark of realization. He said, "You know, I volunteer a lot. When Mt. Penatubo exploded I spent a week helping out at an Air Force camp—helping to take care of the children while the mothers got their lives together. And I flew back from Mexico to help out after the big earthquake in the Bay Area." There were other relief stories—two or three others—and then he added, "And in prison I ran a welding shop and spent my time teaching others a trade other than drugs." It was as if he had just learned something about himself.

I smiled inside and calmly said, "That's who you are." He nodded. My friend Danny Siegel has a poem that says, "You should always treat the man sitting next to you on the subway as if he could be the messiah." I was sitting next to a *lammed-vavnik* in recovery. He really was a strong and sinewy man.

We shook hands as the bus pulled into the L.A. terminal. I had left my annual Egypt adventure behind. Matzah was over, I was on my way to a doughnut. He was done with jail, heading back to a new life—boat building in the Pacific Northwest. We had shared a one-hour Greyhound road story. That night my dream was filled with sparks—black fire on white fire. It was spiritual white heat. We saw each other briefly one more time; I was leaving the men's room and he was entering. We nodded and smiled. There was nothing more to say.

Epilogue: How much of what I was told actually happened, I'll never know. Even his face is lost in the obscurity of too many thoughts and meetings that followed. This much I do know—all of it was true. Even if it could never be verified as part of any résumé or character report, it was soul truth, mythic truth, the true expression of who he hoped he could be and therefore had the potential to become. It was an L.A. story, night in the Naked City of Angels.

O Leerie I go round at night and light the world with you.

10
The Miracle of Loneliness

It may reveal a lot about my own working that only here did I drop the pretense of the midrashic form and just tell a story. Maybe form means everything. Maybe nothing. Maybe it is just a story that feelings can carry without the need for any Midat ha-Din.

Raph (pronounced Raaa-f not Ray-f) Lieb has a hunger. He is obsessed with God. Haunted by God. Actually, or more clearly, he is obsessed with not-God. He is on a spiritual quest to discover why he doesn't believe. He is looking for proof that non-belief is okay. In other words, Raph has no God-answers, only God-questions. In other words, he is a perfect, enlightened sixteenish-year-old—doing just what he is supposed to do. Reading, thinking, doing theater, and arguing about all life's great questions—God, beauty, meaning, and finding a girlfriend. He is one of those rare opportunities in life. I am privileged to do a lot of learning because I am his teacher.

Yesterday I was sitting in his family's all-black (stealth) swimming pool, and after his father asked me the correct *brakhah* for planting a new grapevine, Raph again asked me (in the twentieth or fiftieth way) if I believe in God (and why). I started to run the "cart" of my God belief answer when suddenly a new one flashed. I started out:

"I don't know if I believe in God or not, but I believe in believing in God. In other words (like Kurt Vonnegut, who says in *Cat's Cradle*, "A perfectly useful religion can be built out of lies"), acting as if there is a God makes you a better person; talking to God (as if someONE is listening) leads to self-revelation." I was being rational, pragmatic, suggesting that at least the illusion of faith has advantages. It was sort of an Ogilvy (the advertising guy) spirituality: "Reason Why—theology!" I suppose it was Joshua Loth Liedman (*Peace of Mind*) does Jewish Norman Vincent Peale (*The Power of Positive Thinking*).

Then I said to Raph, "But there is another side to my God belief. While I can't think my way to God, sometimes I feel that God is there." He asked for an example, and I retold the story of the Palm Springs Phantom Welder Ex-con Recovery Mensch, which was the core of the previous proem, *Weld*. Then the lightning hit. As we were leaning on the edge of the cold hot tub, both of us shivering as the sun was in its last minutes, I had a new answer.

I said, "The other reason I know there is a God is loneliness. It is loneliness that drives the *Midat ha-Din* to risk losing control, risk being absolute, and making itself vulnerable enough to connect to someone. It is loneliness that teaches the *Midat ha-Ra*h*amin* to let loved ones go, take risks, be free, in order to retain them. It is loneliness that teaches people that winning arguments isn't always finding happiness. It is loneliness that makes the growth and compromise necessary for relationship, family, and community.

"Loneliness proves that there is a soul. It is loneliness that takes us past being an animal. It is loneliness that teaches us that real hunger can never be satisfied by eating, or having, or owning, or dominating, but only by sharing. It is loneliness that teaches people delayed gratification—and spiritual truth and ethical living are all rooted in delay.

"It is the feeling of being alone that teaches us that we need not be alone. The steps involved in being with others in a permanent, on-going, satisfying way teach meaning, not gratification; commitment to struggle, not being right; the need for balance, not monolithic truth. Suddenly I knew that when I feel alone, I know that there is God. Loneliness is the 60-cycle hum of the human soul being plugged in, but not yet in motion."

Then, in a flash, I had one more image: When Adam and Eve ate the fruit of the Tree of the Knowledge of Good and Evil, the Tree that was also in the middle of the Garden, the Tree of Life, the force that changed them, that told them that they were naked, that forever changed humanity, that was the retrovirus of loneliness. For it is loneliness that always motivates first the search and then the finding.

We got out of the pool, changed, then went on to other things. Later Raph said to me, "I now know why I told one of my three best friends that I loved her—loneliness." I didn't say anything. I nodded. I probably didn't say enough. Because I, still lost in the power of my truth, wasn't ready for anyone else's deep insight yet. I did nod. I did affirm. But I probably didn't do enough. Later that night, alone, replaying the day, it was his comment that was the deepest truth, much more than mine. For me, other people's words often have to boil in my gut for a while before I can absorb their full power and meaning. When Raph, who kept on wishing we had tape-recorded our conversation, reads this, I hope the depth of my affirmation and confirmation of his feelings and faith will be felt. At least he knows what the word "grok" means. He is one of those who reads.

Now, every time I feel lonely, I know that God is there. I didn't know the "right" *brakhah* for planting a grapevine, so I suggested (with clear uncertainty) *she-he-he-yanu*. I wonder if that works for loneliness, too.

11

The Zohar of the Wave— The Zohar of the Particle
Dancing Toward a Quantum Theology

Pre-Text 1: Physics is not religion. If it were, we'd have a much easier time raising money. (Leon Lederman with Dick Teresi, *The God Particle: If the Universe is the Answer, What is the Question.* New York: Houghton Mifflin, 1993, p. 198.)

Pre-Text 2: A FRAGMENT OF DIALOGUE FROM TOM STOP-PARD'S *HAPGOOD:*

KERNER: Every atom is a cathedral. I cannot stand the pictures of atoms they put in school books, like a little solar system. Bohr's atom. Forget it. You can't make a picture of what Bohr proposed, an electron does not go round like a planet, it is like a moth which was there a moment ago, it gains or loses a quantum of energy and it jumps, and at the moment of the quantum jump it is like two moths, one to be here and one to stop being there; an election is like twins, each one unique, a unique twin.

HAPGOOD: Its own alibi.

KERNER: Look at the edge of a shadow. It is straight like the edge of the wall that makes it. Your Isaac Newton saw this and he concluded that light was made of little particles. Other people said light is a wave but Isaac Newton said, no, if light was a wave the shadow would bend round the wall like water bends round a stone in the river. Now we will do an experiment together.

In this experiment you have a machine gun which shoots particles…which we call…bullets. You are shooting at a screen and I have put a wall of armor plate, so of course none of the bullets get through. Now I open two slits in the armor plate. (*He gestures to indicate the two slits a few inches apart.*) Now you shoot many times. Now you stop shooting and examine the screen and naturally it has bullet holes where some of the bullets came through the two slits. Opposite each slit there is a concentration of bullet holes, and maybe just a few holes to the left and right from ricochets. This is called particle pattern. If your gun was a torch and light was bullets, as Isaac Newton said, this is what you will get.

But when you do it you don't get it. You don't get particle pattern. You get wave pattern. Wave pattern is like stripes—bright, dim, bright, dim across the screen. This is because when a wave is pushed through a little gap it spreads out in a semi-circle, so when you have *two* gaps you have two semi-circles spreading out together. and on their way to the screen they mix together…where a crest from one lot of waves meets a crest from the other lot of waves you get a specially *big* wave, and where a crest meets a dip, the wave is cancelled out—strong, weak, strong, weak, on the screen it looks like waves. …

So now light was waves, Isaac Newton was wrong about the bullets. But when light was waves there came a problem with a thing called the photo-electric effect, a real puzzle, which I will describe in detail with historical footnotes… But this puzzle was a puzzle because everyone knew that light was waves. Einstein solved it. Or rather, he showed that if light was bullets after all, there was no puzzle. But, how to explain the stripes on the screen, the wave pattern. Wave patterns happen when light from the two slits mixes together but your particles can't do that—your bullet of light has already hit the screen before the next bullet is even fired. So there is only one solution.

What is that?

Each bullet goes through both slits.

That is silly.

Now we come to the exciting part. We will watch the bullets of light to see which way they go. This is not difficult, the apparatus is simple. So we look carefully and we see the bullets one at a time, and some hit the armor plate and bounce back, and some go through one slit, and some through the other, and of course, none go through both slits.

I knew that.

You knew that. Now we come to my favorite bit. The wave pattern has disappeared! It has become particle, just like with real machine-gun bullets.

Why?

Because we looked. So, we do it again, exactly the same except now without looking to see which way the bullets go; and the wave pattern comes back. So we try again while looking, and we get particle pattern. Every time we don't look we get wave pattern. Every time we look to see how we get wave pattern, we get particle pattern. The act of observing determines the reality.

How?

Nobody knows. Einstein didn't know. I don't know. There is no explanation in classical physics. Somehow light is particle and wave. The experimenter makes the choice. (Tom Stoppard, *Hapgood*. London: Faber and Faber Limited, 1988, pp. 10–12.)

Mashal L'Ishah B'Tzelem Elohím: A Parable about a woman who is the image of God: Imagine a woman who is a skilled tightrope walker. That isn't hard; most of us cross various tightropes every day. Imagine that this woman has a particular problem—crossing the wire while carrying two buckets filled to the brim with water. That is harder, and in a sense, that is more the way our lives often feel. But for our mothers, crossing the tightrope—even carrying two buckets of water—is no problem. They always do it with grace.

Our fathers can do the trick, too, but when that kind of work needs to be done (except on weekends), they always seem to be away at work. But the truth is, this parable can work just as well with a father as the star. The deeper truth is that right now I'm just thinking more about my mother—even if this is a "men's book." But honestly, the gender of the parable is no big deal. Maybe that is why even my mother makes that point.

This is what I know. When we walk the tightrope, our mother often rides in one bucket; our father rides in the other. Other times when I walk my walk, my mother supports one of my buckets while my father carries most of the weight of the other.

However, the main problem for the woman in our parable isn't crossing the rope, but figuring out how to see to it that her grandchildren's grandchildren's grandchildren will still be able to perform the feat—because this feat is no mean feat; it is a matter of life and death. The sad truth is that the only available source of water is across the gorge, across the wire. Life requires balancing two buckets.

Commentary: I am teaching a lesson we have often used in this book to my juniors and seniors. It goes like this: in the first chapter of Genesis we have a long shot. God, who goes by the name *Elohim*, is nowhere to be seen. God works over the P.A. system. We hear The VOICE, we see the results, but God is off-camera. In the second chapter of Genesis we move in for a close-up. We are going to see the same story (more or less), but this time we are going "up close and personal." This time God's name is hyphenated, God (Who may have gotten married) is now *Adonai— Elohim*. This God is hands-on, shaping humans with hands, blowing breath in their mouths, and going for long walks.

I try to explain that many modern Bible readers say it is just "two stories," "two different people" writing about their experiences of God. But for Rashi it is a big deal. His belief that the Torah all came from God means that he needs One God to have dictated the whole thing to Moses in forty days. For him, two conflicting stories is a huge problem. He solves it by using the "blind men feeling an elephant" trick—stating the formula we have studied. *ADONAI* conjures the *Midat ha-Raḥamin*, *ELOHIM* evokes the *Midat ha-Din*. One God—two aspects. We go back and forth on this a while.

Interpreting the same text more than one way is confusing to them. I make it more confusing by trying to create a "c," which is the place that understandings "a" and "b" meet. In the resultant chaos of no-comprehension I start to dance around the room and try to embody three different interpretations all at once. Out of synch with where I was, but at the perfect place in the lesson, Justina Nemoy said, "**It is sort of like parallel universes.**" It took awhile for me to hear, a while longer for me to understand, but she was on to something. The *Elohim* of Creation and the *Adonai* of Creation are indeed like parallel universes.

A Review: In the course of this book we have learned that God seems to have at least two sides: the *Adonai* experience and the *Elohim* experience. (Two buckets, get it?) *Elohim* is connected to law and order. *Elohim* is transcendent. *Elohim* is equally in all places for all people. *Elohim* is big on boundaries, limits, hierarchies—a place for everything and everything in its place. *Elohim* is a King. *Elohim* is indeed the *Midat ha-Din*. *Elohim* is probably German.

Adonai is God with a womb. *Adonai* is the "up-close-and-personal God." The God who is "in your heart" and who shares your pain. *Adonai* is immanent. *Adonai* is God who has favorites—even if everyone, each in his or her own way, is a favorite. *Adonai* is God Who is a parent (and, to my way of thinking, The Mother). *Adonai* is the essence of *Midat ha-Rahamin*.

Most men are deep into the *Midat ha-Din*. Most women center themselves in the *Midat ha-Rahamin*. As a category, "man" is all about rules, status, freedom, and boundaries. As a category, "woman" is rooted in intimacy, shared experience, and connection.

Human intimacy and Divine imminence are two different levels of the same experience—both connected to the *Midat ha-Rahamin*. Human freedom and Divine transcendence are also two layers of the same experiential vector—leading to and from the *Midat ha-Din*. What we experience in our interpersonal life as the duality of male and female we experience in our spiritual life as the duality of *Elohim* and *Adonai*.

Davar Aher: Another tack: In this proem Albert Einstein is going to be one of our teachers. With him we will explore the Torah of light, and through it—the light of Torah. To do that we need to skim the surface of quantum mechanics. Quantum mechanics is the thing that really freaked Einstein out—it destroyed his sense of order. We are interested in his "freakout." We will learn from it. Therefore, we need to learn just a little about quantum mechanics.

Quantum mechanics is not the fellows who repair automobiles in Mr. Quantum's garage. Quantum mechanics is a branch of physics. A "quantum" is a quantity of something, a specific amount. "Mechanics" is the study of motion. Therefore, "quantum mechanics" is the study of the motion of quantities. Quantum theory says that nature comes in bits and

pieces (quanta), and quantum mechanics is the study of this phenomenon. Quantum mechanics does not replace Newtonian physics; Newtonian physics is still applicable to the large-scale world, but it does not work in the subatomic realm. Quantum mechanics resulted from the study of the subatomic realm, the invisible universe underlying, embedded in, and forming the fabric of everything about us. (Gary Zukav, *The Dancing Wu Li Masters.* New York: Bantam, 1980, pp. 18-19.)

Here is Einstein's central problem with quantum mechanics: light sometimes acts like a wave. Light sometimes acts like a particle. Light sometimes seems to have a spectrum. Light sometimes seems to come in quanta. The big *kuntz*[18] in the cosmic plan, is that when you do an experiment to prove light is a wave, it acts like a particle. When you do an experiment to prove that light is a particle, it turns into a wave. It is always the one you don't want. **The act of observing determines the reality. *How?* Nobody knows. Einstein didn't know. I don't know. There is no explanation in classical physics. Somehow light is particle and wave. The experimenter makes the choice.** (Tom Stoppard, *Hapgood.* London: Faber and Faber Limited, 1988, pp. 10-12.)

Commentary: Albert Einstein once said: "**For the rest of my life I will reflect on what light is!**" I feel exactly the same way. However, old Albert and I were and were not talking about the same light. The message of this chapter is simple. It is also impossible to grasp fully. (What else would you expect—especially for the end of this book?) In the simplest possible terms, that message is: "**Every truth and its opposite are equally true and unequally false.**" In this collage of dancing irreconcilable opposites, the light and the shadow of The CREATOR are slowly revealed.

Our Torah Text: Consider Einstein more than one man. Consider him an archetype. Both the man and the archetype are always screaming for order in creation. Our Einstein piece is always demanding a "unified field theory." He wants a clear sense of purpose (even if he has to be relative). He is the fulfillment of the enlightenment and the industrial revolution—and so our Einstein voice declares, in his words, "**God doesn't play dice with the universe**" as it says (Genesis 1.1) "IN THE BEGINNING, GOD CREATED...."

---

[18]Hebrew, Yiddish, Jewish camp slang for a prank.

Our Proem Text: The part of our inner voice that opposes and debates our inner Einstein in this proem is performed by Rabbi Nachman of Bratslav. That voice sees the world as not quite random chaos. Rabbi Nachman teaches, **"The world is a spinning die."** With it he anticipates Bruce J. Friedman's play, "Steambath." In our cut-and-paste virtual theology, Nachman's God turns to Einstein, as to a Puerto Rican steambath attendant, and says, **"Pick a card, any card!"**

Commentary: Einstein is the perfect symbol of the moderne. He is the godfather of the atom bomb, the king of relativity, the archetype of genius. He is, despite the warp in some of his time-space distortions, the very model of the modern, rational, scientific man. Just think Sam Jaffe in *The Day the Earth Stood Still* and you've got the Einstein archetype. (Even given the pop mysticism "*Gort Varada Klatu Nictos*.")

On the other hand, think Sam Jaffe in *Lost Horizons* and you begin to understand Reb Nachman of Bratzlav—the manic-depressive Hassidic myth maker. Nachman was the one Jewish storyteller whose Torah edged unabashedly into the mythic. Consider this proem a contrasting study of Sam Jaffe as wave and Sam Jaffe as particle. Whereas Einstein said, **"God doesn't play dice,"** Nachman teaches, **"God's creation is dice—reality spins like a dreidle."** Listen to more of his rap:

Our Proem Text: Almost complete: **The world is a spinning die.** Life is like flipping a coin. Tom Stoppard in *Rozencrantz and Guildenstern are Dead* has already taught us that sometimes flipping a coin is a random truth; sometimes it is uncertainly predictable. **The world is like a dreidle: everything is a cycle.** We know from cycles: life cycles, year cycles, wash cycles, etc. When we think of cycles we usually think pattern and predictability. When Nachman thinks cycles he is playing roulette. He is spinning the dice. He knows that everything has two sides— its basic nature and its opposite. That is why he says: **"People become angels. Angels become people."** He could as easily have said, "Sometimes a man's got to do what a woman's got to do. Sometimes a woman needs to stand by her inner man." And amazingly, he could have taught, "And all the time, all of us are sometimes Godlike." That gives you pause to feel! Pause to think, too! **Head becomes foot. Foot becomes head.** Rapport talk becomes report talk. Micro and macro do-si-do. *Halakhah* melts into *aggadah*. Frozen *midrash* becomes law. **Everything goes into cycles. Especially spin cycles. It revolves. It alternates. All things interchange—one from another, one to another—lifting up the low, setting down the lofty.** That sounds like total chaos. Then Nachman says: "**All things have one root.**" So far we have learned life always has two sides (both Sam Jaffes) and life has one common origin. That makes perfectly no sense. It is the truth of saying men tend to do this and women tend to do that, and all of this is in imitation of the same image of God. This chapter is all about learning how to make that kind of no sense. It is about taking chaos' order: "Sir, which particle do you wish to wave?"

This is why we play with a dreidle on Hanukkah. For Nachman, dreidles are going to teach us about God! So let's think dreidle. **Hanukkah explains the deep meaning of the Temple. The Temple (in Jerusalem) is like a dreidle. It is a tumbling die.** The Temple, too, is two truths in one. **The Temple is the embodiment of what should be above** (the *Midat ha-Din* God) **being below** (acting like the *Midat ha-Rahamin* God), **of what should be below being raised up.**

God, who should be in the heavens, who should be a male, transcendent, thunder-making Sky God, a God of War Drums, **dwells in the Temple, below,** as an intimate, immanent Neighbor, as our Mother. In other words, God in a heartbeat.

And vice versa. Sometimes we find that the breasts that nurtured us, the breasts we were comforted by when in our tears, belong to an all-powerful Warrior God.

The pattern of the Temple, as we have learned before at Beztalel's Bar Mitzvah,[19] **is replicated in the structure of the heavens**[20] because the Temple is really a spiritual planetarium.

---

[19] See Fragment B, *Coming of Mitzvah*.

[20] It is a well-known Jewish perception that the language used to create and establish the Tabernacle is a direct echo of the language of the creation of the world. Extrapolated from this insight is that the Cosmos and the Temple are reciprocal macro- and micro-cosmos. The best simple place to find this clearly explicated is in Nehama Leibowitz's *Studies in Shemot* (WZO, 1976, pp. 471ff). Here Nachman's reversal of the image is an ironic expression of his central message.

Nachman's own students footnote the following texts as deeper explanations of this idea: *Tanhuma, Pekudei, I*, and *Zohar* 1:80b.

This is an example of something that should be below being raised to a higher level. And the deeper spiritual truth is that we are like the Temple, too. We have our own holy of holies. We have our own ark and our own eternal light. We have our own veils and curtains and set-aside areas and more. We make our own sacrifices and smell their sweet savor. And, like the Temple, in each of us the need for both freedom and intimacy topples like a spinning coin. In our Temple, too, we constantly spin and whirl our senses of immanence and transcendence—of Albert E. and MC Nachman. **The Temple is therefore like a dreidle, like a tumbling die, where everything revolves and everything is reversed.** So Albert, throw those dice because the **Temple refutes logic**—it is both wave and particle. But that is just a building.God is even more so. **God is above every concept.** Break it down! **God is *transcendent*. There is no logic that limits God.** That is where science, rationalism, modernity fall apart. **God is beyond all boundaries.** God is primal, primitive, post-modern, post-rational. To talk of God experiences, we need to get mythic. **It is impossible, illogical to believe that God could limit God enough to fit into the vessels in the Temple.** A myth is like a vessel. In fact, a myth is a vessel. A myth is nothing more than a truth frozen in a story. To talk of God, even though it is incomplete, we need to capture God's light—the way the Chelmites did in the dark surface of a tub of water—in the sacred water of our stories. God's captured image fills the two buckets the woman carries across the tightrope.

Break it down! **But God is also *immanent* in the Temple.** When we get up close and personal, light can be a wave. When we get up close and personal, light can be a particle. When we step back, the dislogic of our experiences becomes clear. The same is true of our God experiences. God can be *AVINU* and *MALKEINU*—Parent and Ruler, Mother and Judge. **This is impossible, but this is also true. God's reality destroys all philosophic logic. Such logic is crushed by the dreidle, the spinning wheel that brings the transcendent immanent and the immanent transcendent.** So, Albert, pick a card, any card. *Rabbi Naḥman of Bretslav, Sichot ha-Ran, 40.*[21]

Davar Aher: Another parallel universe: Martin Buber

begins an explanation of the world this way: To man the world is twofold,

---

[21] This is a very loose, not precisely literal, translation by your author, which extrapolates the actual wording to clarify meaning and connect some of the language to parallel terms we have come to invest with meaning. It is not a very "precise" rendering. I do believe it is a very "truthful" one.

in accordance with his twofold attitude. (His version of two buckets). **The attitude of man is twofold** (wave and particle), **in accordance with the twofold nature of the primary words he speaks.** He says people can have only one of two relationships with the world. **The one primary word is the combination I–Thou. The other primary word is the combination I–It;** Buber, too, divides reality into two halves. He calls them I–Thou and I–It. I–Thou is a reality of meaning, of connecting to those things that are eternal, that connect to the spirit. Buber, however, makes a big deal out of teaching that I–Thou isn't only person-to-person. He writes a whole big thing about how he used to do I–Thou with the tree across the street. Buber says "tree," and I think of Margo and her tree. He says I–Thou, is not a druid thing. It is not a pantheist thing. It is what Reb Nachman would call being in touch with the Creator. Years ago, two or three realities ago, one of my students, Margo Louis, once studied Martin Buber's tree thing with me under a tree at camp. She obsessed on it. She went crazy with it. She talked about her tree for a long time. Twenty years later we still kid about Margo's tree. She taught me the power of the I–Thou idea. I–It is his *sitre aharah*, his other side. It is all about relating to objects. Treating trees as objects and treating people as objects is I–It. A lot of people have taught me the power of that perception.

Commentary: I–It doesn't equal male conquest. I–Thou doesn't equal female connectedness. I–It is not patriarchal. I–Thou is not sisterhood. I–It is not all bad. I–Thou is not all good. Think of the cosmos of human experience as being a pie. We always need to yang-yin the pie. Our experience is always two sides of the pie. It is male and female. Light and shadow. Moses and Aaron. Wave and particle. *Din* and *Rahamin*. Immanent and transcendent. Intimate and free. Connected and commanded. Free and predetermined. Predictable and chaotic. *Adonai* and *Elohim*. Laurel and Hardy. Any dichotomy, every dichotomy. The big mistake is assuming that any two halves are ever the same. That is the dance of the electron. The truth of the quanta. Sometimes there is overlap, sometimes there is congruence. The only truth I know is that evil comes when we forget the balance.

Davar Aher: Another aspect: Remember *Tikkun Olam*? Remember the Lurianic creation myth? Our world is divided between spark

and shell. This is probably where Martin Buber learned his Torah of the *I–Thou* (spark) and the *I–It* (shell). The bottom line is the same. The more sparks you gather, the more of God's light you have. The more *I–Thou* relationships you have, the more you know of the Eternal, Ultimate, Divine, First and Last, and Only Thou. The more light, the closer we get to redemption. What is evil? When we treat "shell" as "spark." What is evil? When we do "*It*" in the name of "*Thou*."

Now here is my big question: is spark the same thing as wave? Is shell the same thing as particle? I just don't know. But what I do know is that the mysticism of light applies to Torah. When we try to make a mitzvah all connection, all Thou, we often turn into the *tzis-tzis* police and make it an "it." (That is forbidding the boys from wearing baseball caps in services and not celebrating the glee in Kent's national magic trick with a *kippah*.) When we lean too hard on the form, on the rules, on the shell of mitzvot, we often drive people into other realms of the thou. (That is Michel asking, "Who made up these rules anyway—and why should I do it if I don't feel it?" It is also Jesse's father[22] rallying against pain caused by the circumcision of his son. In passing on Torah, in trying to check and measure and assure Torah, it usually becomes just the opposite. I also know that the physics of Reb Nachman works for light. Wave becomes particle and particle becomes wave. Predictable becomes unknowable. Unknowable becomes truth. Why? I can think of only one thing: The Creator.

Davar Aher: Another parallel universe: In many ways, good and bad, Joseph Campbell is the godfather of this book. (Though Jung and Otto Rank, and even Frazier sit somewhere in his background.) Bly and Hillman and the other mythopoetic guys who set my resting body in this motion were in turn set in motion by his work. Campbell suggests that there are men's religions and women's religions. In a lot of ways, it all comes down to penis and womb. Women's religions are centered in the moon. They are of the universe of the cycle. They are always dying and rising. Growth and rebirth are at their center. Men's religions have to do with change. They are vectors through history—straight lines. Men's religion, starting with Marduk, starting with the Axe Cultures, is all about heroes. It is all about owning, con-

---

[22] You will meet him in the commentary to "*Cut From the Team*" in the Geniza.

quering, changing. Is Judaism about circles or lines? The answer is yes. It is *Adonai* and *Elohim*. It is *Rosh Hodesh* and Redemption. **Among the hunting tribes** (think Abel, Ishmael, and Esau) **whose life style is based on the art of killing, who live in a world of animals that kill and are killed and hardly know the organic experience of a natural death, all death is a consequence of violence and is generally ascribed…to magic** (something a man actively does that determines his fate and the fate of others). **For the planting folk of the fertile steppes and tropical jungles** (think Cain, and Jacob, and Boaz), **death is a natural phase of life, comparable to the moment of the planting, for rebirth** (in other words, death, just like shit, happens). (Joseph Campbell, *The Masks of God: Primitive Mythology.* New York: Viking Press, 1959, pp. 125–27).

But Judaism, which does have its moments of magic and its mandalas of rebirth, does a third thing. It talks about shepherds. Are shepherds men or women? Yes. Do shepherds connect like hunters to the sky or farmers to the earth? Yes. Do I know the deep meaning of a religion whose major metaphors grow not from the land, not from the hunt, but from the wave–particle-like task of constantly trying to confine sheep on a field without boundaries? No. I only know that shepherding is a cyclic task in which one must constantly move and balance. I only know that shepherding is very mystical. I only know that shepherding is all about light. I know that shepherding is like moving a whole host of inside feelings and urges in the same direction—balancing *Midat ha-Din, Midat ha-Rahamin, Yetzer ha-Ra, Yetzer ha-Tov* (and your sense of humor). Einstein was a shepherd. So was Reb Nachman.

Davar Aher: Now for something completely different: A STORY.

Scott was seventeen, a basketball player, taking my post-confirmation class because he wasn't protesting his parent's demand that he do so, destined to go to junior college. Sweet kid. Thinking kid. Not a book kid. (There is a difference.) Most of the girls also thought he was profoundly cool. One day, when I was trying to teach something complicated out of the Talmud, Scott interrupted me and asked the same question Raph Leib would later ask me: **"Do you believe in God?"**

I gave Scott my standing response, compact and too cute, **"It depends on what time it is,"** and looked at my watch. He looked totally perplexed.

So I said, **"It's like the blind men and the elephant."** That, too, was cryptic, so I retold the story. **"Three blind men feel an elephant. They say in turn, "An elephant is like a roof." "An elephant is like a tree." "An elephant is like a rope."**

Scott asked, "So what does that have to do with believing in God?"

I explained, **"When it comes to God, we are all like blind men feeling an elephant. Sometimes God is immanent enough for me to know God is there. Sometimes God feels so transcendent that I think of God as only a good idea."** He looked puzzled, and it was clear that I had two problems. One, he had no idea what immanent or transcendent meant; and two, he had no idea how my God belief could be ambivalent. I tried out this explanation:

Joel:**"How do you feel about your mother?"** Scott: **"I love her."** Joel: **"How else do you feel about your mother?"** Scott looked around. He checked the room for bugs. He checked the room to see if it was safe. Then he said, **"Sometimes I want to kill my mother."** Joel: **"One mother, two feelings—get it? That is how I feel about God. I've just learned that my feelings about God are more important than my ideas."**

We talked about that for awhile and then moved on to the immanence–transcendence thing. Again I used Scott. **"Scott, how would you feel if your mother was in the back seat every time you went out on a date?"** With less then a millisecond's hesitation he said, **"I would never go out on a date again."** I said: **"That's immanence,"** and I gave a further explanation. Then I said, **"How would you feel if your mother was gone, nothing more than memory?"** He said, **"I don't know how I would go on."** Then he said, **"Transcendence, right?"** I nodded. The class discussion went on.

Eventually Josh asked, **"Where do you think evil came from?"** I went back to Scott to explain my answer. **"Scott, where does the feeling 'I love my mother' come from?"** He thought for a moment and asked, **"From God?"** I don't know if he really believed that answer or had psyched out the answer I wanted. I didn't care. I let my pedagogic trap swing shut. I asked, **"And where do you think the feeling 'Sometimes I want to kill my mother' comes from?"** There was silence. I was proud. I said, **"I think that feeling comes from God, too."** We went on to redo the **"Yetzer ha-**

Ra can be VERY GOOD" lesson. I ended it in a very Freudian way, explaining, "**If you didn't love your mother, you'd be a feral child, a wild child raised by the wolves. If you didn't sometimes want to kill your mother, you'd wind up never leaving home, never growing up. We need both feelings. We need them at the right times and in the right balance.**"

Commentary: I have retold this story and this dialogue often. In many ways it has become the cornerstone of my gender work, because it reveals a very deep problem. That problem is polytheistic psychology. Simply put, polytheistic psychology (something Jung creates and James Hillman talks about a lot) is the understanding that our psyche is made up of a lot of conflicting voices. As Bly often says, "**There is a platoon in there.**" So why is that a problem? Simple. It is a macro–micro thing. We tend to want that which is inside of us to be the same as that which is outside of us. (We wanted the atom to look like the solar system.) That is why all god systems look a lot alike.

Imagine a bunch of plastic collectible god sets with a fancy shelf you could put them on. (Maybe they would be sold by the Franklin Mint on a monthly basis.) They certainly would have lots of little labels. On one shelf the Greco-Roman gods, on another shelf the Norse gods, on another the Ten Spherot of the Kabbalistic Tree of Life, on another all the angels in that heavenly pantheon. If you look closely, the shelves all line up, more or less. We can line the gods up by column. Each shelf has a *Malkhut*—a patriarchal Thunder God, an Ultimate King. Each shelf has its Athena (in the Jewish tradition we call her <u>H</u>okhmah, wisdom). Human nature works that way. If we hear a voice, we think it is connected to an outside pull. It is a tidal thing. That is why people's reaction is always to create gods. God may be more rational, but gods feels truer. All of us feel eight to ten (or so) of these voices.

So what does a monotheist do with those feelings? We play the "three blind men and the elephant" game—we create a lot of parallel universes. Except for the Bible, Jewish thought has always been busy breaking God into attributes and experiences, making God mythic. But as we have learned from *Adonai* and *Elohim*, priest and prophet, Moses and Aaron, the Torah may have tried to purge the mythic, but it always kept on growing back.

Rational Judaism, modern Judaism, scientific Judaism wanted to believe in monotheistic psychology (that the central personality could control not only the actions of the other voices, but their feelings as well). That Judaism, the Judaism of logical positivism, the Judaism of everything is getting better and better every day, the Judaism of progress, wanted to make God an idea—or at least a lot like an idea. It wanted evil to be the absence of good. It wanted, ultimately, to understand Hilter as a sad victim of abuse. It wanted to believe that not dating a non–Jew prevented trichinosis. This was the thought pattern (if not the lifestyle) that held that men and women were the same. But we know better. We now live in an era in which everyone wears sneakers, jeans, and T-shirts. We've run the grand experiments in which Lucy and Desi trade jobs for the day. We know that ideas and feelings are not always the same. We've changed our models of gender along with our models of the atom. We are now dealing with the uncertainty of quantum theology—the study of the motion of qualities. While this work has dealt with issues of maleness, it really has been a study in "post-rationalism." (I think post-rationalism is to post-modernism as rationalism was to the *moderne*.)

This is the simple truth. The secret of this work has been the application of mythic thinking to classic Jewish texts. I don't think this is a new thing to do. I believe that it is the core of that which is Talmudic, that which is mystic, that which is spiritual. Mythic thinking is knowing that the Temple is always inside of us, part of our experience, as well as something we could rebuild and actually visit. It is a place in us as well as in the world.

Here is the other mythic secret, learned from Robert Bly in an audio tape called *What Stories Do We Need?* Mythic figures always come in pairs. Every character has its shadow. Every character has its opposite. Dwarfs and giants always go together. Jacob needs Esau. I can't talk of my father without explaining my mother. Moses is balanced by Aaron. Hell, invite Abbott and you get Costello. Spin *Adonai* and you get *Elohim*. Every cosmic pie has two halves. Mythic is knowing the Torah of the Shadow as well as the Torah of the Light.

Finale: This book started one rainy Thanksgiving weekend when listening to an audio tape of *Iron John* set off a feeling and a thought. The feeling was profound sadness, a deep mourning for a relationship with my father that could now never be healed. And the thought was that this men's stuff was both powerful and pagan. The two together sent me on a three-year journey through rabbinical literature, through lots of classes I then taught, through my soul, and through the Jewish tradition. In the process I have learned some and I have healed some. The record of both can be found in these pages. And I am still turning the crank on my mythic science fair project, collecting sparks as electrons try to find their way home.

This book's final answer—wisdom relearned and echoed by my friend and teacher Rabbi Ed Feinstein—is in the words, **"What you're really trying to say is just** '*Elu v'Elu D'vrai Eholim ha-Hayim*'—THESE AND THESE are all the words of the living GOD." The Talmud teaches: **Hillel and Shammi were three years into an argument.** They were getting nowhere fast. Little John and Robin Hood were at it again with their staffs. Kent and his father each knew that the other was one hundred percent wrong. My dad worked on the science fair project while I was sent to my room. Carol said, "Are you pulling my chain?" And just about everyone else knew that I was wrong for some independent and personal reason. **Each said, "I am right." Each said, "The law should be my way."** Then a *Bat Kol*, the voice of a daughter of heaven, **said:** "*Elu v'Elu D'vrai Eholim ha-Hayim*—**THESE AND THESE are all the words of the living GOD.**" Sometimes truth comes in two buckets.

THE GENIZA

When you write the name of God, it's supposed to be forever. That is a core Jewish concept. That is why we kiss fallen siddurim and protect every scrap of writing. A geniza was a box, often a place in the wall, where any holy writ could be preserved once it was no longer useful. A geniza is a spiritual junkyard—and as a man who still contains the boy who picked up and played with rubbish on the way home from school every day—I know that junkyards are often repositories of hidden treasures. The Whimshurst Static Generator was once such a find.

Geniza has been an important metaphor for this book. I have often called the pit in my stomach where all the uncomfortable feelings go my geniza. Memory is another geniza. The Torah itself is a geniza for lots of Torahs that have gone before. So it goes.

Therefore, it is very logical that this book, too, has its own geniza. Consider these last few pieces discarded treasures from other visions of this book. Things thrown away, yet preserved, as Jews do with all their holy writ.

Fragment A

Cut From the Team
A Just So Midrash about Male Initiation

When this book contained a full set of essays on the male life cycle, this story midrash opened a long and necessary discussion on Brit Milah. It was cut because a long discussion on the ethics of circumcising and uncircumcising, of the meaning of male initiation rituals, the pagan and the pure, got bogged down and became difficult.

It also got bogged down because every time I "performed" this story, which basically starts with the word "penis," a lot of women acted as if it were an act of rape. I like to be gentle. (Passionate, but gentle. . . .)

It was saved because I like it as a story, and because the notes that follow it contain the important essences of the discarded sixty-page chapter that originally followed it.

"You've put in too much penis," the angel complained. God looked up from the electron microscope and said, "Igor, am I creating this monster or are you?" The angel heard his cue, immediately grew a hump, and said, "Yes, Master," rolling his eyes and doing his best Marty Feldman.

You may want to suggest that to consider God as a mad scientist when He created man is either rude or sacrilegious (somewhere between belching in public and taking His Image in vain). I'll admit the truth right now: God is not a mad scientist, but He does like to play a mad scientist.

You may want to suggest that this is just a metaphor. It could be, but it isn't. You see, the long and the short of it is that "mad scientist" is one of God's favorite roles. He thinks it is funny—ironic—better than playing an attendant in a *Steambath* who does card tricks. In the midrash we are told, "God created people because God loved stories," but that is only half the truth. Paul Simon is closer when he sings, "That's why God made the movies." In fact, God and the angels often live out their own movie fantasies—the metaphysics of astral projection are a little bit complex, but we are, after all, talking about God. The bottom line is that Dr. Frankenstein is one of God's favorite parts, especially when He is feeling creative. When He feels like telling stories, God does a mean Mark Twain.

After a minute or so, the angel said, "You're still mixing in altogether too much penis—you're going to make every man into Jack the Ripper."

Without looking up this time, God said calmly, "Do you want to splice this gene for Me, or will you let Me do it Myself? I am mixing in just enough penis to allow for either Amos or Ben Franklin."

"It looks more like Caligula or de Sade to me."

"Rabbi Akiva or Socrates," God retorted. "You expect them all to have the sex drive of Buddhists?"

"You're making Hitler," the angel priggishly responded, sounding a lot like Edward Everett Horton. They had already played this scene a lot of times—God had been experimenting with the formula for man for a couple of weeks already.

"Hitler's problem," God said, "will be penis envy, not too much penis. Besides, I'm working on the raw materials that will turn into Darwin or Bar Kokhba. Do you want Jewish history without King David? A David takes a lot of penis!"

Then, to prove their points, God and the angel said in unison, "The Kennedy brothers." Both of them laughed.

The angel asked a new question. "Why blend in so much anger? That much penis and that much anger together scares me."

God said pedantically, "Good penis blends take a lot of anger, right-eous anger. Martin Luther King takes anger. Jeremiah takes anger. Sure, there is a secret, hidden womb in every man, a source of nurture and comfort, but a real man has anger coursing down his spine. As gentle as he seems, you can't have Pete Seeger's intensity without anger—penis and anger together."

"But Martin Luther King, Jeremiah, and Pete Seeger are all pacifists, not rapists. Why do they need that much penis?"

"Trust Me, penis is an important part of the blend. You can't have Pete Seeger—and all of his refusal to quit, all of his energy—without anger. Penis anger. (Cut back on the penis anger and Pete Seeger becomes Arlo Guthrie, funny but nowhere near as intense.) Listen, I need the Weavers. They're part of my plan. They all will have a lot a penis in them; even Ronnie what's-her-name, the woman in the group. I will not create the world without a hammer of justice. Pass Me that complex protein, will you, please?"

The angel sighed. He said, "I know that you have to make Elvis in order to get Kurt Vonnegut—but I wish the first man wasn't just a bread-boarded approximation, a first draft."

It was then that God spoke the fearful words, "Don't worry so much about the hardwiring. This is just a prototype. We're just laying out the basic archetypes. We'll fix any problems in the next iteration of software." (To my way of thinking, evil entered the world from the moment there was a possibility of upgrading the software.)

"I have the biggest penis of anyone." That was what Ishmael used to tell everyone. Eleazer would always counter, cutting him down to size, "Close. You are the biggest prick of anyone around here." Truth be told, Ishmael was rather well-endowed for a twelve-year-old. It was four inches long, with a lot of hair and three more inches of foreskin. Ishmael used to brag about having seven inches and would fight anyone who challenged his prowess. Remember, Ishmael was really tough. Remember, he was a real wild man. God remembered.

Circumcision started out as a joke. Not one of those "rub it and ..." things, but an off-hand comment by Satan. Once, when he and God were sharing the afternoon shift watching the security monitors, Ishmael once more launched into his "I'm the greatest" routine, and Satan joked, "God, you ought to let me pull the Pinocchio shtik with him, except let it shrink by an eighth of an inch every time he tells a lie. The problem will be gone in no time."

God laughed. God has a great sense of humor. Then God screamed, "Eureka!" "By Jove, you've got it!" "Great Caesar's ghost!" and a lot of other stuff. Then, in his best Don Ameche, he said to Mikha-el, "Come here, Mr. Watson, I need you." Mikha-el grew his Igor hump, and they went to work. They worked all night. By dawn the next generation of covenant software was ready. Satan, God's investigating angel, had done it. He had figured it out: to run the covenant through a man's operating system, a minor alteration to the hardware was necessary.

God phoned Abraham. ABRAHAM WAS NINETY-NINE. GOD SAID, "I'M EL SHADDAI. WALK IN MY WAYS AND BE PERFECT. I WILL ESTABLISH MY COVENANT BETWEEN ME AND YOU, AND I WILL MAKE YOU VERY MANY."

Abe said, "Deja vu! God, haven't we done this before?"

God said, "We are going to install the 3.0 covenant software." For those of you who are now counting on your fingers, the 1.0 beta test was given to Noah and his family after the flood. That was the first covenant. The first Jewish edition, 2.0, was given to Abram in the *Covenant of the Pieces*. It was here that cutting and covenant were first physically related—but what got cut up was only a lot of holy props. This was the 3.0, Abraham's final edition. Here a minor operation was performed, teaching every man that part of the covenant was learning to cut back on the penis by themselves. It was through the 3.0 edition that penis became holy (as well as fun) and could now be blended more easily. God liked the innovation. This is where He would teach Israel that performance rather than size was the essence of good Jewish practice. He would start with the penis, connect the covenant, and then move to the rest of the *mitzvot*.

The 4.0 release was scheduled for Mt. Sinai. It would be a big release—a lot of advertising dollars would be spent on that campaign. Then the final release, 5.0, the one that added the *t'shuvah* windows package, would follow the Golden Calf Event. From there the covenant would only take a few minor additions over the ages.

Five iterations of covenant. God liked the number five. He could count it on His Mighty Hand, and Israel could see it on His Outstretched Arm. He liked things that were a handful. This is why there were five uses of

137

light on the first day of creation. Five blessings given to Abram. Five books in the Torah. Five ways the Egyptians would persecute the Families of Israel. Five ways the Families of Israel would multiply in size. Five Commandments on each tablet. And a lot more. God thought of a bad pun. He decided not to say it out loud. It was beneath him. God is almost never crude. I, however, have promised to tell you everything. The pun that God rejected was: "Five is Good. I like taking this penis thing into My own hand."

"No way! Forget it! Not a chance!" were the only clean things Ishmael said when his father told him about God's latest religious innovation. Abraham tried each of the good arguments.

He said: "It's a mitzvah!"

He said: "No, It's mutilation."

He said: "It's what God wants—a way to be holy."

He said: "No, Dad, it's what your God wants—my mother's goddess offers religious alternatives."

He said: "My God has promised to make you the father of a great nation."

He said: "My mother was right. Sarah is a castrating bitch."

He said: "Leave Sarah out of this. It's healthier. I mean you won't have to wash as often."

He said: "Given the choice, I'll get close to God by washing more frequently."

He said: "Without the foreskin you'll be more sensitive. It will feel better."

He said: "I do just fine right now! If it ain't broke, don't fix it."

He said: "I'm your father!"

He said: "If you try to make me, you won't have a son. I'll run away."
He said: "It will make me proud."

He said: "Can't you love me for who I am—not who you want me to be?"

He said: "I'll give you a big party." That answer met with silence. Abraham saw that he had an opening. Ishmael wasn't ready to give in yet. But Abraham went on. He talked about showing courage and being a real man—a man others would follow. Ishmael's foreskin was almost in the bag (so to speak) when Abraham made the mistake of talking about greatness. Abraham was speaking about character. That isn't what Ishmael heard.

He said: "How can I be a great man with only four inches?"

Abraham should have stopped with the party. Abraham thought of telling his son that with four inches he could be great at foreplay—but he knew that wouldn't work. Then inspiration struck. He said, "Son."

Ishmael said, "What'ya want now?"—not "Hineini."

Abraham said: "Son, what happens when you prune a tree?"

Ishmael thought for a moment. He was afraid of being caught by a trick question. "When you cut a tree back, if you do it right, it grows back thicker and stronger. It grows better."

"Right," Abraham said, and he offered his kid a beer. No, don't be skeptical, this isn't an anachronism. Of course it wasn't in a can, but Abraham did offer the kid a real beer. The Egyptians were among the first brewmasters there ever were—we are, after all, talking about the Bronze Age—not the Stone Age, and making copper tubing was a breeze. Hagar, Ishmael's mother, the Egyptian Handmaiden, knew how to mix up a great brew. Normally, or at least up to now, Ishmael wasn't allowed to drink. (Sarah, not his own mother, objected.) But today Abraham was treating him like a man. They talked about manhood, great battles, fast deals Abraham had pulled—all kinds of man stuff. Three cups of beer later, Abraham said, "When Sarah made me send your mother away when she was pregnant with you—something I deeply regretted—God sent an angel to her. The angel told her, 'YOU WILL HAVE A SON, YOU SHOULD CALL HIS NAME ISHMAEL.' You know that Ishmael means Eyl—my God—listens to you. You know you can trust Him. Anyway, Eyl's angel told your mother: 'I WILL GREATLY MULTIPLY YOUR SEED, YOUR SON WILL HAVE ENDLESS OFFSPRING. HE WILL BE A WILDASS MAN—HE WILL LIVE IN EVERYONE'S FACE.'" Then Abraham lifted his cup and said, "Here's to you, my in-the-face wildass son." They both drank again.

139

Finally Abraham said. "You're going to be really great. God has promised. Kid, where does your family tree begin?" Ishmael lifted up his robe and showed off his seven inches. Then, casually, Abraham said, "What do you say we prune it and watch it really grow?" Ishmael just said the local shepherd equivalent of the surfer exclamation: "far out."

Rashi explains that each of them had a different understanding of what had just happened. Abraham thought he was being honest. He had waited over a hundred years to have a kid with Sarah. God had just told him that if he had a little minor surgery the fertility problem would be solved. He figured if pruning would work in his family tree, it would do wonders for Ishmael. When he said, "watch it really grow" he was talking about Ishmael's future family. That wasn't the way Ishmael heard it. He figured that if he gave up three inches of foreskin he would grow back four or maybe five inches of real penis. That was his idea of greatness.

It was a hell of a fight the day that Sarai told Abram that Hagar had to go. The Torah makes it all sound too simple. But read closely and you can see all the pain. Come and hear the true story. It stands there ready to unfold. SARAI, ABRAM'S WIFE, HADN'T CONCEIVED A CHILD FOR HIM. We know that Sarai is Abram's wife. We've already followed them through lots of adventures. Why remind us of the relationship? The answer is obvious— it was at risk! Was Abram threatening to take another wife? Did he just stop visiting her tent? Was it her own unhappiness? Reach into your own imagination to find the truth. But this much is clear: ten years after leaving H̲aran, ten years after the first promise to have a huge future family, Sarai still can't get pregnant. SHE HAD AN EGYPTIAN HANDMAIDEN NAMED HAGAR. Why tell us she was Egyptian? Was it because Sarai intentionally picked an Egyptian? Was it a clue to the future? We don't know—but we do know that Hagar's Egyptian identity is important. Twice in a row the Torah identifies her as such. (And in the Joseph story we learn about the meaning of things that happen twice in the Torah. It says: "THIS HAPPENED TWICE BECAUSE IT IS TRUE AND FROM GOD" (Genesis 41.25). Abram and Sarai have been to Egypt. They got rich there. Abram passed her off as his sister (in truth she

140

may have even been a half-sister). Perhaps Abram was trying to pimp her, perhaps not—but in any case, he denied their relationship. PHARAOH GAVE ABRAM because of what Sarai almost did SHEEP, OXEN, ASSES, MALE AND FEMALE SLAVES, SHE ASSES AND CAMELS. Maybe that's where Hagar came from. The midrash is fond of suggesting that Sarai's new handmaiden was Pharaoh's daughter. Is Sarai taking revenge? Is she throwing that wife-sister thing back in Abram's crotch? I don't know, but the possibilities are interesting.

Or is it something else? In the 2.0 edition of the covenant, Abram and Sarai are told, "KNOW WELL THAT YOUR FUTURE FAMILY WILL BE STRANGERS IN A LAND WHICH IS NOT THEIRS, THEY SHALL BE ENSLAVED AND ABUSED FOR FOUR HUNDRED YEARS, BUT I WILL EXECUTE JUDGMENT ON THE NATION THEY SHALL SERVE, IN THE END THEY SHALL GO FREE WITH GREAT WEALTH." God keeps the location secret. God doesn't say "Egypt." He just says their kids will be strangers and will come away wealthy. Did Sarai figure it out? Did she make the connection to her own Egypt experience? Had she singled out an Egyptian for revenge in advance, taking God into her own hands? I don't know—but the possibilities are interesting.

SARAI SAID TO ABRAM: "ADONAI IS KEEPING ME BARREN. MAKE IT WITH MY HAND-MAIDEN AND THROUGH HER I'LL GET BUILT UP." Sarai blames Adonai. Later she will blame Abram for what has happened; for now it is God's fault. But that isn't entirely unfair. After all, it does demonstrate faith.

The interesting idea here is Sarai's statement, "THROUGH HER I'LL GET BUILT UP." It suggests a lot. The scholars like to blame it on the example of Assyrian marriage contracts and Hammurabi's law codes, both of which order barren women to buy their husbands slave-women to be surrogate mothers. They like to explain that Sarai was just following the common practice. I figure she hated the idea from the start. Maybe she thought that she was supposed to do it—maybe she thought it was the grand gesture—but Abram, the old fool, didn't read between the lines. Listen and think. She says, "ADONAI IS KEEPING ME BARREN—so let's follow pagan wedding contracts. Because ADONAI is responsible for everything—why don't you sleep with an Egyptian nonbeliever, and that way we'll have kids?" Abram just didn't get it.

In my more subtle moments, I think Sarai had an even slicker plan. She figured he couldn't do it. She figured he was the one who couldn't have kids. Her idea was this: he would sleep with the Egyptian slut (her with all the family secrets her descendant Cleopatra would later use to hook two Caesars). He could do it as many times as he wanted, and still he wouldn't be able to get her pregnant. That was the meaning of "I WILL BE BUILT UP." It wasn't a surrogate she wanted—she wanted vindication, proof that it wasn't her. It appears that he fooled her.

However, in the same moments in which I believe that the C.I.A., the Mob, and the Cubans all working together conspired to kill Kennedy, I figure Hagar got someone else to knock her up—after all, it was her way to the top.

ABRAM LISTENED TO SARAI'S VOICE. SO TEN YEARS INTO THEIR TIME IN CANAAN, SARAI, ABRAM'S WIFE, TOOK HAGAR THE EGYPTIAN AND GAVE HER TO HER HUSBAND AS A WIFE. Listen to the language and you'll know from the start what is wrong. After ten years of trying, Abram gives up. He hadn't figured out that tens were important. Then the text rubs it in—SARAI, ABRAM'S WIFE, GAVE HER TO HER HUSBAND AS A WIFE. If you listen to all those words, you can feel the pain.

Other times I blame the whole thing on Sarai. She is the active party. Maybe she is the one who is making Abram do it. Maybe all the emphasis on wife and husband in the text are the echoes of his words. He said, "God will take care of the child. I am your husband. You are my wife. That is good enough for me. Husbands are supposed to be faithful. I won't sleep around with a slave—it isn't right." "Okay," Sarai replies with great anger, "then we'll make my Egyptian handmaiden your other wife."

Whatever happened, it was love gone awry. Whether Sarai compromised herself for Abram's sake, or whether Abram gave in because he thought it was what she wanted, or whether this whole incident is a warped version of *"Gift of the Magi"* the way Arthur Miller would write it, it goes wrong. What was supposed to correct the situation only makes things worse. Families are like that.

HE MADE IT WITH HAGAR WHO GOT PREGNANT. WHEN SHE REALIZED THAT SHE WAS PREGNANT SHE REALIZED THAT SHE HAD IT ALL OVER HER MISTRESS. The scene is easy to imagine; just think of Hagar with Bette Midler's affect and drive. Do that, and you know how Sarai felt.

142

Sarai said to Abram, "This extortion is your fault. I put my handmaiden in your lap. Now that you got her pregnant, she realizes that she has it all over me. Let Adonai be the judge between me and you." So what did Abram do wrong? Why is Sarai blaming him? Didn't he just follow her lead? There are lots of possibilities. Maybe he was supposed to say no and was now getting blamed for taking the bait. Maybe he gave Hagar credit for the kid, rather than counting him as Sarai's. (Later his grandson, Jacob, would have children with his wives' handmaidens, Zilpah and Bilhah, but he would be smart enough to credit the kids to Leah and Rachel.) Maybe he was treating her as his new favorite wife and encouraging her. Maybe Sarai was now blaming herself for her barrenness and taking it out on him. Or just maybe, because Abram had forgotten to exercise his *Midat ha-Din* and treated his two wives like sisters, not realizing that two wombs can experience sibling rivalry the same way two penises can. Whatever it was, Abram gave up. Abram said to Sarai: "Your handmaiden is in your hand; do to her as you see fit." He walked away from the whole thing. We can suspect that he was hurt and confused and not good at sharing his feelings. If he could have, he would have gone bowling with the guys or spent the weekend painting the garage.

Sarai abused her and she ran away from her. Sarai abused her. The echo is loud. Sarai abused her, the same way that God promised that foreigners would abuse her children. In fact, she abuses her with the same verb and root that the New Pharaoh would use on Israel when he made them slaves. The Torah is clear that this is measure for measure. All that is lacking is clarity about what is cause and what is effect.

Sarai thought she had solved the problem. Abram had let Sarai solve it her way. They both thought it was over. Unfortunately, families don't work that way. The solution only lasts eight verses, then she is back and Ishmael is born. Yes, families are like that.

V.

It was the next morning. Or several next mornings later. Ishmael didn't know. He only knew that his head hurt a lot—down there hurt a lot more.

Ishmael's coming-of-age event would have been worse if this hadn't been a good three thousand years before George Eastman. At least there was no candle lighting ceremony. The day had started out with three or four cups of beer, and there were a lot more cups to follow. That afternoon, in the midst of lots of drinking, drumming, dancing, shouting, and general bravado, every man in the camp "had his spear sharpened." The women called it "The Blunting," but never to the men's faces.

But we are getting ahead of the story. God had SAID TO ABRAHAM, "AS FOR YOU, KEEP THIS *BRIT* THING, YOU AND THOSE WHO COME FROM YOUR SPERM AFTER YOU—IN EACH GENERATION. THIS IS MY *BRIT* WHICH YOU SHALL KEEP—BETWEEN ME AND BETWEEN YOU AND BETWEEN THOSE WHO COME FROM YOUR SPERM AFTER YOU— TO TRIM EVERY PENIS. TRIM AWAY THE MEAT OF YOUR FORESKIN AND THIS WILL BE THE *BRIT* BETWEEN ME AND BETWEEN YOU. Abram had a hard time keeping a straight face when God dropped this particular mitzvah on him. Not only was it ridiculous and scary—it hurt to even consider it—but he thought it was funny that God wanted him to cut his "zab" and then used the word "between." It would be days or weeks before he could be between anything. ANY **MALE MEMBER** WHICH DOESN'T TRIM THE MEAT OF THE FORESKIN—HIS SOUL WILL BE **CUT OFF** FROM HIS PEOPLE—HE HAS BROKEN MY *BRIT*. Abraham heard the pun and wanted to laugh. He knew he couldn't. But he did know that God didn't waste words. With all this meat being cut off—with the whole camp "covenantized" in one day—they weren't going to be hunters anymore.

Ishmael had been the hardest sell. Everyone else was more scared of Abraham getting angry than of some minor surgery. Everyone else had written it off as a workplace requirement, a "man's gotta do what a man's gotta do" kind of thing—they were committed to work through the pain. Ishmael was different. He was the wild ass. He was always out of control. He was terminally angry. He would not be an easy stallion to geld—and gelding was what Abraham suspected this "covenantizing" was all about.

AND WHEN HE WAS DONE SPEAKING WITH HIM, GOD WENT AWAY—UP FROM ABRAHAM. God knew what was coming. He didn't want to see it. Boys will be boys and all that. God was getting too old for all of this. He left Abraham to finish the job and take care of the crew. God went home to get some rest.

Everyone got drunk. Everyone carried spears. Everyone beat drums. Then they sent the women away. THEN ABRAM TOOK HIS SON ISHMAEL AND ALL HIS HOMIES AND ALL HIS PURCHASED HELP AND HE CIRCUMCISED THE MEAT OF THEIR FORE-SKINS ON THE SAME DAY GOD HAD SPOKEN TO HIM. Ishmael went first. Abram set out to make him the hero. He went on talking about how brave and vir-ile his man-son was. He set Ishmael as the example. He challenged every-one to be half the man his son was. By the time he was done, Ishmael had no way to back out.

He stood naked on the rock in front of the all-male gathering. He was held up by Eleazar and another. He bit down hard on the leather-wrapped stick. He was very drunk. His raging hard-on pointed up in anger in heav-en—and he fainted before Abraham's flint knife ever touched it. It was a long afternoon. The flint knife went in and out of the fire between every act of spiritual affirmation. Abraham saved himself for last. Long before sundown the camp was silent. The women sneaked out of their tents. They tried to clean up the mess—and clear their minds of the madness that had struck the whole camp. Sarah alone understood the full meaning of the day. She had her own little moment of laughter—a great surprise—her own blood was among the things she got to clean up that afternoon. Now she believed God's promise.

VI.

The next morning Abraham was the only one moving. Even he was not too mobile—just sitting in the doorway of the tent, hoping for a breeze. He hurt too much to sleep. Everyone else hurt too much to feel. You know the story. Three visitors show up. Abraham runs to make them welcome. Now, if you think about it, you know why—the rest of the staff had the day off. The big question is, why and how did he run? The answer is "out of will" and then "out of joy." When Abraham discovered that most of the pain was in his fear, and the rest of it could be managed, he got excited. He lost himself in company, good manners, and gossip. As soon as he real-ized that covenantizing was not gelding—that he would heal—that every-one would heal and be strong—he found a lot of strength and joy.

By the end of the story, when Sarah laughs and God comments—we now know the secret—Sarah laughed, and God celebrated that laugh, because both of them shared a secret. Both of them knew that the possibility of that future was now coming true. The Torah tells us: Sarah was listening at the entrance to the tent. Abraham and Sarah were old in years, but not in spirit. Sarah had stopped having a woman's period—but we know the secret: she had stopped but suddenly started again. Sarah laughed and said to herself, Now that I am wrinkled, am I still to get it on with my old man? Sarah wasn't being sarcastic. She wasn't doubting anymore. She just sensed that a miracle was in process and didn't have the words to communicate her total joy. She laughed and stuttered at the amazing contradiction. God echoed her joy and her laugh. God couldn't resist teasing her a little now that her bitterness was ending. God said to Abraham, making sure that Sarah could hear, "Why is Sarah laughing and saying, 'Am I really going to get knocked up—old broad that I am?'" Sarah knew in her heart and her womb the answer was yes—after so many years of thinking it was no.

I do have one question. In the middle of this story an unidentified servant boy dresses the calf. Who is he? How come he can stand? What happens to him? We do know that every male in camp was circumcised the previous day. I figure the Messiah is still in the gates of Rome, bandaging and unbandaging his wounds, one at a time.

VII.

Circumcision was supposed to teach Ishmael a lesson. It did. The wrong lesson. It hurt for days. Every time he tried his usual way of feeling better, it only made it hurt more. His rage grew. He made himself lots of promises. He decided to use it as much and as soon as he could. It took awhile.

A couple of weeks later it still worked as good as new—maybe even better, because it was more sensitive. Nine months later, when Isaac was born, it still hadn't grown any. Four inches were still four inches. Ishmael figured exercise was the thing. He developed a new motto: "Anywhere it fits and feels good is fine." He proved himself a real wild ass. Abraham had a lot of apologies to make—it cost him more than a few sheep (some of which also fit and felt good).

Almost no one stopped Ishmael—except for Sarah. The day he lifted his robe to show her his worth she poured a jug of cold water over him and then told everyone he had a bladder problem. Things were tense, but, like his mother, he learned to keep his distance from his father's Queen Mother. He had his hobby to keep him busy.

Isaac was circumcised on the eighth day. That's the way God wanted it. On his second, third, fourth, fifth, or thirteenth birthday (depending on which rabbinic or archeological source you want to believe), Abraham threw a big party, and the kid was "weaned." Here they might have done a candle ceremony.

Right after that, in the next verse, the Ishmael story rushes to completion (he was having enough climaxes on his own). We are told: SARAH SAW HAGAR THE EGYPTIAN'S SON WHICH SHE BORE TO ABRAHAM—PLAYING. We know what he was playing with—the only question is where and with whom. We can suggest lots of possibilities (most of which include Isaac), but it really is all the same. Sarah reached her limit, even for Abraham's sake—now she had Isaac to think about. SHE SAID TO ABRAHAM: DIVORCE THIS SLAVE WOMAN AND HER SON, BECAUSE I WILL NOT HAVE HIM SHARE AN INHERITANCE WITH MY SON, WITH ISAAC." The story plays out from here. Abraham again is trapped. God again tells him to do what Sarah says, promising, "ALSO, THE SON OF THE HANDMAIDEN, no longer considering Hagar a wife, I WILL MAKE HIM A NATION, not a people, BECAUSE HE IS FROM YOUR SPERM."

Mother and unmarried son, who is at youngest fifteen—and may be twenty-six—go on their desert outward bound adventure. To become a man, Ishmael should have gone alone. You know what they suggest about Elvis's mother. Then the angel shows up and renews the promise. The funny thing is, he talks to Hagar, not Ishmael. I've never understood why.

IX.

Up in heaven, God, Mikha-eyl and Satan were settling their bets. Satan said, "You're right, the 'eight-day control group' did a lot better than this 'big-warrior-manhood-become-a-real-hunter rite-of-passage.' That way it showed parental concern, rather than encouraging rage." They looked at the security monitors and watched Ishmael hunt. "He does it with a lot of grace," Mikha-eyl said to God. "You should be proud." God said, "Yeah, but you were right. With that much anger in the blend we got to make sure the covenant takes."

"By the way," Mikha-eyl said, "you know what else he does with that bow—"

"So that's why you sang the message to the mother," Satan interrupted.

God started to hum a Weavers tune. "I dreamed I saw Joe Hill last night."

BLOOD AND WATER

An Extended Footnote on *Brit Milah*

PROLOGUE: His name is Boris. In the former Soviet Union he was a professor of drama; here he is still looking for real work. His nine-year-old son, thanks to resettlement money, is studying in a *Chabad* Day School. The school has been putting pressure on the boy and on the family to have the son circumcised. They have said that he can't observe his Bar Mitzvah without a *Brit Milah*. According to the father, the boy has de-cided that he wants the surgery, he wants "to have" a Bar Mitzvah just like his cousin. The father is in agreement—he is manifesting lots of positive Jewish feelings. At the moment, the part-time work that gives his life meaning is serving as a Jewish teacher. He is presently seeking full-time employment. Still, he has some doubts. According to Boris, the one big problem is the maternal grandfather. The grandfather is a Holocaust survivor who felt continually at risk because of his own missing foreskin, and who swore that none of his descendants was ever to be in similar danger.

I answer a lot of Boris's questions. I ask a lot of questions for those sharing the conversation, but who are afraid to ask for themselves. Everyone at the table is talking on tiptoes. I understand—I, too, don't want, in any way, to be responsible for creating a torture scene from a Fu Manchu movie. The situation is truly awesome, awe-inspiring, both spiritually powerful and deeply shadowed with the dark edge of pain. When I finally am sure that what I am hearing is a decision requesting both approval and expanded background information, I share ways that the son's choice can be honored as an "heroic" action. However, the most important part of the conversation is the sharing of a simple fact. I inform Boris that some 90% of the 125 million men in America are circumcised (something he was not likely to know, having escaped all the showers that followed gym classes in high school). This fact allows him to prove to himself that his wife's father's fears are not rooted in an American reality. That is the truth he needs. Not any other kind of spiritual or intellectual insight. That allows his already-made decision to be self-accepted.

That lunch was haunting. My knees were a little weak as I walked away. I was in awe of this phantom nine-year-old's courage—and I could emphatically feel his pain. I knew that I hadn't recommended the operation—I hadn't imposed it—but I had affirmed this test of honor and identity. It *thought* better in my mind then it *felt*—given the sympathetic pains I was experiencing. My heart was palpitating with a syncopated backbeat.

What I don't tell Boris is that that number is rapidly declining. That growing in America and elsewhere is an anti-circumcision movement (both in and out of the Jewish community) that defines *Brit Milah* as "child abuse" and lobbies actively for "the intact penis." Later that night, the "Woman from Northern California" confronts me at this conference. She attacks (aggressively, not assertively). She demands to know how I could suggest condemning a child, especially a nine-year-old child, to this kind of ritual mutilation and primitive torture. This note is my long personal response to that confrontation and that juxtaposition of stories. It again is braided truth.

îî.

DAVAR AHER: From Deborah Tannen's work. **Eve had a lump removed from her breast. Shortly after the operation, talking to her sister, she said that she found it upsetting to have been cut into, and that looking at the stitches was distressing because they left a seam that had changed the contour of her breast. Her sister said, "I know. When I had my operation I felt the same way." Eve made the same observation to her friend Karen, who said, "I know. It's like your body has been violated." But when she told her husband, Mark, how she felt, he said, "You can have plastic surgery to cover up the scar and restore the shape of your breast."**

Eve had been comforted by her sister and her friend, but she was not comforted by Mark's comment. Quite the contrary, it upset her more. Not only didn't she hear what she wanted, that he understood her feelings, but, far worse, she felt he was asking her to undergo more surgery just when she was telling him how much this operation had upset her. "I'm not having any more surgery!" she protested. "I'm sorry you don't like the way it looks." Mark was hurt and puzzled. "I don't care," he protested. "It doesn't bother me at all." She asked, "Then why are you telling me to have plastic surgery?" He answered, "Because you were saying *you* were upset about the way it looked."

Eve wanted the gift of understanding, but Mark gave her the gift of advice. He was taking the role of problem-solver, whereas she simply wanted confirmation for her feelings. (Deborah Tannen, *You Just Don't Understand: Women and Men in Conversation*. New York: Ballantine Books, 1990, p. 49.)

For classical rabbinical literature, circumcision is a *solution*. We see in many of the texts that follow that *Brit Milah* cures the *Yetzer ha-Ra*. This theme is repeated over and over. Circumcision is seen as a solution—the final act of "sweetening a man."

A Story: The wicked Turnas Rufus asked Rabbi Akiva, "Whose deeds are more beautiful, God's or people's?" Rabbi Akiva answered him, "People do the prettier work." When Turnas Rufus questioned the answer, Akiva had grain and flax brought. Then he had bread and linen brought. He said, "Is not the bread more beautiful than the grain, the linen nicer than the raw flax?"

Turnas Rufus then asked: "If God wants circumcision, why aren't babies born already circumcised?" Rabbi Akiva answered him, "God gave the *mitzvot* to Israel as an opportunity for Israel to purify themselves" (*Tanhumah, Tazria*).

Turnas Rufus and the anti-circumcision movment ask the same question. "If God wanted men circumcised, why did God give them foreskins?" is the same question as "Why can't we treat our son (in regard to birth ritual) as if he is a girl?"

This midrashic story is a great expression of the classic "male" (rabbinic) position on *Brit Milah*. *Brit Milah* has to be understood as "radical spiritual amputation," a necessary treatment in the battle against evil and assimilation. To understand this, think of this classic "type-scene" in western, war, and action-adventure movies.

The hero takes a swig of the bottle of whisky and then hands it to the poor wounded guy, who takes a deep swig, too; maybe even two or three. Someone then puts a stick or a piece of leather in the victim's mouth and tells him to "bite hard." The hero then cuts out the bullet, or cuts off the leg, or does whatever is necessary to save the victim. Then he takes another gulp and pours the whisky over the wound to sterilize it. Often, the wounded guy shows up a couple of scenes later, wearing the bullet as a good luck charm (and a badge of honor).

In the world of men, wounds, and whisky, no one wants the pain.[23] The victim doesn't get burned on purpose. The hero doesn't look forward to the surgery. Both of them drink to numb the pain. The whisky is a pragmatic tool—anesthesia and antiseptic. This movie scene is typical of men facing pain because it is necessary and because it is dysfunctional to back away from the only solution. The act of courage in operating and being operated on is celebrated because it is the only logical solution, a difficult solution—not merely as a proof of the ability to endure pain. Rabbinic literature works with *Brit Milah* in the same way. For them, it is never the removal of a foreskin; it is always the act of cutting a covenant. *Brit Milah* is a spiritual treatment, not simply the absence of a flap of skin.

"When God created the *Yetzer ha-Ra* God had already created the Torah as an antidote against it" (*Bava Batra* 30b). Man is born with a "problem," the *Yetzer ha-Ra*, which can be overcome only through Torah and Covenant. Circumcision is the act of cutting away the evil and accepting Torah. *Brit Milah* is a heroic gesture—a necessary (not desirable) test of courage and commitment. In other words, like John Wayne, we're supposed to take a deep breath, bite down hard, perhaps take a swig of whisky, and then just do it.

This is more clearly expressed in a parallel midrash when a philosopher asks Rabbi Hoshayah the same question (If God wants *Brit Milah* why the foreskin?). This time the answer is: **"Plants must be sweetened, wheat must be milled and even man needs to be perfected (finished off)"** (*Genesis Rabbah* 11.6). The notion here goes back to the "bread is better than grain" piece of the story. It is the power of doing the "action" (the process), not the result, that makes the final difference.

This is further explained in an interesting midrashic exposition. **Adam, the first man, was created circumcised** (*Avot d Rabbi Natan* 2.5). In other words, because God thought the first man was going to be perfect, God didn't add a foreskin—it wasn't needed, because God didn't intend a covenant. The need for both would come later, when God saw that given free will, lots of people didn't automatically choose the good. This is the way the story continues. **Rabbi Judah said in Rav's name: "Adam was a heretic."** How so? **Rabbi Isaac said, "He practiced *epiplasm* and pulled his foreskin back down to hide his circumcision"** (*Sanhedrin* 38b). The lesson here is both deep and political. In Greek and Roman culture a lot of Jews died for the sake of circumcision. When Antiochus Epiphanes (the Darth Vader of Ḥanukkah) made it a crime, Jews risked their lives to have their babies "entered into the Covenant of Abraham." In fact, a lot of mothers gave up their own lives (despite the fact that they were under no Halakhic obligation to do so) when they presented their sons for entry into the covenant. Circumcision was a real John Wayne–Clint Eastwood kind of thing

[23]There may be some "deep level" at which men seek the opportunity to prove they can conquer pain. They may even invite the pain, but what they are really welcoming is the opportunity to be tested—not the suffering.

in those days. In contradistinction, many Jews practiced epiplasm and had their foreskins restored in order to "pass" in the naked Greek world of baths and gyms. While some Jews were dying for the mitzvah of *Brit Milah* (a question of Jewish identity and religious freedom), others were pulling a cover-up and leading the good life. They were doing the *Europa Europa* thing, dreaming of entering the Olympics, winning the gold, and taking home some blonde Aryan babes. This is Boris' son's story again come to life.

Brit Milah was the ultimate boundary act. Do it and you could die. Remove it and you could make it in the real world. This was a hell of a lot more powerful an identity issue that "clipping" a long name to get through Ellis Island. Or, as my teacher Harold Schulweiss once wrote, "Cutting off one's nose to spite one's fate."

The dangling question is: *Why did Adam do it?* Why would the only man in the world think of and then ever desire a foreskin—especially if the original "intact penis" didn't have one? Growing up in the fifties, I was in seventh or eighth grade (and started taking showers in gym) before I ever knew what a foreskin was. I can't imagine how Adam found out. Of course, the rabbis had a political agenda, but they explain it this way. When Adam hides from God after the "sin," he is performing spiritual epiplasm, epiplasm on his heart, covering up his true potential. The rabbis take the "metaphor" of undoing the actual circumcision to stand for unmaking of the covenantal relationship with God. For the prophets, and then later the rabbis following their lead, hearts, too, needed to be circumcised and therefore entered into the covenant. Adam's denial of wrongdoing—his hiding from God—is Jewish original sin—not the sex, but the alienation, the recession from responsibility. In that sense, Adam lowers himself to the level of the pagan—he is traitor to God's gift, just as the Jews who tried to pass were traitors to their family covenant.

Here is the rabbis' meaning. Sin and assimilation are exactly the same thing. Both are breaking rules, crossing borders, denying the "rule of law." In *Brit Milah*, a man cuts the boundary between his knowledge of the right thing to do and his tendency to be an animal, to be free of law. "Even the organ that represents man's worst animal-like urge was totally harnessed to God's service." (Rabbi Nosson Scherman, editor's introduction to Rabbi Payasch J. Krohn, *Bris Milah, Cicumcision—The Covenant of Abraham: A Compendium of Laws, Rituals, and Customs from Birth to Bris, Anthologized from Talmudic, and*

Traditional Sources. Brooklyn: Mesorah Publications, 1985.) Before we are done talking about circumcision, we'll ultimately have to talk about intermarriage, because they are one in the same. That is the way the *Midat ha-Din* sees things, those calling for the intact penis come from someplace else.

These midrashim about *Brit Milah* (and Torah) as a cure for the *Yetzer ha-Ra* also speak of free will. The truth is that freedom, responsibility, self-discipline, and pain all go together. This is why "grain-into-bread" is directly connected to making *Brit Milah* a mitzvah. These midrashim suggest that it is better or even necessary to do "it" ourselves rather than having God do it for us. It says *Brit Milah* is about the cutting, the "covenantizing," not just the absence of the foreskin.[24] It is a "freedom to be responsible" thing. *Brit Milah* is "the good cure" because it allows us to be responsible for taming our own animal urges. We bring ourselves under control, rather than being controlled. Without a *Yetzer ha-Ra*, free will would be gone—there would be nothing to choose. We would be as intimate as hell with God—we could have all the nurture-oriented immanence you could stand (and perhaps more), but there would be no distance, no free will, no sense of independence, and no transcendence. *Brit Milah* is, in essence, men telling God, the Parent, "Let me do it myself."

What is missing in most classical rabbinic sources is the voice of the *Midat ha-Raḥamin*, the voice that can sit in empathy rather than solution. Consider this text: **I bent over to pick up Jesse's diaper off the floor and saw the spots of blood. Falling onto my knees, sobs and tears suddenly shook my body as I clutched his diaper to my face. I looked up at Elizabeth, who was holding Jesse on the bed—the bed he had been born in eight days before. I felt we had violated a blessed new soul.**

Before Jesse was born, Elizabeth and I talked many times about "If it's a boy, should we circumcise him?" Elizabeth felt strongly that "Nature knows best;" leave the baby the way God created him. I was in conflict. In my heart I agreed with her, but coming from a strongly traditional Jewish background, I feared that if Jesse was not circumcised I would

---

[24]In Jewish law, a child who has been circumcised in a non-ritual way is still obligated to shed a drip of blood (*tipat dam*) in a ritual circumcision. The importance of actually "cutting" the covenant, not just being circumcised, is informed by this practice. Likewise, a child born without a foreskin is also obligated to have a ritual circumcison—making it clear, that for the Rabbis, the act and the drop of blood, not the absence of the foreskin, are the essence. Finally, a stillborn infant is also circumcised before he is buried—*Brit Milah* is seen as a connection to grace.

be "exiled" from my family and closed to or alienated from Jesse…I can still hear Jesse's crying…begging for someone to stop the pain…screaming of being violated. Elizabeth, with tears streaming down her face, soaked a washcloth in wine, which Jesse intermittently sucked…Twenty-five minutes passed. A sacred boundary had been crossed. Never again will a son of mine be circumcised…as was traditional, we said a few blessings and served cake and wine. To me this seemed barbaric. What had Jesse gained from this "tradition"? What meaning could this have for him? How could Elizabeth and I justify violating his body? We couldn't and we can't. Ignorance? (M. Pickard-Ginsberg, "Jesse's Circumcision," *Mothering Magazine*, Spring, 1979, No. 11.)

This is perhaps the most famous text utilized by the anti-circumcision movement, and to be fair to it, it stems from a richness in the *Midat ha-Rahamin*. The "Woman from Northern California" summed up her position, angered at what she thought I had told Boris: "I don't believe that God wants to cause children pain or have the human body marked with a sign of ownership." As she explained her theology of circumcision, the Woman from Northern California is echoing the teaching of Michael Zeldin, who had his son circumcised privately, explaining, "We were not interested in inviting people to hear our child's pain."

When I listen to this position, I am reminded of another type-scene that is common to a lot of wagon train movies—though it happens elsewhere.

A woman's baby is sick. She does everything possible to care for it. Everyone does. In the middle of the night it dies. She continues to hold it and comfort it. She refuses to give it up. She holds on to the connection. Eventually some man comes and, as gently as possible, removes the baby, believing that the "solution" that grieving offers cannot begin until the separation is started.

My friend Carol teaches: "This is just like men who always wanted to keep woman from mourning fetuses that were lost before they were brought to term, or babies that died in the first thirty days. Repression (biting down hard) was their solution to the grief." It wasn't till women became rabbis that an understanding of the need to mourn was brought into conservative law. Now both men and woman's tears were liberated.

ііі.

Davar Aher: In his *The Memory of Earth*, Orson Scott Card creates a planet where men and women have very different (but intertwined) cultures and religions. Each group tries to cope with the collapsing world order. Listen to his contrasting description of men's and women's religion—it will prompt our discussion of *Brit Milah*. The men's scene comes first. It happens in the sunlight, in the afternoon: **Since Nafai was here to pray, the priest didn't jab him. Instead he let him reach into the golden bowl of prayer rings. The bowl was filled with a powerful disinfectant, which had the double effect of keeping the barbed prayer rings from spreading disease and also making it so that every jab stung bitterly for several long seconds. Nafai usually took only two rings, one for the middle finger of each hand, but this time he felt that he needed more…so he found prayer rings for all four fingers of each hand, and thumb rings as well.**

"It can't be that bad," said the priest.

Nafai walked to the center of the courtyard, near the fountain. The water of the fountain wasn't the normal pinkish color—it was almost dark red. Nafai well remembered the powerful frisson the first time he realized how the water got its color…It was a strange and powerful feeling, to pull off his sandals and strip off his clothes, then kneel in the pool and know that the tepid liquid swirling around him, almost up to his waist if he sat back on his heels, was thick with the passionate bloody prayers of other men.

He held the barbed hands open in front of him for a long time, composing himself, readying himself for the conversation with the Oversoul. Then he slapped his hands vigorously against his upper arms, just as he did in his morning prayers; this time, though, the barbed rings cut into his flesh and the sting was deep and harsh. It was a good, vigorous opening, and he heard several of the mediators sigh or murmur. He knew that they had heard the sharp sound of his slap and seen his self-discipline as he restrained himself from so much as gasping in pain, and they respected this prayer for its strength and virtue. (Orson Scott Card, *The Memories of Earth*. New York: Tom Doherty Associates, Inc., 1992, p. 245.)

Comment: While I have no desire to personally enter that pool of blood and inflict pain on myself, there is a power and dignity in the passage I respect, much as I respect the courage of the nine-year-old Russian boy who is choosing to self-consciously cut a real covenant with the Jewish people. I love Card's worship model as myth, if not as real practice. It postulates one mythic vision of spiritual runners "hitting the wall" and then finishing the prayer marathon. Ritual blood is its central feature; the act of conquering pain is its prime vehicle. With these images Card taps into some deep aspects, subrational aspects, of the male pysche—the "challenge of pain" and the power of "warrior blood." In our hearts and our sociology we know these things. There are clear similarities to a lot of "stigmata"-oriented self-denial rituals of primitive Christianity. It also echoes many of the training exercises that Cain (of "Kung Fu") went through to become a Chau Lin priest. Even Tony Robins and his New Age pseudo-religion, N.L.P., made it big by centering on the ritual of firewalking. I find my own personal connection to this passage in my boyhood meditations, which often involved picking scabs time after time, bursting pimples, wiggling a loose tooth until it was finally ready to come loose; and in my adult manifestation of the same need, picking my teeth (to keep them clean) until my gums bleed. There is something inside of "men" that likes to face the pain challenge and emerge the victor. This is the celebration of biting down hard and overcoming. Judaism has these stories, too, though they have been minimized.

These are the very stories I hold out to Boris as the way to affirm his son's commitment. We have two dramatic moments, both only just more than implied in the Torah. (Only a residue of the original seems to remain.) The clearest is in the beginning of the book of Joshua, where all of the males born in the desert are circumcised at one time, at Gilgal, just before they become warriors and conquer the Promised Land. The Bible tells us nothing of the story, just saying: "THIS DAY I HAVE ROLLED AWAY THE TAINT OF EGYPT FROM YOU" (Joshua 5.9). It is a pun: *Gilgal*, the name of the place, means "roll away." Those of us who know our men can imagine it as the drunken type-scene where all of the marines or sailors get their first tattoo together on a shore leave. It is a warrior's challenge—a test of pain—an act of initiation. Then the people celebrate their first Passover since the Exodus. My internal midrash paints a vivid scene: a lot of off key singing, a whole cadre staggering arm in arm, and a lot of bravado and camaraderie. To call it bonding would be both trite and accurate. We can, however, imagine that they are singing their own version of "The Army Keeps Rolling Along." Also implied in the text is that a similar kind of mass circumcision may have taken place on the eve of *Pesah Mitzrayim*, the seder night before the actual Exodus from Egypt.[25]

This is Orson Scott Card's portrait of women's religion. It happens at night—it happens by moonlight. **We (women) do our worship nearer to the other end, where the lake is fed by ice-cold mountain streams. Some go into the coldest water. But the visions come to most of us when we float in the water at the place where the cold and hot waters meet. A turbulent place, the water endlessly rocking and swirling, freezing and searing us by turns. The place where the heat of the world and its coldest surface come together. A place where the two hearts of every woman are made one."** (Orson Scott Card, *The Memories of Earth*. New York: Tom Doherty Associates, Inc., 1992, p. 245.)

Comment: What I love about his portrait of women of faith is the strength and power of both their bodies and their souls. These are not simply dominated, subjected women who whisper a few silent prayers. Rather, their worship, too, is filled with danger and challenge—but coming from a very different place than his men's vision. For women it is water. Women wash blood and pain away—they do not draw blood, they do not

---

[25]Stanley Gevirtz, "Circumcision in the Biblical Period," *Berit Milah in the Reform Context*, Ed. Lewis Barth (New York: C.C.A.R., 1990).

In this paper, my teacher, Dr. Gevirtz (Z"L) suggests that these two examples of mass circumcision represent the primal form of Israelite practice, a collective ritual held close to "social puberty." This is a priestly modification—almost all scholars agree that eight-day *Brit Milah* is a "P-Source" innovation (the period of Hezekiah and Josiah), or perhaps something underlined by "R," the final redactor during the Babylonian Exile. Gevirtz points out that there are two features of this transformation that are important: (a) that circumcision in and of itself is essentially a secular act, not an entry into the covenant, and (b) that it was a collective act, performed without regard to age. I personally believe that my teacher was wrong in both of these conclusions. My understanding of Savage Religion, to use a term we will encounter later in this chapter, is that no actions are "secular." While the action is not rooted in ethical monotheism, something we might recognize as religious, it is clearly religious in their context. Secondly, the cross-cultural work of Arnold van Gennep (*The Rite of Passage*, Chicago: University of Chicago Press, 1960 [1908]) teaches that "social-puberty" is not the same as "physical-puberty." Initiation rites tend to take place for a group of youngsters who are collectively entering "social puberty." It is logical that if circumcision was a mass right of puberty—as it is in every other culture—it would normatively take place at a collective point of social puberty. However, I do believe that Dr. Givertz is correct in understanding that the individualization of *Brit Milah*—the de-tribalization—is an important feature of *Brit Milah*, and one of its sharpest breaks from other Near Eastern examples of circumcision—perhaps even more dramatic that the modification to infant circumcision.

honor pain. Women endure pain and women heal pain. I know for certain that if women had written the Jewish tradition, birth rituals would be baths—they float and endure—and, as we will see, that may take more strength and more courage. It is not just "baptism" but mikveh and Moses that emerge from women's rituals. Orson Scott Card's work is fiction, not anthropology, but he suggests some interesting marked contrasts in men's and women's souls and psyches. In many, many ways, mikveh as a ritual both opposes and balances *Brit Milah*.

Davar Aher: In an issue of *Moment Magazine*, by accident, I saw an article by my faux "son," Rabbi David J. Meyer, which talked about the circumcision of his son.[26] **"During the past five years, I have shared more than one hundred baby naming and *Brit Milah* ceremonies within our growing congregation. A few months ago my wife and I celebrated the birth of our first child. So, for the first time, I presided over a *bris* not as officiant, but as parent. Rather than delegate that assignment, I asked our expert *mohel*, Dr. Eric Tabas, if he would allow me to perform the *milah* personally, under his supervision …. He would position the simple, yet effective, *morgen* clamp, and then I would fulfill the *mitzvah*….According to the midrash, the wicked King Ahab, under the influence of his Phoenician wife, Jezebel, abolished circumcision. Elijah…intervened to restore the observance of *Brit Milah* (*Pirke de-Rabbi Eliezer*, 29). Therefore, Elijah is present at all circumcisions, so that he might witness …. In the midst of that tense, dangerous moment emerges the prophet Elijah, whom the Bible tells us will arrive "TO TURN THE HEARTS OF THE PARENTS TO THE CHILDREN AND THE HEARTS OF THE CHILDREN TO THE PARENTS" (*Malachi* 3.23–24) . …I recall my own deep feelings of nervousness at that awesome time. The moment was at hand. I looked into my son's wide-open eyes as he quietly sipped some wine-soaked gauze. His face**

---

[26]The "son" part needs explanation because it is relative to my emotional involvement. Years ago David was my camper. He later spent a summer and some other times living with my ex-wife and me in order to spend time in the larger Jewish community of Chicago. He took to calling me "Dad" as a joke, and I returned his comments with "Son." Our rhetoric had a profound impact on an already defined deep mentorship that grew into a friendship.

was remarkably trusting and serene. He was not even crying. The scalpel felt steady in my hand. And in the presence of Elijah, with the words "Who has commanded us regarding the *mitzvah* of circumcision," whatever apprehension existed quickly vanished as I brought my son into the covenant community of Israel." (David J. Meyer, "Doing It Myself," *Moment Magazine,* February, 1992.) When you lay the story of David Meyer's performing the *Brit Milah* of his son next to the M. Pickard-Ginsberg account of Jesse's circumcision, they are opposite but equal experiences. Both are sensitive and caring fathers who want the best for their sons. That caring breaks down the fantasy that the circumcision controversy is exclusively a question of gender—though it is rooted in gender tendencies. We have the spirituality of blood and the spirituality of water.

Secondly, it is interesting to note that David, too, reduces the battle over circumcision to a battle of origins—his choice being Elijah, who "TURNS THE HEARTS OF THE PARENTS TO THE CHILDREN AND THE HEARTS OF THE CHILDREN TO THE PARENTS." When I got as far in my pursuit of the "meaning" of circumcision as David's story, I realized that the battle over circumcision was not a new battle, not a new conflict—it was ancient and archetypal.

Davar Aher: Another explanaton: In *Kiddushin* 29a the Talmud makes *Brit Milah* a "man's got to do what a man's got to do" thing. It is a father's job, *not a mother's*, to circumcise a son. The Talmud makes it "law" that if the father doesn't or can't do it, *the mother can't take over.* The Bet Din (the men's court) becomes responsible. If they don't do their job, *the mother still can't take over;* it becomes the responsibility of the boy himself to find someone to do it when he is thirteen (and legally responsible). Rather than letting *the mother take over*, the Talmud asks this hypothetical thirteen-year-old to walk up to the barber-surgeon-Kohen and say, "Go ahead, DO IT TO IT—I can take it." This is very deep into "a man's got to do what a man's got to do." The Talmud bases its proof on a literal reading of a collection of biblical texts. It essentially comes to say, "God told Abraham to do it. God didn't command Sarah to do it." Because it was only Abraham's mitzvah (and this silence speaks louder than words), Sarah and all Jewish women after her are cut out of this mitzvah, and then, in turn, out of lots of other Jewish ritual involvements.

Commentary: Savina Teubal, in a challenging book called *Sarah the Priestess*, retells the story of Isaac's circumcision with a very different spin. (Savina J. Teubal, *Sarah the Priestess*. Athens: Ohio University Press, 1984, pp. 38-40.) In her version Abraham is the liar, Sarah the betrayed woman. She tells the story this way. Sarah was a Sumerian priestess who took drugs to keep from getting pregnant (in those days, pregnant women couldn't give prophecies). When Abe wanted a kid she exercised the handmaiden option. The correct way of doing this, the way Jacob did it, was that when the boys were birthed the handmaiden (surrogate) sat on the mother's knees and delivered. The "mother," not the father, not the surrogate, then named the child and was credited as his parent. Abraham and Hagar co-opted this process with a series of Egyptian customs. Hagar was credited as mother, and Abraham named the child. Later the boy was circumcised. In the process matrilineality was subsumed in patrilineality. This, according to Savina, was why Sarah freaked out and had them exiled. Later, having learned the lesson, Sarah went off the drugs and birthed her own boy. Having learned the lesson, Abraham named and circumcised the child at day eight. Jewish identity may be determined by the mother, but to be a Jewish male, as we have noted, you have to be entered into the covenant by another man, your father being first choice. Howard E. Schwartz states, "In other words, it takes a member to be a member." Savina Teubal provides at least one answer to the question, "Why didn't God tell Sarah?" Why? Because the men were stealing the boys away from their mothers, contrary to the wishes of the goddess.

Her work falls in concert with a lot of feminist historians who teach the "myth" of the axe people. In their reconstruction of HIStory and HERitage, original religions were all women's religions. **"In the beginning, people prayed to the Creatress of Life, the Mistress of Heaven. At the very dawn of religion, God was a woman. Do you remember?"** (Merlin Stone, *When God Was a Woman*. San Diego: Harvest/HBJ, 1967, p. 2.) Such is the way that Merlin Stone begins her pop reconstruction of religious history. She is one of a group of feminist historians who believe that buried under male history is women's true story. One of their key texts is this: In the *Enuma Elish*, an Akkadian creation myth circa 1700 B.C.E., is the story of the god Marduk killing the primordial goddess, a sea serpent, his great-great-great-grandmother, and then using her corpse to shape the world.[27] We are told: "He released his arrow and it tore her belly. It cut through her guts and split her heart. Having thus conquered her, he extinguished her life…He paused to view her dead body that he might divide the monster and do artful works. He split her like a shellfish into two parts. Half of her he set up and ceiled it as sky…he pierced her eyes to form the sources of the Tigris and Euphrates…Her tail he bent up into the sky to make the Milky Way and her crotch he used to support the sky."[28] This is the way the Bronze Age ends, but it is not the way it begins. Listen to another piece of ideological history. The Bronze Age…seems to be named in the image of conquest, commemorating not its culture but its technology. For the invention of bronze—an alloy of copper and tin—made possible not only more flexible and durable tools, but also weapons that would not break in battle. So in the river valleys of the earliest civilizations bronze was molded not just to the shape of the plough, but also to the shape of the battle-axe and sword.

Yet the momentous discovery of the Bronze Age was the art of writing. Now, for the first time, massive stone columns and walls of the temples are carved with images and hieroglyphs, which tell the stories that had been handed down through countless generations by word of mouth. On tablets of clay and strips of papyrus so fragile that their survival seems miraculous, pictures and words appear together, bringing to life the soul of long forgotten people.

Now we read everywhere of goddesses and gods who take their being from one Primordial Goddess who is the origin of all things. We can recognize her as the Great Mother Goddess of the Paleolithic and Neolithic eras. In other words, our mothers civilized us as far as the Bronze Era, gifting us with civilization, agriculture, writing, and religion, and then when their sons took to playing with war toys much was lost. The universal

---

[27]This is the true origin of Shel Silverstein's novel of obsessive motherly codependence, *The Giving Tree*. In both, the mother is destroyed in order to give a better quality of life to her offspring.

[28]This translation of the *Enuma Elish* is adapted from Prichard, ANET, p. 60f.

mother (earth) with her son-consort disappeared into a victimized female who is consumed by technological progress and territorial needs of the male ego. The Bronze Age comes to an end when Marduk, like the boy in Shel Silverstein's *The Giving Tree*, cuts his mother into little pieces to gratify his needs. In real historical reconstruction we can see it as the male "battle-axe cultures" invading the Middle East circa 2000 B.C.E. and fathering such civilizations as the Hittites. Goddess-son consort myths have now been replaced by "heroic stories." History now has a direction. The circle has been broken. We are now moving toward a progressive future.

Sabina Teubal casts the circumcision of Isaac into this moment and this process. In this way she echoes The Woman from Northern California. Just like Marduk, Abraham uses his knife to cause pain, not only to the infant, but also to the mother–child relationship. If Sabina is right, and I am sure there is a "truth" if not an actuality to her reconstruction, then gender conflict over *Brit Milah* is not only archetypal (cut on the matrix of pain) but historical as well.

Davar Aher: Another interpretation: But let's step back to the earliest reaches of civilization. Chris Knight is a social anthropologist. In a radical book, *Blood Relations: Menstruation and the Origins of Culture*, he suggests that women invented morality and symbolic culture by collectively synchronizing their menstrual periods and refusing sex during menstruation. This is another version of "how women started religion." His argument: (Chris Knight, "The Bloodiest Revolution," *Tikkun Magazine.* May/June 1992.*) (1) human women were at constant risk of rape because they don't physically indicate their ovulation and therefore don't drive all males into heat at the same time. If men can always desire women, rape is probable, and men have every reason to collect harems and subjugate women; (2) when women live together their menstrual cycles tend to coordinate; and (3) when the Ice Age came, humans had a need for meat. He suggests that human females (collectively) refused to have sex with males—inventing the idea of blood taboo—when they were menstruating. They would send the men off hunting during their "impure" times of month and allow only men with meat to return. Women then "purified" the meat (probably by "cooking" away the blood) from its "polluted state," and then they all could eat. When all women were only available one or two days a month (at the full moon) there was no point to rape (because it was now bad karma) and no point to a harem, because you couldn't have sex more than a couple of days a month anyway. In the process, families, communities, and religion were created.

The *Tikkun* editor conducting the interview makes this comment. **Your account provides a different framework for thinking about the kosher laws, which absolutely prohibit the eating of blood…It also gives us a new view of the menstrual laws that prohibit sexual contact with women while they are menstruating…Originally, the Torah says that woman are supposed to be "outside the camp." If women were coordinating their menstruation with the moon, and were supposed to be outside the camp (and hence outside the sphere of male authority), then we probably expect that this would have become a great women's celebration, coordinated with the new moon.** (*Ibid*, p. 91.)

And, in fact, we now do have these stories coming down to us. In *Miriam's Well, Rituals for Jewish Women Around the Year,* Penina V. Adelman offers the following feminist midrash for the month of Heshvan. **In our wilderness wandering we learned to speak to the heavens and find answers written in the shapes of the clouds. The rocks taught us to be patient. The scraggly bushes taught us how to save the rain, embrace the earth. The palm trees clustered together like children around a green pool, showing us how to join them on our knees to drink the blessed water. The desert sustained us all with the same umbilical cord.**

Is it any wonder that we who had emerged from the Sea of Reeds together into the wilderness of Sinai all began to live by one rhythm? And is the wonder any greater that the cycles of the moon reverberated in every woman at the same time, in the same way? As soon as the moon was born anew in the sky, each woman began to bleed.

Without saying a word to each other, we women knew it was time to separate ourselves from the men. As if the moon was calling us, we

*Reprinted from TIKKUN MAGAZINE, A BI-MONTHLY JEWISH CRITIQUE OF POLITICS, CULTURE, AND SOCIETY. Subscriptions are $31.00 per year from TIKKUN, 251 West 100th Street, 5th floor, New York, NY 10025.

left camp and hiked together to a wadi a half-day's distance…We bathed very carefully in different ways. The moon bathed us with her light. Our mothers soothed us with the lullabies they had sung to us when we were children. We felt purified with a green fragrance which seemed to emanate from the rocks…From a rock a spring trickled forth." (Peninna V. Adelman. *Miriam's Well.* New York: Biblo Press, 1990, pp. 32–33.) While the women are celebrating their cycle of creation, their men are ending the Jewish Bronze Age by making the Calf. Once again we are soaking in the pools of swirling waters of Orson Scott Card's women's religion. There is a connection between moon, land, menstruation, and agriculture that first connected people and God. While men wound themselves and soak in the blood, women use water to wash away their menstrual blood and pain.

Davar Aḥer: Another hypothesis: In a really interesting book called *The Savage in Judaism*, Howard Eilberg-Schwartz teaches us some pretty powerful lessons about the probably real origins of *Brit Milah*. This is a simplification of his thesis:

(1) Circumcision is connected to progeny. It is a symbolic act of "pruning" the male "tree" so that it will be fruitful. Here are his big proofs: (a) Abraham is able to father children only after he enters into the "Covenant of Circumcision," (b) "seed" and "sperm" are the same Hebrew word, and the Torah keeps talking about being fruitful and multiplying, (c) one who is not circumcised is "cut off" from his people—many commentators sense that this means he becomes infertile, and (d) fruit trees are considered "uncircumcised" for the first three years, and their fruit during that period are called "foreskins," which must be sacrificed in order to allow the tree to be utilized. He concludes: **"Cutting away the foreskin is like pruning a fruit tree. Both acts of cutting remove unwanted excess and both increase the desired yield. One might say that when Israelites circumcise their male children, they are pruning the fruit trees of God."** (Howard Eilberg-Schwartz, *The Savage in Judaism: An Anthropology of Israelite Religion and Ancient Judaism.* Bloomington: Indiana University Press, 1990, p. 153.)

(2) Circumcision is a way for men to claim the lineage of their sons. Maternal identity is always self-evident, and Jewish tradition honors that truth by defining the "Jewishness" of a son only in terms of the mother's identity. With *Brit Milah* (as traditionally commanded, a father circumcises his own son), paternity becomes legally and ritually evident. Schwartz states, **"Men thus associate circumcision with the desire to deny the connection between mother and son and emphasize that between father and son."** About this process of separating the woman from the boy, he also writes: **"The priestly writers suppress the names of women in their genealogies…as if women played no role at all in the continuation of the generations. Circumcision is one of the rituals that justifies this fiction…It creates opposition between male and female."** (*Ibid*. p. 171.)

(3) The deep connection between circumcision and the covenant started with the Kohanim in Babylonia during the exile. Circumcision was a way of cutting a boundary between Israel and their non–Jewish (and uncircumcised neighbors). Babylonians were not circumcised. By controlling circumcision, Kohanim were able to control membership in the Jewish people. Schwartz explains it this way: **"As the progenitor of a new lineage, Abraham had to be distinguished from all humans who had come before. But he also had to be connected to all his descendants. Circumcision solved both of these problems simultaneously."** When the Babylonian priests got their hands on *Brit Milah*, it became a whole new thing. **"Belonging to that community meant having a place in lineage and having the obligations that go along with perpetuating the line and keeping it genealogically pure. To make these points, to themselves and those beyond their community, the priests adopted circumcision as a sign of the covenant. Circumcision had previously been a sign of belonging to God's people."** (*Ibid*, p. 167)

In other words, like Savina Teubal, he catches a stratum in the biblical stories about *Brit Milah* that reflects the same kind of gender conflict we first found manifest in *Kiddushin* 29a—that *Brit Milah* is a "man's thing" and mothers don't have any say in the matter.

VIII.

The Braided Truth: In the Maccabean era, when *Brit Milah* marked the boundary between persecution and economic success, we have a series of stories about mothers who risked their lives to have their children circumcised. In Egypt, when circumcision was abandoned, we have the midrashic suggestion that the women (at least of the tribe of Levi) were the ones who kept the mitzvah of *Brit Milah,* along with procreation and Hebrew names. The notion of why these two traditions credited women with the courage to do a man's thing really confused me—until I had an epiphany.

I thought of the other Egypt, slavery in the South, and saw generations of women holding together families while the men were missing. I know the same story from Nicaragua, from Bosnia, from Palestinian camps, etc. Suddenly I saw a truth about pain and courage. Men are like the X-15; they know how to soar. Men challenge pain. Men conquer pain. Men become heroes, or martyrs (who are posthumous heroes). Men know how to make goal-line stands and dive into the end zone. They can do the "when the going gets tough" thing. The question is, what happens when the going gets impossible? What happens when there is no way to win—not even symbolically? What happens when things are too desperate for a martyr to make a difference? I suspect that men throw down the ball and go home. This is when the women take over. Women are like eighteen-wheelers— built for the long haul. My mother calls herself the "Bulldozer." She knew and loved my father. But she also knew this truth. My mother often had to be a Maccabean mother. When you have to challenge pain, you want the *Midat ha-Din.* To endure pain, to be in labor a long, long time, to keep the faith, not win the faith, you need the *Midat ha-Rahamin.* There are times to shed blood; there are times to soak in the water.

Gunther Plaut taught: **"The command to Abraham shifts the practice away from young adulthood to the eighth day after birth and thereby from sexual to spiritual significance."**(Gunther W. Plaut, *The Torah: Genesis.* New York: Union of American Hebrew Congregations Press, 1981, p. 118.) Now it is time to understand the full significance of this lesson. At a gift

167

show I saw an item called the electric parents. They were boxes designed to be taken away to college, to be "electronic" *in loco parentis*. Each had six buttons to push. Each button made a different comment. The electronic mother's comment was: **"Be careful, you'll shoot your eye out."** That is also her base attitude toward *Brit Milah*. The electronic father's first retort is: **"When I was your age, I used to walk three miles through the snow to school."** That is most dads' starting take on *Brit Milah*— "If I could take it, you can take it." It is stereotypic truth, but a truth nonetheless. But we know more. Maccabean women taught us more! Jesse's father taught us more.

A father who could circumcise his son at age thirteen could easily castrate him. We all know those tensions and feelings. A father who is required to perform the *Brit Milah* on his eight-day-old son learns just the opposite lesson. He is deep into his womb. He is aware of how much damage he can do. He needs to limit the pain while creating the boundary. *Brit Milah* teaches a father to be gentle, to understand and fear causing pain, not to recall walks through the snow. Likewise, on day eight, a mother who has just gone through the greatest separation from her son that she will ever know has faith that pain does end, that pain can be endured. Fathers learn to swallow their anger and be gentle. Mothers learn to live with their fears and allow for independence. Fathers hug. Mothers let go. The message of the eighth-day *Brit Milah* is in the irony, the needed irony.

The midrash teaches that Isaac circumcised Jacob on the eighth day, but Esau's circumcision (because of his red color) was postponed until his thirteenth birthday. By thirteen, Esau was out of control. By thirteen Esau was filled with anger and strength and independence. Esau quit Hebrew school. Esau intermarried. Esau left home. Esau was never circumcised. Esau was lost to the Jewish people. This was the lesson The Woman from Northern California failed to appreciate—that while, as Jews, we want to limit the pain in the world, sometimes pain forms connections. Freud called it cognitive dissonance. The rabbis called it spiritual sweetening. We can think of John Wayne and take a slug of the rotgut whisky before we bite down hard and accept this notion.

The Epilogue: I do not know the resolution of Boris' dilemma. I do not know if his son was circumcised. I never followed up. But

I did start to write this chapter. I then published a much shorter version of it in the premiere issue of *Jewish Family*. As a result, I got a lot of hate mail. My favorite read, "**Yours is the most pitiful magazine we have ever ever read, *especially* your article on circumcision. We are a group of teachers and parents and are telling everyone not to subscribe to your periodical. It lacks substance and merit. Tell Joel Grishaver to get a life. He needs one.**" Half the world thought I was telling mothers to "win" the battle and therefore empowering them to keep their husbands from "entering their sons into the covenant." The other half of the world accused me of ordering fathers to give up their patriarchal commitment to "mutilate their babies." Almost no one understood. But this letter did come in the mail, too. "**This letter is in reference to an article I recently read written by you regarding circumcision. I am a single Jewish parent adopting a non–Jewish boy child who is now nine. I have had this child for three years and the adoption will be final in a few months.**

"**He has been attending religious school since the fall of 1991 and has begun Hebrew studies this year. He is very happy about being a Jewish person but as the time gets closer I am very scared about having him circumcised.**

"**I have spoken to my rabbi, and he has told me how he feels and what to expect. I just wonder if there are any good books that you know of? I am feeling so very guilty and my family is mixed. I love this child and do not want to do anything that will hurt him due to his early abuse.**"

We had a wonderful phone conversation. I made all the right suggestions, asked all the right questions, listened empathically, and never made a hard recommendation. (It was all very socially correct.) We had a good time. It felt close. Almost a year later, this second letter came in the mail. "**Thank you very much for following up on our communication earlier in the year. My son had his circumcision on August 27—after his adoption on August 12, 1993. I moved quite fast since the process took 3 1/2 years. My rabbi will conduct a service at the University of Judaism when his calendar allows. I am presently on my way to Nashville on business and will be back on Wednesday. I would really like to meet with you and tell you the whole story. I was sitting in temple last Sunday and heard Doug Colter's song "Isn't it Amazing" and I know in my heart that**

my son was a gift from God and he is turning out to be such a terrific Jewish soul.

We talked again, and the family agreed to tell me their story. According to mom, son was more than willing to talk. We met, had dinner, and talked for a while. I was expecting a great "It bled for a while, but I could take it" kind of thing. Like everyone else, I had a voyeuristic interest in the bloody details—I wanted to know about THE PAIN but, per usual, that is not what I learned.

This was the story of a child who was circumcised at age nine. It is a story of pain and healing. But the surgical pain is only one small part.

They are now mother and son. It didn't start out that way. They are also very good friends, in many ways more like a couple than a child and a legal guardian. Both of them were adopted. She, when she was a child. Then he, in turn, when she, as a single adult, sought to fill a void in her life. They both say "we" a lot, even when it is syntactically awkward. When you hear her say, "We are both very proud of how well he is doing in Hebrew school," it sounds forced, almost like a health teacher saying "We are going to eat our vegetables." Is sounds awkward, but that is not the way it feels. When you listen for a while, you know that "we" fits their emotional syntax.

Each has experienced a lot of pain, though it doesn't show, even in very honest conversation about painful things. It doesn't show, except when you listen very carefully. The boy—along with his mother—enters my loft, which is filled with books, electronics, guitars, pool table, workout equipment, computers—all the right toys for today's middle-aged adolescent single male. He, just ten, is impressed with "all the stuff," especially the books. Most kids I allow to enter my sanctum sanctorum go crazy, wanting to play with everything, wanting to live there. But within a minute or two, realizing that I live by myself, he asks, "Doesn't it get lonely?" He sees through the pretense. He knows his truth. When you listen carefully, you can hear a wisdom grown in the healing from pain.

The outline of their story is simple. The details are enough to fill a week, maybe a week and a half of your favorite soap opera. He is an abused child, product of a birth family that divides and reemerges into new units like paramecia. Most of the parents, step and birth, are in jail. She, a professional woman, lost a child before it came to term, and then, years later, but still in that emotional vortex, separated from the baby's father. With a single will and determination she established herself as a short-term foster parent, waiting until she could position herself to provide care for a child who—because of the legal situation—a single woman might well be allowed to adopt. We all know the cliché that adoptive babies are told, "We chose you." In this case, he knows that she planned, organized, plotted, conspired, and, in lots of other ways, did just about everything to get him. He knows it. She knows it. It shows.

He came into her house at five. From day one she chose to raise him as a Jew. One, maybe two Easters and Christmases were part of their combined life as she eased the transition to High Holidays, Shabbat, and then, when he was six, Hebrew school. From the beginning she planned on a circumcision and a conversion—he was going to be a real Jew. Legal processes take a long time. A boy who was six became an almost ten-year-old before the cycle of convictions, relinquishment of custody, and then adoption could be completed. Circumcising any child is not emotionally easy. It is harder at six. It is much harder at almost ten. (I am afraid to think of it at fifteen!) She talked with rabbis and doctors and even saw a psychiatrist eight or nine times, just to clarify her feelings. She is that kind of self-aware, responsible, professional-type parent. And, as she put it, "I wanted to make sure that he wouldn't kill me when he was a teenager." Then, within a week or two of the legal window opening, she and he talked about it for the first time, then talked with the rabbi, talked with the doctor, and just did it.

He said, "It was no big deal" (while making eye contact with an adult sandbox on my coffee table, not with me). Few other facts were forthcoming. It was done in one day, outpatient. He used gas, not a local, because he hates shots. He spent the next three days "on the sofa." When I said, "That's when you were ready to kill her," he said, earnestly, "No, I didn't want to kill her," giving an answer far more serious than the question. I made a comment about his actions being heroic, brave—all that macho stuff. With a deep smile that said "I don't know what other emotion to put on my face," he shook his head and said no. Not saying, but echoing, "No big deal." Finally, looking for a way to end an interview that was awkward for him and therefore painful for me, I asked, "If some other nine-year-old boy was facing a *Brit Milah* and asked your advice, what would you tell him?" He looked up at me and started to answer slowly: "I'd tell him to do it. I'd tell him it was no big deal." Then, as if he had found the answer to avoiding not only the embarrassing parts of my question, but also the embarrassing parts of life, he said, "And if he asked what they did to me"—the smile now huge— "I'd tell him to go ask his mom." That was his ultimate answer.

What did it teach? One thing: pain can be healed, washed clean away, with love.

Fragment B

Coming of Mitzvah
Bar Mitzvah as a Faux Coming-of-Age Ritual

The standard question today is "How can we make bar mitzvah more meaningful?" The real problem is that this is the wrong question. We should be asking, "How can we make bar mitzvah less meaningful?" Bar mitzvah is a case where Jews have kept the bathwater after having thrown out the baby. Moses never had a bar mitzvah. Neither did Spinoza, Jeremiah, Hillel, Rashi, Rambam, the Baal Shem Tov, Abraham, or King David. There was no candle lighting ceremony for Amos, Jacob, Rabbi Akiva, Benjamin from Tudelah, Samuel, Isaac Luria, Rabbi Judah Lowe of Prague, the Vilna Gaon, Samson or anyone else born, bred, or raised Jewishly before 1400 C.E. or so. A lot of them turned into great Jewish men anyway.

This essay was the first piece published from this book. It has had a life of its own as a bar mitzvah essay freed from the gender/man's context. Unapologetically, this is an essay about a man's coming of age; I don't feel qualified to make it gender-neutral. I invite my "matching side."

From My Hebrew School Diary: Last night
was Daren's bar mitzvah—the first in the class. It was an astounding event. It revealed much. Recently, Eugene Borowitz has been commenting on the "end of the ethnic agenda." He suggests that as we are hitting the 1990s, the cultural and ethnic Judaism that made Israel a center, and that cared a lot about Jewish pride and belonging, was now over. Larry Hoffman, another Hebrew Union College professor, has been talking about "ethnic suburban" as the passé trend in North American synagogue design. Last night's bar mitzvah clarifies their insights.

Daren's technical performance was poor. The limited chanting he did was much more connected to unsyncopated rapping than to any melodic endeavor. It was not off-key—it was non-key. The Torah and Haftorah portions were performed as a series of unconnected single words—each uttered as an individual statement. The English parts were read with as

173

little affect as possible, and eye contact was never made with anyone—not his parents, not the rabbi, not the congregation. Even so, there was a basic dignity to Daren's performance. Knowing that he was not going to do well, he ran the graphemic-phonemic gauntlet with an inner sense of pride. It was the bar mitzvah equivalent of playing the last five minutes of the last period with a broken leg—made more interesting because Daren has no faith in, nor any commitment to, the Cosmic Gipper.

The temple service involves the parents' saying a few words to their child before passing him or her the Torah he or she will read from. Daren's mother said the following:

"Daren, over the past several weeks, while we were driving to your meetings with the Rabbi, your practice sessions with the Cantor, or your work with your tutor, you would ask me: "What is the purpose of a bar mitzvah? Why do I have to have a bar mitzvah?" You said: "I'd rather be home playing my guitar or doing architectural drawings on my drawing board." I hope that someday you will understand why a bar mitzvah is important. (There was a big pause.)

"Maybe someday in the future you will be traveling abroad and you'll, by chance, find yourself in a synagogue, and something will be familiar—and you will make a connection.

"Or maybe sometime when you are playing your guitar, you'll write an important Jewish song.

"Or someday, if you do become an architect, maybe you'll design a synagogue—

"And then you'll decide why a bar mitzvah is important."

A few niceties followed. All the time, Daren never looked her in the eye. I hope someday she figures out for herself why this bar mitzvah was important.

Daren's father said a few words. Identity and values were prominent words, but it was a generic speech. It could have been given by any adult to any child at any event. It wasn't personal and it wasn't Jewish—except by the twofold use of the word "Jewish."

Daren's own *D'var Torah* was equally revealing. His Torah portion included the story of Jacob's dream of the angels going up and down the ladder. Daren didn't talk about heaven. He didn't talk about angels. And, he didn't talk about dreams. Instead, his access to the story came from being chased by his brothers. He explained that just as Jacob was running away from his brother Esau, he, too, often found himself running away from his brothers. It included statements about how brothers can chase each other, scare each other, and still love each other. Then he pointed out that all through his life his parents had used his bar mitzvah as a milestone, listing things he couldn't do until he was thirteen. He put them on notice that he now expected to begin doing those things. He ended by talking about hoping that his brothers, his parents, and his friends would help him climb the rungs toward being a "responsible adult." Once again, neither the word "Jewish" nor any mention of "tradition" in either a personal or an abstract sense was ever voiced.

The rabbi gave a wonderful *D'var Torah*. He talked about how the rabbis said that Jacob was the first person to pray the evening service. He then pointed out that to the modern mind, the reference to Jacob praying was clearly "reading into the text." Then he reversed the image, pointing out how logical it was for a man on the run, alone, to turn to God in prayer. His culmination was that Jacob discovered God, saying, "I didn't know that God was in this place." He ended his sermon by wishing Daren the opportunity to invent prayers and find places where God could be discovered. It was a really nice homily—it was directed to the wrong family and the wrong kid. He was more on target later, when commenting that, having been at Daren's *Brit* and at his bar mitzvah, he hoped to be at his wedding—emphasizing that there were things that Daren still wasn't permitted to do until then. That, too, got a laugh.

A former temple president also spoke of being at Daren's *Brit* and then reflected on how her own daughter had grown. Not a substantive word was said about Judaism, Daren, or his family.

As I left the party several hours later, his mother thanked me for everything I had taught Daren. And then she said, "Now you'll have a chance to really teach him some Hebrew." Then, as I said "*mazel tov*" to Daren and he shrugged it off the way he had shaken and wiped off each and every kiss and pat he had received on the *bimah*, he asked: "What are you getting me for my bar mitzvah? A camera?" There was no joking or irony in his request.

The event itself was indeed a *simḥah*. A good time was had by all. It was joyous. It was a celebration. It could have been so much more.

Proem Verse: On a tape called *The Dance of Gender: The Men Went One Way, the Women Went the Other,* Michael Meade teaches: "**When the myths die, the rituals come unglued. Myth is the glue which holds rituals together. Ritual is the acting out of myth—myth speaks to the meaning of ritual. Ritual (in turn) validates the myth. It is ritual which points to the old men and gives the elders their importance—they are the ones who tell the stories and teach the dances. The myths broke, in part, because the teachers ceased to be elders.**"

Real Jewish bar mitzvah is rooted in rebellion, not conformity. Real Jewish bar mitzvah is energized by the rejection of parental authority. **The Torah teaches: "**IF A MAN HAS A REBELLIOUS AND DISOBEDIENT SON...HE SHALL BRING HIM TO THE ELDERS IN THE COMMUNITY IN A PUBLIC PLACE...AND THE MEN OF THE TOWN SHALL STONE HIM TO DEATH" (Deuteronomy 21.18–21). The Mishnah takes this text and then asks: **When is it possible to execute a boy for being a stubborn and rebellious son? He is liable for capital punishment from the time he first grows two pubic hairs** (sometime after age twelve) **to the time he grows his lower beard** (hair that fully surrounds his testicles, the last of his body hair, which often comes in the early twenties). They explain their clarification of the boy's age this way: **Because the Torah says "son," this is applied to a son and not a daughter. And because it says, "son" and not "man," an adult son is obviously exempted. And any boy who is still a child, and is therefore not responsible for fulfilling the *mitzvot*, cannot be liable for his actions** (*Sanhedrin* 8.1/68b ff).

Commentary: The single most overstated, oversimplified, profound truth taught by the men's movement is that modern Western men lack an initiation ceremony to help them leave their childhood behind and successfully enter manhood. In *Iron John*, Robert Bly states: "**Mick Jagger still puts on war paint and tights and runs around a stage screaming— because he is waiting for someone to initiate him—waiting for someone to tell him he is legitimately a man.**" The whole pantheon of patriarchal prophets—Keane, Bly, Hillman, Gillete, Moore, Meade and their camp followers—cries for a reestablishment of male initiation. Rooting themselves in Campbell's interpretations of Freud's and Jung's interpre-

176

tations of myths, hearth stories, fairy tales, and sacred texts, they call for a return to the archetypal patterns of mythic male initiation. And they are somewhat right. If you're a Jew, their work points you directly at bar mitzvah.

Their simplified (mytho-poetic) truth of male initiation is that first a boy breaks with his mother, cutting the apron strings. Then, a short time later, a boy breaks with his father, too. When he is ready, and when the cosmic cycle dictates the right moment on the ritual calendar, he is taken away by the old men and initiated into manhood. Classically, this initiation begins with a kidnapping. Classically, it is both a test and a teaching. Archetypally, the boy receives a wound—a mark—a sign that activates the transformation. Then the "hero's journey" begins. Not as well articulated, but equally true, is that the initiation of a pubic male is not the entry into manhood, but rather marks the end of childhood, the beginning of the quest that leads to manhood. Initiation is the time of two pubic hairs, not the time of growing a beard (upper or lower). To be authentic, a bar mitzvah boy should say, "Today I am no longer a boy."

At the beginning of *Iron John*, Bly writes: **By the time a man is thirty-five he knows that the images of the right man, the tough man, the true man which he received in high school do not work in life. Such a man is open to a new vision of what a man is or could be.** Here he is echoing an old rabbinic insight that teaches: **Judah ben Temah taught: "At five a boy is ready to study Torah, at ten he is ready to study Mishnah, at thirteen he is ready to be responsible for the *mitzvot*, at fifteen he is ready to study Talmud, at eighteen he is ready to get married, at twenty he is ready to pursue a living, at thirty he reaches full strength, at forty he reaches understanding"** (*Pirke Avot* 5.22). Bar mitzvah is only entry into the corridor of manhood—a hallway we have forgotten to light ever since we forgot that bar mitzvah only gets you through the door and there is somewhere much deeper you have to reach.

Davar Aḥer: So where are the bar mitzvah myths? Michael Meade's Torah taught: **When the myths die—the rituals come unglued. Myth is the glue that holds rituals together. Ritual is the acting out of myth—myth speaks to the meaning of ritual.** We need to ask? In bar mitzvah, where are the bar mitzvah myths, and where are the old men? When

I originally started this chapter I had assumed that there were no bar mitzvah midrashim. I had never heard one. Rabbis never tell them. The rabbi of the synagogue where I was Daren's and Kent's teacher is fond of building his bar mitzvah experiences around a *Sefer* Torah saved from the Holocaust and renewed for the congregation. It's not one that sings to me, "I've already been overdosed on Holocaust guilt and I am somewhat immune—it does, however, speak to a number of my kids." Lots of rabbis have fabricated lots of sources for their bar mitzvah messages, but in the course of writing this book I found six wondrous midrashim. They are authentic myths that honor courage and independence—and which also are deeply dipped in the shadow, acknowledging the dark side of the *Midat ha-Din* and its potential to be very good. These are mythic midrashim that empower real boys with their shirttails hanging out, not the perfect posed forms in the picture album. These are stories for the masters of two-pubic hairs who are just leaving the halls of childhood, not for those who are bearded, ready to enter full maturity. These are stories that find the best aspects of rebellious sons. To start with, here are three:

Abram Destroys His Father's Dreams:

In *Pirke d'Rabbi Eliezer*, a midrashic collection, we learn that Abram was thirteen on the day that he smashed his father's idols. Now that's a myth that Daren could live with. He could easily take Abram's Louisville Slugger and smash his father's accordion to bits—and with it the sense that he must like the same music, achieve the same academic pattern, follow a whole realm of expectations. Daren's running is one way of establishing independence. That is why he wanted to think himself safe now that he had passed the boundary of thirteen. He never saw any responsibilities coming. He still has a lot of false idols to smash first.

Isaac Abandons His Kids:

In *Genesis Rabbah* (63.10) we find this story of Jacob and Esau. Until they were thirteen Jacob and Esau were sent to school, and their life was controlled by their parents. When they were thirteen their parents set them free. Jacob, the one who would become "the God-Wrestler," Israel, continued his studies and remained true to the One God. Esau immediately left school and found a string of Canaanite women. He was the wild man. He followed them into idolatry and paganism. When that happened, Isaac became the first Jew to say the bar mitzvah *brakhah*: **"Praised are You, Adonai, our God, Who has liberated me from the liability of being punished** (for the horrible things) **this** (kid) **does."** Many bar mitzvah kids, especially during the horrid fights that happen in the last two weeks before the ceremony, discover that they have both a lot of Jacob and a lot of Esau in them.

Levi Renders His Enemies Impotent:

In Genesis 34, Dinah, Jacob's only daughter, is seduced by a Canaanite, Shechem, the son of Hamor. Later he asks for her hand in marriage. Simon and Levi, two of Jacob's sons, take the lead. They make a deal: if every male in Shechem's house is circumcised, the marriage will go through. Shechem is in love or lust. Two days after the surgery, Simon and Levi take their swords and slay the whole family, avenging their sister's honor. An obscure commentary (*Tosefot Yom Tov* on *Pirke Avot* 5.2) tell us that Levi was thirteen when this took place. This last midrash, especially, is Kent's story.[29]

A Story: Kent is my private puer—the boy I was never brave enough to be. He is my access to all that is heroic. I say that knowing full well that true heroes are boyish creations—that mature men become "warriors" only when necessary. Still, Kent's courage and excitement sing to my child within. I never would have understood coming of age without him. I wrote the piece that follows immediately after Kent's bar mitzvah. It tells half this story.

Early in the year the class had pizza in the Sukkah. Josh started listing who would and would not be invited to his bar mitzvah. It started a very mean conversation. You (Kent) waited for him to finish and then strongly said as a challenge, "I'm inviting the whole class to my bar mitzvah." Someone then said, "Even the Erics?" You shot back with a sneer, "Yeah, more presents." It was as good as Clint Eastwood saying, "Go ahead, make my day." I learned then that standing up for justice can be "cool" as well as right.

---

[29] Louis Ginzberg, in *Legends of the Jews*, Vol. 1, (JPS), Philadelphia, 1909, page 315ff, pieces together another junior hero bar mitzvah story, that of Elifaz. Elifaz is Esau's son, who goes after his uncle Jacob and forcibly takes back the fortune he believes was stolen from his father so many years before. Ultimately, his father Esau is more civil and reunites with Jacob in order to return the money and make *shalom bayit*—family peace.

179

When Brian and Bob got into an argument about who pissed on the bathroom floor, I was unsure of what to do or say. You burst in with an instant solution. "We'll solve it the mishnah way—each of them needs to take an oath that no more than one half of the piss on the bathroom floor is his."[30] Not only was it funny, but it taught me, in ways that I never could have made up on my own, that Jewish law really does help us solve our own problems.

When you stood up at the end of that school *tzedakah* assembly and on the spot invented "Milk and Honey" (a program where kids give candy to homeless kids, because you knew that in their hearts they needed that joy as well as the protein), I saw a depth of insight that was profound. You really did find a level of understanding of human need that practical adults missed. Regardless of the future of the project, I was inspired by your thinking, feeling, and thoughtfulness.

When we were studying your Torah portion (just because I wanted to), I told you, "If you need any help with the speech, I'm available." You shot back, "No, I want you to hear it." Not only was I proud of your independence, but you echoed an old midrash. I finally understood it. It says that God taught Torah to Moses on Mount Sinai, first by saying it to Moses, then by the two of them saying it together, and finally by Moses saying it alone. You let me learn about how students grow to say things alone.

That's half the story—all the innocence and boyish joy. Kent is my direct connection to Tom Sawyer. But Kent casts a deep shadow, too. Kent is the kid in all those Dead End Kids movies who could wind up a cop, a gangster, or a priest. He used to want to be a navy fighter pilot and go to "Top Gun school." Today his active choices are either policeman or district attorney. He also mentions "president"—talk about shadow! His life is all about off-road vehicles and paint-gun battles. Violence is also a major theme— it fills the times between fights with father, chores, and homework.

The day the Scud missiles hit Israel for the first time, we had a class discussion. Kent couldn't sit in his chair. When it was his turn to speak he was jumping up and down. He banged the table and began his talk.

---

[30]Earlier in the year we had studied the first Mishnah in *Bava Metzia*, which says that the right thing to do when two men both claim to have found a single coat is to divide the coat after each takes an oath that he found no less than half. That formula assures that neither is calling the other a liar, but honestly voicing his own truth.

"I'm for war—you all know that." The next night his mother called me to ask for a rabbinic text to study with her son (yes, she is a great lady). He was standing in front of the TV set, cheering the bombing reports like they were basketball scores.

After a class art project I made the class clean up before they could leave. I handed him the broom. He threw it at Erin, saying, "Sweep it, bitch," or something like that. She gave it back to him and said something nasty—I didn't hear. He turned and belted her, and other kids dragged them apart.

Kent called me on the phone, anticipating a fight at home. He wanted me to render a "mishnah verdict" he could use in his defense. This was the story: he and a friend had been playing around with paint guns. The car of their ex-fifth-grade teacher (whom they both hated) was parked across the street. The friend wanted to pelt it with paint pellets. Kent told him not to because everyone would know that they had done it. The friend insisted. Kent told him he couldn't do it from his property. The friend walked across the street. Kent cheered as each and every pellet hit. He asked me about his culpability. I asked his opinion and shared some thoughts. Later, he confessed—rather he bragged—that half of the paint pellets his friend used were his. He had never heard of accessory before the fact.

Commentary: In a great essay called *The Long Bag We Drag Behind Us,* Bly explains Kent. **When we were one or two years old we had what we might visualize as a 360-degree personality. Energy radiated out from all parts of our body and all parts of our psyche. A child running is a living globe of energy. We had a ball of energy, all right; but one day we noticed that our parents didn't like certain parts of that ball. They said things like: "Can't you be still?" Or "It isn't nice to try and kill your brother." Behind us we have an invisible bag, and the part of us our parents don't like, we, to keep our parents' love, put in the bag. By the time we go to school our bag is quite large. Then our teachers have their say: "Good children don't get angry over such little things." So we take our anger and put it in the bag. By the time my brother and I were twelve in Madison, Minnesota, we were known as "the nice Bly boys." Our bags were already a mile long. We spend our life until we're twenty deciding what parts of ourselves to put into the bag, and we spend the rest of our lives trying to get them out again. (Robert Bly, *A Little Book**

on the Human Shadow. New York: HarperCollins, 1988, p. 5) Kent gives off a lot of light—and also casts deep shadows. Any bar mitzvah that will work for him and set him on a course to Jewish manhood has to honor both aspects. His has a big heart filled with both courage and a strong *Midat ha-Rahamin.* He has a very young, undeveloped *Midat ha-Din* that still thinks right and wrong are essentially about being caught. They need lots of blending. The self-indulgent sensitivity of "Milk and Honey" has to meet the macho posturing of "Yeah, more presents."

Davar Aher: *Avot D'Rabbi Natan* is a commentary on *Pirke Avot.* It asks, **Why is thirteen the right age for the *mitzvot?*** Then it gives a very simple answer. **Because thirteen is when a boy should begin to be able to control his own *Yetzer ha-Ra.*** Everyone is born with the *Yetzer ha-Ra.* We all know how to be animals. Thirteen is when the *Yetzer ha-Tov* kicks in. America thinks that thirteen is the age of hormones, but the rabbis knew a second truth: it was the age to seek wisdom. That is why another bar mitzvah midrash teaches that while Solomon became king at fourteen, for his thirteenth birthday, when God did the three wishes thing, his first request was for wisdom. I think of bar mitzvah as when you get a learner's permit to begin to drive your own anger, urges, needs, and desires. When I do workshops on teenagers, I warn parents that three out of every two teenagers who get their license will dent the family car within the first year. And even though I made up this statistic, it has a great truth. Drivers' licenses are risks we have to take. Drivers' licenses are ways of growing past childhood toward adulthood. When it comes to driving their own *Yetzer ha-Ra,* most thirteen-year-olds have a lot of Parnelli Jones in them. We must expect scratches, accidents, and tickets.

Commentary: If I could redesign bar mitzvah, I would imprint on the model the Torah verse our mishnah text utilizes: "IF A MAN HAS A REBELLIOUS AND DISOBEDIENT SON...HE SHALL BRING HIM TO THE ELDERS IN THE COMMUNITY PUBLIC PLACE...AND THE MEN OF THE TOWN SHALL STONE HIM TO DEATH (Deuteronomy 21.18–21)." I would have fathers drag their sons into the synagogue courtyard. I would have each elder stand with a cinder block in his hands as the charges against the rebellious son were detailed. I would have each father admit that his son was dangerous on some level. Next, the elders would lift the cinder blocks and get ready to pelt the kids. Then, at the last moment, each parent would stop the action and say, "No, despite everything wrong with him, I want to keep him." Then the *brakhah,* **"Praised are You, Adonai, our God, Who has liberated me from the liability of being punished** (for the horrible things) **this** (kid) **does,"** would have lots of meaning.

Davar Aher: A tale of two blessings: Let's consider a

much greater shift. Once a father said these words at a bar mitzvah ceremony: **"Praised are You, Adonai, our God, Who has liberated me from the liability of being punished** (for the horrible things) **this** (kid) **does."** It is really a wonderful blessing. It acknowledges that thirteen-year-old boys are nasty creatures—still awfully wolflike. It sets the kid free, saying, "I've done my best—now it is your turn to solo." And, in an "ass-wipe" to "butt-head" kind of locker-room way, it is an intimate confession— "Kid, you may be a rebellious son, but you're my rebellious son. I love you. I want to say a blessing over you." It honors the boy in the emerging man. It says, "there is a lot of trouble ahead—let's be honest about it, but I set you free to face it on your own—I trust you. You want me—I'm here, but you're own your own."

Compare and contrast that moment with the pseudo-rituals of Suburban Ethnic Chic. Mommy and Daddy come up on the *bimah* and dress the kid in a *tallit.* Remember, *tzit-tzit* are something a boy should achieve right after toilet training. Dressing himself is also something he should be able to do by now. A private moment is now made public. We all get to see the mother take her handkerchief, spit on it, and wipe her son's face. The *tallis* ceremony is just that kind of gesture—an act of independent manhood that has now been trivialized by making it public. We allow parents to say emotional words in public—because we don't trust them to speak those words authentically in private.

But then we get to the big change. Today most parents in most synagogues say this *brakhah*: **"Praised are You, Adonai, Our God, Who has sustained us, kept us alive, and brought us to this moment."** By itself, without the other *brakhah,* it is 180 degrees in the wrong direction. It takes the spotlight off the kid—it talks about the parents. It says, "Thank God we made it to this point." Now we're adults. Even the "we" of this *brakhah* is oppressive. It keeps the kid at home. It loses the male "I–Thou" of the other *brakhah*.

Too many bar mitzvah ceremonies involve the parents leading their son onto the *bimah*, each holding him up by a pubic hair and asking everyone, "Isn't he a cute little emerging man?" and then saying, "Enjoy the party? Tomorrow you will start in on the thank-you notes or else you won't be able to go out to play." Think of what a bar mitzvah would mean if every parent took the bar mitzvah *brakhah* seriously: **Praised are You, Adonai, our God, Who has liberated me from the liability of being punished** (for the horrible things) **this** (kid) **does."** What if it meant: "Kid, I will never punish you again. No more docking, no more grounding—you are on your own. I will bug you—I will tell you when I am happy and when I am not proud of you—but you are responsible for the consequences of your actions. From now only you will punish you." That would change Kent's whole life.[31]

Davar Aher: And now a search for the old men. Bly states, and all of the rest of the "men's guys" echo: **A mother can't make a son into a man. A father can't transform a boy into manhood. Only the old men can initiate a boy into manhood.** Enter the role of the mentor, or what the mythological types call the male mother. The man who serves as the transitional figure—the teacher and initiator of a boy into manhood. Think of *Camelot* (or *Sword in the Stone* or any version of the Arthur cycle); remember Merlin and Wart in the woods, and you've got the concept of mentoring. If that doesn't do it for you, recall Manuel in *Captains Courageous* or M. Miyage in all the *Karate Kid* flicks. (How good are you at catching a fly between your teeth?) Mentoring is something the Zen folk understand—they are big on their masters. Mentoring is something Jews understand, too—we have our own masters. Translated into Hebrew, *sensai* comes out *rabbi*. The Talmud teaches: **He who teaches Torah to his neighbor's son will be privileged to sit in the heavenly academy** (*Bava Metzia* 85a).

---

[31] **"Thank God for liberating me from this responsibility"** is a *Midat ha-Din* kind of thing. It is a legal formula that acknowledges the *Yetzer ha-Rah* as a real part of a boy. It is a masculine kind of honoring—a granting of freedom and status. **"Who brought us to the time"** centers in the *Midat ha-Rahamim*. It is about sharing and connection and affirms the *Yetzer ha-Tov*. It is all about inti-macy and roots in feminine aspects. A bar mitzvah—to be a true expression of growth into manhood, needs both kinds of blessings.

The archetypal male mother, the mentor-with-a-womb, in the Jewish tradition, is Moses. Listen to this speech: "YOU HAVE LAID THE BURDEN OF THIS PEOPLE UPON ME. DID I CONCEIVE THIS PEOPLE? DID I BEAR THEM? DIDN'T YOU SAY TO ME: 'CARRY THEM IN YOUR BOSOM AS A NURSE CARRIES AN INFANT'?" (Numbers 11.12) As with the question, "AM I MY BROTHER'S KEEPER?" we know the answer is yes. Moses gives good breast. He is a great mother to the Jewish people. He is nurturer as well as lawgiver. That is why *Moses Rabbenu*, Moses, is the first and quintessential rabbi.

A Story: My real mentor was a wonderful man named Earl Auerbach. He taught me Torah in a way my father never could have, even if he had known the same Torah. My actual bar mitzvah tutor was a very nice man named Mr. Horowitz. He was really good to me, a kind man who helped me do a nice job, give a good performance at my ceremony. But I never knew anything about him. I don't recall ever really talking to him— it was all business (at least that's the way it remains in the truth my limited memory tells). Today I recall no more than his name and a memory of standing in my bedroom and using the dresser as a practice podium. I can't even remember his face, though he wore a well-worn corduroy coat with patches. On the other hand, often when I am studying, Earl's face, with its day-old Saturday-afternoon growth of gray beard, leans in toward me the way he always did when we were studying together.

At my bar mitzvah, Earl, a family friend, gave me a Hertz *Humash*. It came with an invitation to come over to his house any Shabbat afternoon and learn how to use it. Earl was a Conservative Jew, *shomer Shabbat*, who my sixth generation Reform family considered almost Orthodox. He was a major Red Sox fan who kept his TV set on a *Shabbas* clock so that he could see the Saturday games. At my bar mitzvah I was a twelve-year-old agnostic who was going one night a week to Ethical Culture meetings. By the time I was fourteen I was reading Martin Buber and Leo Baeck, and preparing to be a rabbi. (That transformation is another story.) In ninth grade I took Earl up on his invitation and spent many Shabbat afternoons during my high school years studying *Humash* with Rashi and then later a *bissel* Talmud. In my memory now, it is a lot like a silent movie. I don't remember specific lessons or insights. I do remember being served tea like an adult, being treated as one of his adult friends. Earl and I never did much more than watch a little baseball on TV (something I tolerated) and study texts. We never went to a movie, never had a long talk about my life or his or ever went to a ballgame. It was an almost pure Torah relationship—made important both because of the feeling of importance I got by being treated as one of his adult friends and because of the joy of unlocking the puzzles the texts presented. Other adults met my counseling and support needs; Earl changed my life forever by redefining for me the meaning of education. More than anything else, his patience and his interest—his unshaven, old-man smile—taught me that I was smart, really smart, something I had never learned in any school. In all my schools penmanship, spelling, and, as you well know, sitting still and waiting my turn got in the way. But with Earl, even though he never said much about my mastery, no verbalized positive feedback was needed. He transformed my self-image by methodically presenting a new text puzzle that replaced the one I had just solved or mastered.

Another Story: Earl was my private elder. Being raised as a Reform Jew, I lack the body of elders I've learned about from my mother's new husband, Harold. Harold was raised in a Conservative universe; I visited it as a boy but was never part of it. For him, and for a few of my friends, bar mitzvah began with a six-month stint at the morning minyan. There, among the regular elders and the elders-in-training who were putting in their time mourning for a parent, they learned by daily practice (or at least a couple of times a week) the regimens of the prayer service, the dance steps of the service's choreography, the art of *tefillin* wrapping, the ritual of the glass of schnapps at *simhah* times, a few good dirty jokes (which they regularly told in school), and that there was a circle of men who would always be there for them. When I think about the life cycle of the morning minyan, I think of the robot grandmother in Ray Bradury's story, "I Sing the Body Electric." She was built to replace the dead mother of a family of kids. She nurtured them through childhood and got them to resolve their grief and find fulfilling lives. She left when they grew old enough to no longer need her. She returned when they were old, feeble, and again needed her to take care of them. It is a beautiful image of the Great Mother. The *minyan*, as a corporate being, is there to celebrate a boy's birth and participate in his entry into the Jewish people, there to nurture a boy into manhood, there to comfort a man when he spends time in the ashes—

mourning his parents and later, perhaps, his wife and, God forbid, a child—there to escort a man as he ages toward the void, there to cry at his funeral, and there to remember him perpetually.

Commentary: When I was a kid they called it a "bar mitzvah special." It was an important folk ritual. Think of every bar mitzvah party you've ever been to—and you will understand. Kids sit in one universe and, as far away as they can get, parents huddle in the other. In between a few dances and the limbo there is a lot of running around and chasing. By the end of the affair there is always a water glass filled with some of everything on the table—the "bar mitzvah special." And that is precisely what is wrong with the reality of bar mitzvah as an experience—it tends to deepen rather than bridge the gap between kids and adults. The message is simple—the ritual elders are missing.

Listen to Bly: **During the nineteenth century, grandfathers and uncles lived in the house, and older men mingled a great deal. Through hunting parties, in work that men did together on farms and in cottages, and through local sports, older men spent much time with younger men and brought knowledge of male spirit and soul to them...Much of that chance or incidental mingling has ended. Men's clubs and societies have steadily disappeared. Grandfathers live in Phoenix or the old people's home, and many boys experience only the companionship of other boys their age.**

Remember *The Waltons*? Fantasize Jim-Bob's bar mitzvah (don't protest—this is a fantasy), and if your imagination matches mine, you'll understand the problem with the "bar mitzvah special." In *Waltons* world, kids still spend a lot of time with other kids. But there is a free-flowing sense of community. Jim-Bob not only dances with his mother and Aunt Martha, but the boys gather 'round to listen to Uncle Chester tell jokes to the other men before they move off. The divide is nowhere near as great—adults are nowhere near as remote.

Bly suggests that one of the reasons that boys never really mature into men is the distance between boys and men. If the gap between a boy and his father isn't bridged by another male, the boy is likely to descend into loneliness and anger. Alexander Mitscherlich teaches that when a boy doesn't make peace with his father, **"Demons move into that empty place—**

187

demons of suspicion." This is the rejection of the elders by the young. It is *Rebel Without a Cause*, *Lord of the Flies*, and especially *Peter Pan*. Mentors are the key. Imagine how the *Karate Kid* would have matured on the island of *Lord of the Flies*. Think how Peter Pan would have made out if he did "wax on—wax off" with Mr. Miyage. Now ask this question: do most bar mitzvah ceremonies move boys toward the world of men—or help to exile them to the tribe of the Lost Boys?

Almost every non–Orthodox man drops out of morning minyan right after his bar mitzvah. Harold did, my friends did. But they all came back later, drawn like a magnet to a source of power when their fathers, mothers, and wives died. From then on their membership in this supportive circle of men was permanent. They knew with surety that they would be back once a year, and that their sons would be there—kaddish would follow in their steps. It is a cycle of coming of age, into real maturity, which is all but lost today in non–Orthodox circles. The carpools killed it, the suburbs did it in. And sadly, the Reform movement never even valued it. They never understood that the Jewish people needed a place for the old men to go.

Once, the American bar mitzvah was legitimately an initiation into an eternal circle of elders who would always be there when life's real tests were faced. Unfortunately, it has now become something else.

Viewed in this context, bar mitzvah comes close to being a true initiation into the corridor of manhood. To start with, the rituals that Bly et al. bemoan as missing in Western culture are present. There is a ceremony. There is the transfer of sacred objects: *tallit* and *tefillin*, the literal trappings of Jewish manhood, are bestowed (along with a kiddush cup from the men's club, a maẖzor from the sisterhood, and a tree planted in your honor by the congregation). Once, at least, there was good access to male mentors, both formally, as one worked with a bar mitzvah tutor, rabbi, and cantor, and informally, as one spent time as part of the standing minyan. (Today, in many settings, in most non–Orthodox settings, this has collapsed into, at best, a *Tallit* and *Tefillin* Club that meets on a Sunday morning once a month or so.) But most important, bar mitzvah was an initiation into a circle of men, a real and symbolic gathering of men who existed to face the very real question of death and how to live after it. The truth is this: without the standing minyan, without the kaddish circle, bar mitzvah is initiation into nothing. And the higher truth is that even though it came close, bar mitzvah was never intended to serve as a significant turning point, a real rite of passage; it never had the foundation to support that significance.

Davar Aḥer: Bar mitzvah is an example of spontaneous generation and probably *immetatio ex goyim*. Honestly, there are no biblical roots to the ceremony. Later, the rabbis, using their best midrash tools, tried to countersink the ritual into the text—but it is not inherently there. It isn't even found in the early midrashim. This is a pretty good approximation of the "True History of Bar Mitzvah":

The Torah, if anything, is anti–bar mitzvah. Only one biblical character is ever mentioned at thirteen. That is Ishmael—and he is overtly labeled as "the failure." The wild-ass boy, the case where the covenant didn't take. If anything, the Torah, in the same way it rejects the mythic symbolism of "golden objects" as eternal truths by throwing the Golden Calf in our faces, rejects a public rite of passage through the example of Ishmael. But Jews don't leave well enough alone.

In the Talmud, bar mitzvah is mentioned only once in the "ages" of man according to *Pirke Avot*—the rabbinic version of "in the morning he crawls." There are also a number of "two pubic hair" texts that try to denote the age of legal responsibility primarily (but not exclusively) for sexual acts. The Talmud is big on wondering "**whose consummation is a real consummation.**" They make such important statements as "**Intercourse with a boy who is nine or younger is as useful as sticking in a finger.**" The laws do, however, extend to the concept of contracts and other legal obligations. However, no myth and no ritual is attached to these statements. And if you look at this passage, you'll see that the rabbis are big on blurring the thirteenth birthday and keeping it from being a focal event. MISHNAH: **One should not "afflict"** (with fasting, etc.) **children on Yom Kippur; but one should start to train them a year or two before, in order that they become used to the practices.** GEMARA: **Rabbi Naḥman said: "At nine and ten one trains them by the hours** ("Can you make it fasting to noon this year?" etc.). **At eleven and twelve they fast to the end of the day based on Rabbinic teaching.** (Because the Bible doesn't prescribe it— but we think it is good for them.) **And at thirteen they are obligated by** biblical law to fast all day" (*Yoma* 82a). Notice, in this model of Talmudic Judaism, thirteen is no big deal. It is not the first time a boy fasts, not the first time he performs the *mitzvot*—not even close. Thirteen is only the first time it counts. Thirteen isn't a rite of passage, a sudden transition of psychic space; instead, maturity is something a boy eases into year by year.

However, to prove that the bar mitzvah ceremony should not exist, or at best should be understated, we need to look at the single exception. (Come on—you know that exceptions always prove the rule.) In *Meseket Sofrim* (a Talmudic wannabe tractate), we are told of a neo–bar mitzvah ceremony that isn't bad: "**In the days of the Second Temple the sages used to bless the twelve- and thirteen-year-olds who completed their first fast.**" This is legitimately not bad as a bar mitzvah model, because it is a rite of passage with a test. If you are man enough to fast all day, you get the blessing. Bar mitzvah is the result of a *mitzvah* challenge. Imagine the modern synagogue today. Who would make the fasting challenge a condition of bar mitzvah (let alone **mandating**, rather than just encouraging, staying out of school and attending services) on the High Holidays?

In *Yalkhut Shimoni* we are told that this fast marked the transition from elementary school to the *beit midrash*. Now hear this—consider this possibility—bar mitzvah is no longer a sign of completion of Hebrew school. From now on bar mitzvah is the entrance ritual to Hebrew high school or a confirmation program. You want to graduate—go on to Hebrew high school—then we'll celebrate your entrance with a rite of passage.

The first formal mention of a bar mitzvah takes place in 758 C.E. and is the bar mitzvah of Rabbi Yehuda Gaon's son (*Baal Oreckhot Hayyim, Brakhot 5*). It is mentioned, I think, as an exception, because Yehuda Gaon was "top dog," the leading rabbinic figure in the world. I sense that it was more akin to coronation—an anointing of the *dauphin*—than a universal practice. We are told that Yehuda's kid was called to the Torah, and that Dad said the *Barukh She-Petarani*, the "thank God I'm no longer responsible" parent's *brakhah*. We have no record of what the caterer used as the theme for the party or whether they had a band or a deejay. The first normative mention of bar mitzvah is not until the fifteenth century (*Sefer Tziyyoni* of Rabbi Menahem Tziyyoni, as a commentary on Genesis 1.5). The Bly guys would argue (I suspect) that bar mitzvah was an archetypal male need that finally burst out of the anti-mythological and anti-pagan repression of the shapers of biblical Judaism. I suspect it was not so much an imitation of High Church ritual as the transition from page to squire as it skewed into the initiation of apprentices. Remember, the Church never adopted a formal public rite of passage, either. In any case, bar mitzvah is a folk creation that finally gets authenticated by this fifteenth-century legal work.

Until bar mitzvah hits twentieth-century America, until Hallmark Cards got its hands on it (the Baal Shem Tov never sent out New Year's cards; neither did the Vilna Gaon), bar mitzvah was a minor Thursday morning minyan enhancement—or a short pause in the Saturday minyan. It consisted of an *aliyah*, and maybe a serving as *Baal Korei* (Torah reader) or as *Baal Maftir* (Haftorah reader). Neither of them were any big deal—about the same significance as getting picked to lead the class in the pledge on your birthday—the year you are in fourth grade. Bar mitzvah was a brief moment, a glass of schnapps for everyone and "a little fish and herring afterwards," with maybe a family dinner. Kids often went to school after their Thursday morning initiations. It took the market-driven religious innovation (florists more than rabbis) to make bar mitzvah a big deal.

If you want to know how much of a big deal bar mitzvah was to the rabbis, or at least some of the rabbis, come and hear this: **a minor who knows how to shake the *lulav* becomes obligated for the *mitzvah* of *lulav*. A minor who knows how to wrap himself in a *tallit* is obligated to observe the laws of *tzit-tzit*. A minor who knows how to look after his father's *tefillin*, his father must get him his own pair of *tefillin*. If a child knows how to speak, his father must teach him Torah and the recitation of the Shema** (*Sukkot* 42a). This is a merit-badge approach to maturity. Mitzvot are acquired one at a time. Manhood isn't a moment. Bar mitzvah isn't an awards ceremony. Rather, Jewish manhood is acquired one competency at a time. This, too, suggests a lot about the reconsideration of bar mitzvah as process rather than moment.

To be honest, later sources undo this text. By the time we get to the *Shulḥan Arukh* (a fourteenth-century law code), when the bar mitzvah ceremony has come into being, we are told, "**Unlike other *mitzvot*, *tefillin*, which is closely related to spiritual maturity, should be put off until shortly**

191

before the thirteenth birthday" (*Orekh Hayyim* 60.37). *Tefillin* becomes the prime symbol of the bar mitzvah transition; its acquisition becomes part of the bar mitzvah process. That was the role of the morning minyan. That is why Shabbat-only (where you don't wear *tefillin*) *minyanim* are doomed to failure as vehicles to initiate boys into men; the symbol of transition stays in the bag.

Davar Aher: I have heard the karate theory of bar mitzvah. It is a "if you can't lick them, join them" approach that says, "Just as students of karate are trained to use their opponents weight against them, we should use bar mitzvah as a way of coercing families into greater Jewish living." The idea is that just as karate experts know that leaning or momentum in any one direction is a moment of weakness, and can use that weakness or that momentum against their opponent—especially a bigger opponent—bar mitzvah is a time of leaning and momentum. I find little merit to this notion (though I, too, am often caught in its flow). The flaw is that while we win the fall, we also often train families never to lean in a Jewish direction ever again. Think of Daren's *simhah*.

Cherie Kohler Fox is one of the visionary prophets and educational practitioners of the North American Jewish community. Some think she understands bar mitzvah better than anyone else in the world. Once she asked me, "If you were a bar/bat mitzvah tutor and you wanted to open a second business to make additional money, what business should it be?" JOEL: "Invitations?" CHERIE: "No!" JOEL: "Catering?" CHERIE: "No!" JOEL: "What?" CHERIE: "Contracting, because no one has a bar or bat mitzvah without remodeling the house. That's because bar/bat mitzvah is a life-cycle event for the parents—not the kids!"

Commentary: That is powerful and that is deep. And here lies the truth: bar mitzvah has become everything it should not be. In a culture where there is no clean way of becoming an adult, a real adult, bar mitzvah is the rite of passage. It is saying to the world, "I, the parent, am adult enough to have raised a kid who can now grow two pubic hairs." Bar mitzvah ceremonies, as we know them, simultaneously make parents into adults while they infantalize the kids. (Just think of the board of embarrassing childhood photos—including the bearskin rug picture—that is de rigueur at such events.)

Almost all of today's bar mitzvah steps move in the wrong direction. Bar mitzvah was supposed to be entry into the world of men—a debut in the public arena, a kind of coming out. Instead, we have moved the ceremony from the Monday–Thursday pre-market day world of men to late Saturday afternoon. The synagogue is no longer entry into the world of responsible commerce—it has become an extension of our own living room. The ritual elders are gone—only invited guests remain. It is a birthday party, not a "going public."

Davar Aher: A word about adult bar and bat mitzvah ceremonies. These ceremonies do a lot of good in the world. This is especially true of women, who are empowered to recapture a moment of which they had been deprived long ago. But there is essentially nothing adult about adult bar and bat mitzvah experiences except for the age of the child participating. I say this without any hostile or sarcastic intent. This is the truth. Adult bar and bat mitzvah heals the inner child; it has nothing to do with meeting adult needs. It is very important. It is healthy. But it has nothing to do with becoming an adult for the adults who are participating, either.

The Braided Truth: Regrowing a mythic bar mitzvah: Robert Moore and Douglas Gillete are the Jungian dynamic duo in the men's pantheon. Their book, *King Warrior Magician Lover,* is the key work that looks at the four primal male archetypes (according to Jung). They are more psychological and less mythic than many of the other men's writers. About initiation they say, **A man who "cannot get it together" is a man who has probably not had the opportunity to undergo ritual initiation into the deep structures of manhood. He remains a boy—not because he wants to, but because no one has shown him the way to transform his boy energies into man energies. No one has led him into direct and healing experiences of the inner world of masculine potentials.** The question we have to ask is, does bar mitzvah today have anything to do with entering a boy into **direct and healing experiences of the inner world of masculine potentials?** In the old days, in the classic initiatory societies, the preparation for the rite of initiation had more to do with mastering the myths and dances of manhood than with memorizing the dance steps and rituals of the rite of passage itself. The questions we have to ask are:

193

(1) is preparation for bar/bat mitzvah time spent with ritual elders who are preparing and teaching about manhood? (2) does the ritual, as manifest in the context of today's culture, any longer make any connection to the transformation from boy psychology to man psychology? (3) in the process of becoming a bar mitzvah, does the boy have any sense that he has acquired any "secret men's wisdom"? I suspect not—in fact, I know in my stomach that bar mitzvah has become a cul-de-sac, neither serving the moment nor providing passage. No one ever talks to boys about "boy-feelings" and "man-feelings." It has nothing to do with the day or the process—we just work on the haftarah.

Gillette and Moore explain it this way: **Boy psychology…is charged with the struggle for dominance of others, in some form or another, and is often caught up in the wounding of self, as well as others. It is sadomasochistic. Man psychology is always the opposite. It is nurturing and generative, not wounding and destructive."** Being a boy is no longer being a child. It is finding the inner strength to break free of Mother and the courage to challenge Father for domination. Being a boy is breaking with dependence and beginning the hero's journey.

Boys are heroes. When you met Kent you understood. On a radio show I once heard Douglas Gillette explain, **"Tom Cruise in *Top Gun* is a hero"** (he is all about bravery and honor). **"Yul Brynner in *The Magnificent Seven* is a warrior—fighting when necessary, but caring much much more about human life."** Remember the scene where he shoots a man from a long distance with a pistol—an impossible shot. The kid compliments him a lot; he just sneers, " **'I was aiming for the horse.' Boys are heroes, seeking honor and courage—that is what they need to individuate. Men are warriors, with the strength to fight when necessary, but knowing there are much more important things to do with life."**

It is wrong for us to suspect that any thirteen-year-old boy is ready for manhood; rather, they are just ready to begin that quest. Bar mitzvah is a time to initiate a boy into his quest for the heroic—it is the time of two pubic hairs, a time of great danger, when the heroic threatens to go off the deep end as an overly rebellious son, one who is out of control. Gillette and Moore explain that most coming-of-age experiences in our culture (football teams, gangs, and other peer-group adolescent breaks with parental control) are pseudo-initiations. These peer groups tend to emphasize machismo and involve, on one level or another, tests of endurance of emotional and physical pain. We tend to make bar mitzvah an end—an imitation in the name of manhood out of childhood. We then tend to abandon teens to the primitive tribes of wild adolescence, hoping they find their own way out of the jungle. Most b'nai mitzvah ceremonies leave the mother in power at home and drive the kid's independence to be expressed in the mall and other tribal gatherings. The ritual elders are completely missing. So is the rest of the journey.

When the hero's quest is over, the boy becomes a man. When the dragon of the *Yetzer ha-Ra* is slain and under control, when the *Midat ha-Din* knows where it ends and the *Midat ha-Rahamin* begins, maturity approaches. Then it is time to grow a beard. **In order for Man psychology to come into being for any particular man, there needs to be a death. Death—symbolic, psychological, or spiritual—is always a vital part of any initiatory ritual. In psychological terms, the boy ego must die. The old ways of being and going emerge. Pseudo-initiation, though placing some curbs on the boy ego, often amplifies the ego's striving for power and control in a new form, an adolescent form regulated by other adolescents** (the bar mitzvah special). **Effective, transformative initiation absolutely slays the ego and its desires in its old form to resurrect it with a new, subordinate relationship to a previously unknown power or center. Submission to the power of the master masculine energies always brings forth a new masculine personality that is marked by calm, compassion, clarity of vision, and erativity.** That is growing a beard.

In Hebrew, the word **zakayn** means beard. **Zakaynim** is the word for elders—the bearded ones. Bar mitzvah is the time of an emerging struggle—real adulthood is its resolution. Kent and Daren have long struggles ahead. Just as bar mitzvah should honor the beginning of the struggle, some point of victory should also be defined.

Near the end of Book of Numbers (27.18–23), God turns to Moses and says, "SINGLE OUT JOSHUA SON OF NUN, AN INSPIRED MAN, AND LAY YOUR HAND UPON HIM...INVEST HIM WITH SOME OF YOUR AUTHORITY, SO THAT THE CHILDREN OF ISRAEL WILL OBEY." MOSES DID AS ADONAI COMMANDED. HE TOOK JOSHUA AND HAD HIM STAND BEFORE ELEAZAR THE PRIEST AND BEFORE THE WHOLE CONGREGATION. HE LAID HIS HANDS ON HIM AND GAVE HIM ORDINATION. This is the myth we need to reincarnate—we need to share the mystery of the extra hand, the adult hand.

When we reinstall the ordination of adults as successful learners, teachers, and mentors, when it is in place as the achievement of the Torah of bearded elders, then we have a fighting chance (because it needs to be a fighting chance) to escort the boys with two pubic hairs toward a mature Jewish destiny. This is the way to tame our beloved rebellious sons.

Epilogue: From My Hebrew School Diary: About a week later I pulled Daren out of class. I took him into the sanctuary by himself, and we redid his bar mitzvah. This is the *D'var Torah* that I wrote, read, and then gave to him. It is not the ultimate statement on bar mitzvah—just one meant for that moment.

Dear Daren,

I really hated what you did in class on Tuesday, but I really respected you for it nevertheless. It is not fun to be told that the very thing you are investing a lot of time and effort in is useless and not worth anything—which is exactly what you said about my giving up 25% of my working time this year to teach your class—but at the same time, you did it politely, with serious intensity and commitment. Even though I disagree with you, I really respect the way you acted out your beliefs. Believe it or don't, it is indeed a mark of growing into a bar mitzvah.

My plan for today, I am sure, will make you angry. I'll bet that you will have already called it "queer" and said "no way." But I intend to go ahead with it anyway. I look at it this way. You are stuck with your parents for the rest of your life. You will be part of this temple (and therefore stuck with the rabbi) for a whole bunch more years. I will disappear at the end of this year. I get a year to teach—then I'm gone. Therefore, I'm going to take today to tell you what I think—we can then talk more about it—or we can drop it, but I want my one shot to tell you what I think—what I feel, and what I believe.

Today we are going to rerun your becoming a bar mitzvah—just you and me. When you ask me why, I'm going to tell you, "Because it didn't seem to work the first time." Then I am going to insist. Last week you very specifically told me that your bar mitzvah didn't mean anything, that it was a waste, that you only did it for the presents. Today is my chance to tell you what becoming a bar mitzvah can mean—my version, Joel's version, not Daren's version or anyone else's. It is just what I think, but it may help you figure out your reasons.

I think that you should be proud to have and be a bar mitzvah for three reasons: because of a roll of film [just like the one I had in my hand], because of a can of underarm deodorant, and because of Adolf Hitler.

Why a roll of film? Because a blank roll of film is going to be my second bar mitzvah gift to you. On one Sunday to come I am going to let you out of class with my camera to spend an hour shooting Jewish pictures. If any of those pictures are good, and I suspect several will be, I will use it (or them) with your name on it in one of our publications. I want to be the first to publish a piece of Daren's work. I suspect that I won't be the last.

A bar mitzvah is a lot like a roll of blank film. You are a lot like a roll of blank film—many images can be engraved on you; the silver nitrate emulsion can turn into almost anything. You were right when you said that bar mitzvah is a starting point—a beginning of things you can do. You were wrong in thinking that it had to do with rules and bedtime and that stuff. My old college roommate, David Ross, used to say all the time, "People aren't human beings, they are human becomings." Bar mitzvah is the beginning of your actively deciding who you become. At your bar mitzvah you came to the head of a line that is two thousand or more years long. Yes, there are a lot of people in that line, but at that moment you came to the front—it was your turn in the light. Whether you walk off alone, whether you get lost, or whether you become part of a two-thousand-year-old team is now your own choice. This is your first moment of becoming.

Why a can of deodorant? Not because of the smell—even though your body is changing, growing hairs, and needing it. Rather, because a can of deodorant teaches us an important lesson. For almost fifty years people used to spray deodorant under their arms, used to spray paint onto rusty metal chairs, used to spray wax onto tables that needed to be polished. Spraying things was easy. It did a lot of work quickly, and there was little to clean up. Then we learned that spraying our underarms so we didn't stink, and the other things we were spraying, were destroying the ozone layer and would ultimately end life on earth. Something as harmless as Right Guard® could end the world. The lesson here is that being a good person isn't just not stealing, not robbing, and not raping—it takes a lot of thought. Just "doing no harm" isn't easy. Learning to make a difference, to be just one person and change the world, is much harder.

I want you to know that you impress me. In Yiddish there is a word, *mensch,* which means "a man." But in Yiddish it means the ultimate a person can be—being a real person (not a poser). In English we think just the opposite; being a human being is a limited thing. We say, "What do you want from me? I'm only human." The Jewish idea is that being a total person is the ideal—that's a *mensch.* I really think that you are a *mensch.* There are little moments, kindness when you, Josh, and I were playing guitar, the way you set up conversations—that show me that you care about other people's feelings—that while you are working on figuring out who you are, you also worry about others.

As far as I am concerned, Hebrew school is not about roots or reading prayers or mapping the Judges' conquests (even though we do all of those things). Hebrew school is about standing in a two thousand-year-old line of people who are trying to be good people, who are trying to make a difference, to leave good images on their film and positive photographs behind and make the world a better place. That is why a bar mitzvah is about underarm deodorant cans. By the way, they changed the stuff in the cans about seven years ago, so now the sprays do no harm—that, too, is a lesson.

Why Adolf Hitler? Last year I did a guest teaching shot in Sacramento. This kid up there asked me at the end of a lesson, "If God made everyone equal, why did God make Nazis?" I believe what he was really asking was, "Why did God make evil people?" I told him that God didn't make people evil—that God gave people the choice between good and evil, between being Mother Teresa or Adolf Hitler or anywhere in between. Then I realized something. I said to him, "You know why your parents make you go to Hebrew school—because they want to make sure that you learn not to be a Nazi. Hebrew school is the place where you learn how to choose not to be Adolf Hitler." I really believe that. That is why treating each other well is so important to me—that is why I am giving up my time.

When you spoke about your Torah portion, you said that the one thing you really identified with was Jacob's running away. That made me sad. Yes, I know about running away. Yes, I've done it a lot. No, I don't always think it is bad. But what made me sad was that you missed the dreams. Your portion is the ultimate artist's portion. You do art, you're learning music, you're learning photography—they're all about dreams and ladders, all about images of what can be. Jews are really a club of people who dream about the future—who work to make those dreams come true. Being a bar mitzvah is having the guts to make the dreams come true. I really respect your guts, and your individuality, and the sense of dignity you manifest. I think that they will take you very far. If I could teach you only one thing, it would be a sense of connection to others in the process. You do not have to stand alone. That is the purpose of standing in a line of two thousand years worth of people for thirteen years.

I know that you have already taught me a lot this year, both in and out of class. I also believe that I have some worthwhile things to teach you—if you will let me. I hope that you will.

If not, I've shot my wad—you've got my three big lessons: a roll of film, a can of underarm deodorant, and Adolf Hitler. Here is the roll of film—I look forward to the images you are going to make both on it and in your life. Amen.

Fragment C

Toward A Theology of The Jewish Family
The Dysfunctional Myth[32] of the Functional Family

An Insight: Here is my latest vision of the truth: Everyone, at least everyone I know, has two families. One is our real family, our birth family (or if you prefer "our families of origin"). It is the one in which we feel stuck. Our real families frustrate and anger us, they embarrass us, they challenge our individuality and maturity—yet we know that they are always there. Each of us also recruits and adopts a "pseudo-family," a group of friends who feel like family. We celebrate our holidays with this pseudo-family (when we can get away with it), we confide our inner lives to our pseudo-families—telling them all the things our real families wouldn't understand. We share vacations and joys with our pseudo-families; yet, we live with a deep insecurity (a hidden, inner-knowledge) that ultimately our pseudo-families will drift away on the winds of mobility, lifestyle change, economic evolution, or just disappear because of the currents of time. It is the very rootedness of our real families which generates much of the tension. We live with the dual knowledge that they will always be there for us—no matter what, and that we can never escape them—no matter what. Likewise, it is the very ad hoc status of our pseudo-families which allow the intimacy and safeness—and in turn, the deeper sense of ultimate loneliness. Pseudo-families, in an ironic sense, offer all the freedom and angst of a one-night stand.

My friend Adrianne Banks argues that this paper should speak of three families—adding "the ones we create." She argues that I am speaking as "author-as-child" and ignoring "author-as-parent." I believe that stuck is stuck. I hear her truth. I acknowledge it, but it is not mine to speak.

---

32 Myth in this essay is used in a Jungian sense of archetypal truth, rather than in the more colloquial understandings of "false assumption." It is best understood within Robert Bly's chosen explanation, "a myth is a truth frozen in a story."

200

Our family lives are lived suspended between these two poles: the classic mythic roots of the family with all its tension and darkness and the "colorized" illusions of the Louis B. Meyer idealized "Andy Hardy" All American Family—which has tried to digitalize away and mask all the shadows. Pseudo-families try to recreate the illusion that our real families cannot but fail to ever actualize. We are trapped between the "dark" myths of ancient Greece and the "lite" modernist truths of popular culture of an era now passing.

Think Oedipus! Think Demeter! All that stuff. Wicked step-mothers, absent or impotent fathers, jealous siblings, mad progenitors, witches, demons, giants, and capricious monarchs are the things which animate the families in "real" fairy tales; these are the mythological family truths. They stand in marked contrast to the free market illusion of hands with better cuticles thanks to a liquid dishwashing detergent. Oedipus is not the "Ultimate Bob" 50s advertising icon Dad with the pipe in his mouth. We live in a time where all the cracks in our real families have broken through our facades. Of the 1950s illusion of 2.2 children, two parents, and a dog, nothing remains but the mirage evoked by retro-suburban chic. It never was. It will never be. Families are not exclusively happy, sunlit, endlessly joyous places that can solve every problem with a punchline in 28 minutes. No one lives at Club Med. Family is not a vacation.

The darkness which motivates Dan Quayle's attack on Murphy Brown is also the fear which is a major motivator of "Jewish Family Education." They both flow from a "panic" that families do not appear stable enough to bear the weight we wish to place upon them. So Dan Quayle argues, in essence, that we must insist upon "family values" because they appear to be vanishing. And, the popular voice of the Jewish community is chanting "family education" to sustain a sense of Jewish family which seems to be all but gone. This is the ultimate darkness—the vortex of our unspoken night terrors. We are all deep into denial, not that the family of our dreams is dying, but that, finally, we must admit that it never was at all.

We now live in a moment where there are no families who live up to the Hollywood myths. Any of the families you think you know which do are actually the exceptions which prove this rule—or the ones with great camouflage. It is a time where all that seems to have been stable in our culture is disintegrating. Into that void, the family educator has charged. We do not know whether he or she is Don Quixote or Diogenes or Sisyphus or Persephone—the beginning of the end or the end of the beginning.

PRE-TEXT: VILLAGE POWER

A child lay in a cradle
The messenger stood beside the cradle
Villagers formed a ring around them both

WHO TAKES RESPONSIBILITY FOR THIS CHILD?

Two parents came into the circle
We will feed and clothe
Bathe and protect
Teach and love the baby
The siblings came into the circle
We will tell the baby the story of our family
And ease the child into the routine

The elders stepped into the circle
We will pass on the history of our people
And give guidance to the parents

The neighbors stepped into the circle
We will watch out for the child
When he leaves the home
And wanders along his life journey

The community stepped into the circle
We will guard the path of the child
Guiding the steps on the pavement
Offering the knowledge we have stored

The children stepped into the circle
We will show the baby how to be a child
Making discoveries
Learning all that we can

The messenger rocked the cradle
And smiled
For the circle on the outside
Had become the inside

Leaning into the cradle he whispered
"I am leaving you to the care of the village.
Your life will be rich."
And his job being done
He left the child
With the village

The fires of the village need rekindling
We must return to the rearing by the village
The cries of the families are growing louder
Let the talking drums speak
Speak to the needs of the village
Bring the babies to the village
Let the rearing begin
With the love of the village!

An anonymous poem, typewritten on the back of a flyer
and then tacked to the bulletin board in my loft complex.

Now this essay can begin ...

PROLOGUE:

Snapshot: It is after class and I am talking to "The Kid" again. Usually we do a couple of rounds of "*My Father the Fascist,*" starring the Kid as "*The Prisoner in the Iron Mask Who Was Eternally Grounded.*" It is a great *Oedipal* Struggle between father and son: epic in its angst, classic in its form, and a lot of fun to empathize with and smile at. (I knowing that both of them will eventually outgrow it—somewhat.) It is the stuff that the first few teen years are made of—especially for boys in the prime of their *puer*. I do my ritual intervention: "He's a father, that is what he is like. You have a lot of other feeling toward him, but you also love him—learn to live with it. Parents are like that."

Today, it is different. Today, the Kid is crying and mumbling to his shoes. From the sounds that emerge one can detect evidence of a fight between parents which had evoked that abhorred curse word, "Divorce." The Kid is in terror. He nobly proclaims that he will stop it. That he will be better behaved—a better student—that he is the only one who can hold it together—that he will stay home from camp—that he will never leave home. This, too, is classic, but I am too close to the situation—too into empathy—to think that this round is cute. Eventually, he faces up to the fearful decision: "The Choice." His answer, a shock to me only at first reflection, is that he will go with his father. I respect him too much to try to wipe away his tears or tell him it will be better. When a pause finally invites my comment, I tell him, "I actually think the fighting is a good sign." His father had been ill for almost a year. While his father's actual life had never really been at risk, all in the family had been living with the fear of his dying. This fight was an omen of good health. It said, "Now we have enough faith to break out of the mourning mode and have the fights over the anger and fear we've been saving up." He cried some more. Then we hugged. Then he went home. A week later, all I heard of the resolution was, "It's better." Then we went on to other conversations—safer stuff.

Snapshot: I go up to Seattle and make Seder with my friend Carol. We clean, cook, actually see a movie in the afternoon before first Seder. Everything is great. Second Seder is designed to be an instant video replay. It spins into a huge fight. Probably it is my fault—that is what the Russian judge says. Late at night, after the mix-multitude have returned home, the tears and the screams break forth. (It is as bad as the "*Thanksgiving from Hell*"—my worst adult attempt to return to the nurturing bosom of my birth family. It was the one time I took the words of Rabbi Shimon seriously. He said (Avot 5.4): **"When three eat together at the same table and have not spoken words of Torah there, it is as if they had eaten dead bodies."** That year, by the time the ritual arguments involved in the preparation had taken place, the turkey tasted like something the undertaker had rejected.) Maybe it was a cornerstone. Carol and I yelled and blamed each other, then hugged and made up, knowing that perhaps the "adoption" had taken—we had blended into a real family—perfectly accessorized with family feuds. We were now a real family; no matter what the fight the resolution would always follow. We, too, could safely be hurt and petulant and needy—and have the fights and gaps of silent self-righteousness every family needs. "The *Thanksgiving from Hell*" was the last time I ever went home. I swore to myself that was the case. I have been there many times since. It is an annual pilgrimage. I earn lots of frequent fighter miles.

Snapshot: I am having dinner with another one of "my kids." His parents have just separated. This meal becomes a game, a game called *"Which One Shall I Choose?"* (He has named the game—not me!) In between trips to the salad, pasta, and dessert bars, I listen and ask just enough questions to allow him to continue uninterrupted. I learn of the competitive bribes each parent is offering. The bottles of wine (for an eighth grade party), the relaxed curfews, the confusion. These stories are intermixed with stories of alternating strictness—when instead of trying to induce the child's affection, each parent is proving to the other their ability to impose stability. When it all comes down to it—the choice is simple— the boy who is just growing his first pubic hairs chooses to be with the father who is losing most of his hair—and who has again taken to wearing gold chains. Adolescence springs eternal. All this takes place between gulping handfuls of colored sprinkles which were intended to be "sprinkled" on the soft ice cream. He just keeps eating them.

A couple of weeks later the couple has reconciled. It is just another offering in the salad bar of family life. I suspect that the kid will not look back too unfondly on this as some of his pasta days.

Snapshot: My own mother and her husband come to visit. They spend eight days. It is my feeling that we usually do well for about three days when we are together. We go to Palm Springs for the weekend. If Robert Conrad could survive his *Palm Springs Weekend*, so could I. This trip tests the limits. On day six we are eating lunch. I complain about the fact that given the cost of housing in California, I will never be able to afford a home. I state, not complain, "That in this day and age, 'homefulness' is an inheritance, not a right." My mother's husband then let's go with both barrels. He means well. I know he means well.

It is important that I tell you that he meant well at that moment. Even then, when his words were hurting me, I knew that part of his motivation was fondly paternal—part was *Oedipal*—I'm never sure of the actual difference. My mother's husband kindly tells me, "I don't want to tell you how to live your life, but it seems to me that its time you stop wasting your time with this fantasy business and earn a real living—then you can move out of that hell hole where you live into a real place."

I was good. I gently protested, asserting my pride in my career and accomplishments, but I didn't fight back. Later, my mother cried, apologizing for him. At the time, she said nothing. He never apologized himself.

The next day, again out of love and concern, my mother asks me about my business partners—my "real" (read "self-chosen") family (in contradistinction to my relatives)—suggesting that they are taking advantage of my skills and creativity. I again let it pass in relative silence. I assert the facts (my view of them) and then drop to silence. The rest of their visit is tense. My mother calls, crying, the day after she returns. She tells me, "I love you." This is followed by a lot of tears and a lot of testimony of affection. I tell her, "I love you, too, I just don't like you a lot at the moment." This cycle goes round a lot of times. I assure her that I will not abandon her. It makes her unhappy that I don't allow my feelings of hurt to dissipate quickly and conveniently. For me, love doesn't conquer gross insensitivity.

The night after my mother and her husband leave, I call the Kid. He is the one person I know will really understand. I tell him we are going to reverse parts. I tell him the story of my *Palm Springs Weekend*. He responds with the appropriate responsive rituals. "They are parents, that is what they are like. You have a lot of other feelings toward them, but you also love them—learn to live with it. Parents are like that." I wonder how long it will be before the next time I will never spend time with my parents again. I wonder how long before the Kid tells his father, "I love you, I just don't like you a lot at the moment."

Snapshot: I sit at a conference on Jewish Family Education, the Whizin Institute, with the world's leading experts. It is lunch. We wind up in a strange kind of confessional. I tell the story of *My Parents' Visit* and the story of *Retelling My Parents' Visit to the Kid*. The flood gates break. Everyone at the table tells the "real" story of the skeleton in their own family educator closet. We are the perfect family collection, with rebellious out-of-control kids, disintegrated marriages, difficult relationships with our own parents—the whole litany. We are anything but a Quaker's Oats commerical; therefore, we have the perfect background to work with real Jewish families. We all breath deeply—we have confessed one shared dark secret.

To unpack this notion of "function" versus "dysfunction," let's braid two post-modern texts together and make family midrash.

Torah Text: Whatever trouble he's in, his family has the right to share it with him. It's our duty to help him if we can and it's his duty to let us and he doesn't have the privilege to change that. (Jarrod Barkley, *The Big Valley.*[33])

Proem Verse: *Lyman*: Oh.— Actually, though, why do we think of monogamy as a higher form of life? *Theo*: Well' it implies an intensification of love…*Lyman*: But how does that make it a higher form? *Theo*: Monogamy strengthens the family; random screwing undermines it. *Lyman*: But as one neurotic to another, what's so good about strengthening the family? *Theo*: Well, for one thing it enhances liberty. *Bessie* (Puzzled): Liberty? Really? *Theo:* The family disciplines its members; when the family is weak the state has to move in; so the stronger the family the fewer the police. And that is why monogamy is a higher form. *Lyman:* Jesus, did you just make that up? (Arthur Miller, *The Ride Down Mt. Morgan*, 1992.[34])

[1] Rabbinic Visions of the Family

Let's go from an idea we understand to one which may be new. Classic Jewish Theology teaches that : GOD CREATED PEOPLE IN GOD'S IMAGE. (Genesis 1.27) Does that mean people are Godlike? No, it means, that given a lot of work, people can become Godlike. How so? What we need to do is take the "GOD'S IMAGE" thing (Genesis 1.27), and modify it with (Leviticus 19.2): "YOU SHALL BE HOLY, FOR I, ADONAI YOUR GOD, AM HOLY. EACH OF ALL OF YOU

---

[33] Jack Mingo and John Javna, *Primetime Proverbs: The Book of TV Quotes*. New York: Harmony books, 1989.

[34] *The Ride Down Mt. Morgan* is a presently unpublished Arthur Miller play which has been performed on the London stage but is still being perfected and rewritten and has yet to open in this country. The author was good enough to fax me a couple of pages of the script to allow its inclusion here.

In other words, "GOD'S IMAGE" contains the raw material to be Godlike, but to manifest it and "BE HOLY," takes a lot of work, a lot reflection, a lot of mitzvot.

Essentially, "holiness" is a fantasy—a mystical quality like an "aura," like "the shining," like "talent," in fact, like "God" whose attributes can be somewhat described, but whose essence is illusive. We can look at whether or not a person does things we pre-define as holy, whether or not a person seems to have a sense of the holy, but there is no holiness meter. Likewise, "functionality" is a similar construct. It has become a mystical essence like "chi" or "the right stuff" which families seem to possess. If I was a therapist or a sociologist, an anthropologist or a statistician, I might try to elucidate a formal definition. But, my role is that of social commentator; I am interested in this essay in the popular fantasy of "functionality," that—like the Holy Grail—like all the black and white ghosts which still haunt us from the golden age of television—families can find a state of grace we call functionality. (The acid test, if I had to give you one, is that functional families can solve all problems from drug addiction to halitosis in thirty minutes with time left over for two commercial breaks). Here, we are talking about the "idea of the functional" and the "myth of the dysfunctional." We are not interested in their truth, but in their mythic role, the way they have worked their way in the fabric of contemporary thinking as the Valhalla and Hades of post-shag rug America.

This is the idea which may be new: I've come to suspect that the "Live up to GOD'S IMAGE" principle can be applied to families. (Because in many ways covenant theology turns God and Israel into a family unit.) Families have the potential for functionality—but it is an act of work—not grace— to achieve it. Families come with tidal forces. Every couple—no matter how much in love, no matter how committed—fights battles between intimacy and freedom. All children—no matter how close—have moments of the Cain and Abel thing. Children regularly accuse their parents of "the Saturn/Kronos eats his children syndrome" when they demand an independence for which their parents are not yet ready. Simultaneously, their parents describe it as a moment when *Dedalus* needs to warn *Icarus* not to take his wings and head too close to the sun. Families always have mythic proportion.

In our times, *The National Enquirer*'s dream family nightmares are becoming real, ordinary, and everyday. Just ask the Royal Family of England. Ask the cast of the *Brady Bunch*, or your next door neighbor, or just look in your own family's closet. Families just don't seem to be what they used to be. The only problem is, families are actually just what they always were—bond groups of people who both soar together and who equally often ravage each other. The ancient stories, whether Greek or Biblical, Chinese or African understand the duality of the family: arenas of light and arenas of shadow—the solarium and the root cellar.

Modernity fostered the illusion that penicillian would conquer disease. But, we now know all about penicillian resistent bacteria, and even British skin-eating bacteria. We fostered the illusion that first radio, then television, and now computers would educate the masses. We ignored the fact that two weeks after the discovery of each new communications technology we have to face its use as a vehicle for the distribution of pornography. Printing brings the Bible to the mass. Printing makes *Playboy* possible. Modernity, with its illusions about nature and technology with its fantasy that "everything is getting better and better every day," thought it could recreate the family in its own image—only light, only functionality. It believed that poverty and disease were the external sources of darkness. In the new womb of suburbia (freed of the evils of city life), with all needs only a short drive away, families could not fail to grow and prosper. The myths—meaning stories to teach truth—of the modern era, really believed that love and science conquers all. Therefore, family life was triaged (in popular usage) into the functional, that which is the manifestation of Dan Quayle's "Family Values," and dysfunctional, that which a mental health professional is hired to exorcise.

What was forgotten, was that the soul of the family, like the soul of an individual, has moments of sunrise and moments of midnight. What is dysfunctional (not productive for family health and prosperity) is the modern fantasy that most families should never know profound pain, loneliness, jealousy, suffering—that only "bad families" have divorces, addictions, and eating disorders. Even though we now know better (because so many of us get to talk about it with our 12 step groups, our therapists, or our favorite talk radio host) we still feel the guilt—and suffer the pain for being more like the Cramdens than the Cleavers. Mythic truth is that we all have moments of being Hamlet, all have moments of acting like Lady Macbeth, and all have moments of being Lucy—of having our impulses destroy our best intentions. The nice thing about *I Love Lucy* by the way, is that every episode is the affirmation of the possibility of repentence.

Thomas Moore comments: "**When I see those three letters 'dys-' in 'dysfunctional,' I think of 'Dis,' the old name for the mythological underworld. Soul enters life from below, through cracks, finding an opening into life at the points where smooth functioning breaks down…In studying the mythologies of the world, you always find evil characters and some sort of underworld; the same is true in the family. It always has shadow, no matter how much we wish otherwise. Its functioning is always soiled by Dis.**" (Thomas Moore, *Care for the Soul*. New York: HarperCollins, 1992, pp. 26-7.)

Family comes from the Latin word *familia*. "**This famous word …is inseparable from the idea of land settlement, and is therefore essentially the house itself, with the persons living in it …And thus the religion of the *familia* will be a religion of practical utility, of daily work, of struggle with perils …It is not the worship of an idea of kinship.**" (W.W. Fowler, *The Religious Experiences of the Roman People*. New York: Macmillan.)

The notorious "nuclear" family of statistics, sermons and advertisements—two parents, two siblings, a family car and a pet—does not correspond with the Latin word from which family derives …*Familia, familias* to the Romans meant primarily "a house and all belonging to it…In fact, a domesticated animal was often considered a familiar. Living together in a familiarity as a psychoeconomic organism—such is the meaning of family. Even the Greek word *oikonomia* (from which come economy and economics) means household management or housekeeping. The family is a function of the house, rather than vice versa…(James Hillman, edited by Thomas Moore, *A Blue Fire*, Selected Writings by James Hillman. New York: HarperCollins, 1989, p. 202)

This notion of family as *bayit,* as house, is one which we see the Jewish tradition also echoes. The first bottom line is that kinship is over-rated. The second bottom line is that ancient families knew that their "homes" had dungeons and demons.

Various gods and goddesses lived with the ancient family: Vesta at the hearth (focus is the Latin word) who must be acknowledged first and daily else the central bonding flames might go out; Janus at the gates so that one remembered the different faces required for inside and outside…The ancient house gave plenty of place to the invisibles that live in a family, propitiating and domesticating its daimones, which it acknowledged as rightfully belonging. (James Hillman, edited by Thomas Moore, "Mythology as Family," *A Blue Fire,* Selected Writings by James Hillman. New York: HarperCollins, 1989, pp. 202-203.)

Ancient cultures knew that families had shadows. That is a truth we hide from ourselves, replacing it with a false myth of automatic familiar functionality. What has been shattered in our age is merely the freckled Norman Rockwell illusion of wholesome family life. Here are three simple pieces of evidence to think about.

(a) Look at any of the family stories from the Torah. They have it all— all of family's greatest shadows—rape, incest, adultery, favoritism, sibling rivalry—all of the dark side.

(b) Look at fairy tales. Before you get to "live happily ever after" there are wicked stepmothers, absent and weak fathers, evil siblings and a whole host of demons, dragons, giants, and other dangers to get through.

(c) Look into your own heart and feel all the ambivalence family in the specific generates when you contrast it with family in the ideal. Every Cleaver Clan has Charley Addam's Family living in the closet, attic and basement.

James Hillman teaches a number of important lessons. First, he says, there are actually no "normal" families left in America. **Seventy-five percent of family units are not nuclear, normal families. (Ninety-four percent of all families may be "dysfunctional.") Twenty-five percent of all households are people living alone. Twenty-five percent of children are now born out of wedlock. Fifty percent of new marriages now end in divorce. Thirty-three and a third of those treated for mental disorders in hospitals are teenagers. Three out of every 100 adult males in the United States are in the correctional system. Three out of five children born will spend part of their childhood in a single parent household— and in the State of Virginia, 44% of children prefer the company of the**

211

television set to their fathers. And, that home with your family is the most dangerous place you can be (it is where you are most likely to be killed or injured—and the perpetrator is usually a relative. (James Hillman, *Myths of the Family*. New York: Sound Horizons Audio Video, Inc., 1991.) And we are now smart enough not to protest with "But Jewish families are different!" We know better.

Thomas Moore reaches the same conclusion this way: "Today professionals are preoccupied with the 'dysfunctional family.' But to some extent all families are dysfunctional. A family is a microcosm, reflecting the nature of the world, which runs on both virtue and evil. We may be tempted at times to imagine the family as full of innocence and goodwill, but actual family life resists such romanticism. Usually it presents the full range of human potential, including evil, hatred, violence, sexual confusion and insanity. In other words, the dynamics of actual family life reveal the soul's complexity and unpredictability, and any attempts to place a veil of simplistic sentimentality over the family image will break down." (Thomas Moore, *Care for the Soul*. New York: HarperCollins, 1992, p. 26.)

E.B. Howe gets this irony down just right when he says: "**The worst thing in the world is the homesickness which comes over a man when he is at home.**"

Moore writes: **Some people believe the images of normality and maintain the secret of *their* family's corruption, wishing they had been born elsewhere in a land of bliss. But recovery of soul begins when we can take to heart our own family fate and find in it the raw material, the alchemical *prima materia*, for our own soul work. For this purpose, "family therapy" might take the form of simply telling stories of family life, free from any concern for chase and effect or sociological influence. These stories generate a grand local, personal mythology.** (Thomas Moore, *Care for the Soul*. New York: HarperCollins, 1992, pp. 28-29.) Rabbi Lawrence Kushner regularly teaches, "**The Torah is the collective unconscious of the Jewish people.**" Let's use some Torah (oral and written) to find and tell some stories which reveal the real Jewish vision of the family.

Let's use a **Mishnah [Bava Metzia 1.5]** to understand part of the rabbinic vision of family:

An ownerless object found by one's minor son or daughter;
an ownerless object found by a man's Canaanite male slave or female slave,
an ownerless object found by his wife
—these belong to him.

An ownerless object found by one's adult son or daughter,
an ownerless object found by a man's Jewish manservant or maidservant,
an ownerless object found by a man's ex-wife whom he divorced,
     but whom he has not YET given her ketubah to her
—these belong to them.

Commentary: First let's redefine family. Let's think walls—not blood. Rather than think of a family as being a kinship group—part of the fantasy of the Norman Rockwell universe—family was once, and is again, a psycho-economic unit that lived and struggled to survive together. The slave, the cow, and even the furniture were part of "the family." That is the Scottish idea of "The Keep." Home is not where the heart is—the heart is, rather, connected to those who live in the home. Familiarity breeds family! That is the Torah of Stephen Stills: **"If you can't be with the one you love—love the one you're with."** And like all good and true emotions, home feeling/family love is ambivalent. A son cannot love a mother without simultaneously struggling for freedom from her. Husband and wife cannot love each other without, simultaneously, often deep in places that are hard to admit, nursing their unfulfilled needs. Each of our relationships struggles with the no-reality of platonic relationships (the cave, not the friendship)—while falling back into being (at best) only the best possible relationship we can manage.

This Mishnah reaches into that ambivalence and paints an interesting portrait of a family. This is the story! A son finds a coin and tries to keep it. The father feels that he is struggling to maintain that whole family—that he needs the coin and every resource in order for the entire family to make it, and that the lazy son doesn't do enough to support the family anyway. The son, meanwhile, feels himself put upon—robbed—

213

infantilized—all at once. They yell at each other. They do a tug of war with the coin. Perhaps, they even throw things at each other. Maybe doors are slammed. Finally, when there is no reconciliation they take the matter to the *Bet Din.* The rabbis give a ruling: "If the kid is a major, he can keep it. If the kid is a minor—Dad gets it.

The matter has gone to court. How do we know that? Simple, because the Mishnah made the ruling. Things which don't need verdicts aren't made into mishnaot. If there is a mishnah—there were court cases. It is that simple, because the Mishnah is basically a guide book for rabbis acting as judges. But why did the matter get to court? Whenever I teach this text, someone, usually a woman, says: "They should just give the money to charity." She doesn't get it. This is not fifty cents or ten dollars—this is the mythic million dollar briefcase which no one can trace—and the family has been reduced, as the rabbis knew that many families are reduced, to a pair of two year olds each screaming, "Mine." Why didn't good conversation work things out? The answer is simple: because, in real families, fathers don't always know best—and when they do, it is rarely acknowledged. Conversations do not always work—and the Mishnah is written for those eventualities, the times when families haven't yet climbed up to hyper-functionality. The Mishnah knows what Louis B. Meyer denied—families often need family courts. (And even that some Judge Hardys molest Judy Garland when Andy isn't looking.) As Tom Bodett teaches: "**What do sex, rock and roll, and family secrets have to do with growing up—just about everything?**" (Tom Bodett, *The Free Fall of Webster Cummings.* Grand Haven: Nova Audio Book, 1995.)

But the universe of family strife is not just between fathers and sons. In this passage, we have arguments between husbands and wives, between masters and servants, between fathers and adult children, between separated and divorced couples. Here is a world where Shakespeare would feel comfortable: a lot of family comedy, a lot of family tragedy, and all situations which take more than 28 and a half minutes—a lot of winters of our discontent. (By the way, if you can't see all that in those few lines of Mishnah, you've got to learn a little about unpacking Rabbinic texts.) Remember, the whole world is a Mishnah, and the people merely actors…

The Gemara: [Bava Metzia 12a ff]: goes even deeper.

In it, a precocious 12 year old yells at the court, "I am no minor." Like Macaulay Culkin he argues, "Judaism needs a Coogan Law—I am earning enough money to be treated like an adult. I take care of Dad (who is the fat lazy—perhaps alchoholic—cretin who regularly spends my money)—Dad doesn't take care of me! I am an orphan with an abusive father."

Slowly, from the argument, (which I will not reconstruct here—because it is too complicated for our purposes) evolves a new concecpt—*m'P'nai Darkhei Shalom*—compromises for the sake of family peace. This Gemara is worth studying on its own both for the insights and for the compromises. But the story of our father and son needs an ending, so know that the verdict goes this way. Adult is redefined by economic status rather than age. An adult child is "someone who no longer eats at the family table (on a regular basis)." Anyone who still sits at the table—even though they have the "legal right" to keep what they find—are told by the rabbi/judge *m'P'nai Darkhei Shalom*—not to push the point, but to give in. And we learn the deep lesson—when it comes to family, being right isn't always smart. That is the Torah of *m'P'nai Darkhei Shalom*—compromises for the sake of family peace.

Davar Aher: A different truth: And then my friend and teacher Sally Weber will always add, but Darkei Shalom (family peace) can also be the gag used to mask a lot of family abuse. Family's souls have shadows and light, just like the rest of us.

In this passage we see that family membership deals with economic interdependence and proximity—not just blood. (Think of the parallel inclusion of slaves, servants, children and wives.) More than that—we see that the rabbinic perception of "dysfunctionality" as normative, is clarified by the amount of "family law" they make explicit and the centrality they place on learning it. The rabbis know and understand the kind of family diversity and potential darkness that Thomas Moore and James Hillman describe. After our fight between father and son—after the chorus' of "Mine," they are still a family. They are just a stressed family. They know Jared Barkley's truth: **Whatever trouble he's in, his family has the right to share it with him. It's our duty to help him if we can and it's his duty to let us and he doesn't have the privilege to change that.** (Jarrod Barkley, *The Big Valley*.)

Stuck is stuck. That is the Torah of *m'P'nai Darkhei Shalom*. That is Robert Frost's truth: **"Home is the place that when you have to go there—they have to take you in."**

Imagine This Situation: A 23 year old daughter, post-college, moves back in at home. She has a fight with her mother and retreats to her room. She blasts some loud, ugly, music on her stereo. The mother yells at her to turn it down. She yells, "It's my room." The mother yells, "Not in my house it isn't." The mother enters the room—without knocking—without permission to continue the fight. She sees on the wall the recently done graphic painting (done by the daughter as a mural) of a couple engaged in a rather athletic act of intercourse. Think gymnasts doing it in space. Mother yells, "Get that off my walls." The daughter yells, "Get out of my room." And in our world—as Mishnaic as this situation is—there is often no longer the knowledge that a *Bet Din* exists—no longer the sense that a "rule" in Jewish Law prescribes a needed compromise. The yelling continues for awhile. Then the two find their own kind of reconciliation— usually. That is the kind of Mishnaic stage most of our families act out.

My friends and teachers, the Wolins, tell this story: Their **seventeen year old daughter left for college in a huff of blame and chastisement. As she left home, she revealed to her parents all the ways they had limited, ruined, and devastated her life. Then she was gone. The next night they returned home from dinner out to find this message on the answer phone: "Where are you? I called and you were gone!"** The Wolins, here and elsewhere in their writing, reveal a lot about the two-stepped tango of the family. They understand that to be family, to live together, is always to be trapped in the dual-edged feelings of protection and confinement, or love and resentment. The very act of living together with one set of people, generates the fantasy that there are others with whom we could bond more easily. That is the duality of the tango between families real and adoptive. The Wolins, in their book *The Resilient Self*, are the first to suggest this notion of the "adoptive family."

The Wolins write: **"Isn't it true that for every resilient survivor there's at least one caring, strong adult who makes a critical difference? ...I am invariably asked this question...My problem with the relationship question is not with the content; it's the emphasis that makes me uneasy...**

216

I have heard resilient survivors attribute their endurance and determination to a "life-saving" figure who came to their aid (The "Adoptor"). But, like all stories, the one about the caring grown-up and the hurt child can be told from other perspectives, and some slants are better for survivors than others. The version I prefer least revolves on the theme of generosity…A reframed version of the "Save-the-Child" (story is) "**The Appealing Child Meets the Potentially Interested Adult." This script depicts relationships as the fruits of your own labor, a rich yield carefully and deliberately cultivated in the soil of despair.**" (Steven J. and Sybil Wolin, *The Resilient Self*. New York: Random House, Inc., 1993, pp. 111-113.)

The Wolin's model originates in pathologically (in response to their studies of addiction). I, like most post-modernists, suggest that a good dose of pathology is always normative, and that their pyschogenic truth generalizes into our own everyday understandings. We can sing Stephen Stills' chorus: "**If you can't be with the one you love, love the one you're with.**"

There are moment's in our life, where we, faced with Tennessee William's mother as our mother, flee to Glenda the Good Witch to protect us—only to find that she really doesn't care the way that "Mom Williams does." As Hillman puts it, in family: "**No one is at fault, no one is kicked out, no one can be helped. In the paralysis lies the profoundest sense of acceptance. Grandpa can go on grumbling, brother attacking the administration, sister introvertedly attending her exacerbating eczema, and mother goes on covering up with solicitous busy-ness. Everyone goes down the drain because family love allows family pathology, an immense tolerance for the hopeless shadow in each, the shadow that we carry as a permanent part of our baggage and that we unpack when we go back home.**" (James Hillman, *A Blue Fire*, 201.) Some Thanksgivings we eat the bear. Some Thanksgivings Kronos eats us. Or as Jonathan Omer-man teaches: "**God was gracious for giving us so many nights of Passover, so that each side of our family can stage their own psycho-drama.**" We can just imagine Shakespeare's quartet of Seder questions.

Davar Aher: Another version of this lesson: We could

have learned that lesson as easily from the Torah itself. My friend and teacher,

Peter Pitzele, has enabled the spinning of a multi-verse of insights and rethinkings of the the Biblical text both with his writing and his facilitating of Biblical psychodrama. His work can be found in his book, *Our Fathers' Wells,* and his influence is all over. **There is no absolute truth in a family system, only the truths of the participants. These truths are often unspoken, sometimes only partially conscious, and conditioned by the perspective and histories, the illusions and convictions, of each family member. Indeed, to be a member of a family is to live among secrets, hidden-motives, suspected alliances, painful exclusions. Psychodrama, by virtue of its ability to voice the various perspectives that conspire in the family, allows us to explore the family system and attend at any moment to its strange polyphony.** (Peter Pitzele, *Our Fathers' Wells.* New York: HarperCollins, 1995, pp. 167-8.)

But let's work with a micro example:

The story of Cain and Abel begins with an innocent line which seems just to be proforma narration (Don Pardo with his hand over his ear). Worked as a "psychodrama," open to the world of human experience cum midrash, it becomes something else. The Torah says (Genesis 4.1): ADAM KNEW HIS WIFE EVE. SHE BECAME PREGNANT AND GAVE BIRTH TO CAIN. SHE SAID: CAIN MEANS I GOT A MAN WITH GOD'S HELP. When I asked the group to "become" Eve and tell us the "story" behind the naming—these diverse family truths emerged.

• Birth was such a miracle.

• God takes away and God gives. God kicked us out of the garden, but God gave us a kid. When we saw the first smile on Cain's face, all the work and all the pain was more than worth it. God is great! Cain is better than free fruit.

• After the Garden thing—there was so much distance between Adam and I, that I thought a child would bring us together. I asked God for that blessing. I got the child, but it didn't work for very long. Soon, Adam again was remote, but at least God blessed me with a companion. I got a new man to replace the one who virtually left me.

• It hurt so damn much to give birth, I thought I was going to die. I was all alone. (I had to bite through the umbilical cord with my teeth.) Adam was busy working his field. Too far to hear my shouts. And neither of us knew what to do—or what was happening. But, I got through it 'cuz God was my co-pilot.

- Hey, we were young. We hadn't yet connected our nights of pleasure to something that happened nine months later. The stork myth hadn't been invented yet, so who else were you going to blame for this crying thing which oozed fluids at all orifices. But, Cain was cute to start with.

Is all of this in the Torah? Perhaps, but regardless of your fantasies of revelation and the connection between oral and written Torah, this much is clear, the Torah's content, and its literary style of allusion and silence, invites exactly such participation. For the past fifteen years or so, Torah teacher after Torah teacher has remarked with the surprise of discovery, that biblical families are "dysfunctional." These days, at those instances, I smile, and say, "Of course, biblical families are families like all other families, struggling up from their worst tendencies toward *kedushah* (holiness/functionality)."

Davar A<u>h</u>er: Another version of this lesson: I am in Chicago with a <u>H</u>avurah called Eitz <u>H</u>ayyim, and we are studying the Torah portion of the week. We find this passage (Genesis 33.1-2): JACOB LIFTED UP HIS EYES AND SAW THAT ESAU WAS COMING WITH FOUR HUNDRED MEN, SO HE DIVIDED HIS CHILDREN AMONG LEAH, RACHEL, AND THE TWO MAIDS. HE PUT THE MAIDS AND THEIR CHILDREN FIRST, LEAH AND HER CHILDREN WERE BEHIND THEM, AND RACHEL AND JACOB BEHIND THEM .... Jacob is using a King's India Defense. Next Esau arrives and the introductions are made. The text reads, "THEN THE MAIDS APPROACHED, THEY AND THEIR CHILDREN BOWED LOW. THEN LEAH AND HER CHILDREN APPROACHED AND BOWED LOW. LASTLY, JOSEPH AND RACHEL APPROACHED AND BOWED LOW (33.6-7)." Rashi reads the passage and asks: **"Why did Joseph step in front of Rachel?"** As is usual, Rashi answers his own question. **"Joseph knew Esau's reputation and stepped in front of his beautiful mother to protect her."** We study the passage. We study the Rashi—and the group evolves this insight. Joseph and Rachel behave in a way we recognize. They are like a single-parent mother raising a son. They are sometimes like lovers, sometimes like siblings, sometimes like parent and child—each sometimes being the parent in the diad. Jacob is such an absent parent, and Rachel and Joseph are so estranged from the rest of the camp, that they are behaving the

way many mothers and the sons they are raising alone behave. There is a lot of Richard the III in the Torah.

[2] Can the reality of family support the fantasy of family values, family education, and family whatever…?

Family education is the latest Messiah in the Jewish war against the demographics of assimilation. It is very likely to become the next in a long standing series of failures, each of which is predicated on a different mythic vision of Jewish survival. In essence, it is a question of cloning. We are trying to "clone" Jewish life, creating new Jews in an artificial and partial environment; we are constantly seeking the minimum amount of ethno-genetic material necessary to spontaneously generate Jewishness. We are looking for an easy way to say: "Let there be Jews" and have there "Be Jews." We would like all of our family education to be a G.T.H.B.A. ("Good Time Had By All") education, to cure the world by blessing and ceremony, never getting our hands bloody, never crawling into the mud.

Once Judaism, Jewish Identity, Jewishness, and Jewish Survival was an organic whole. Judaism was a closed ecology—it was a living organism. The idea of factoring out individuals or individual elements was not a consideration. Only when we put a little "English" on the ball and ricocheted ourselves off the bumpers of modernity did pieces begin to break off. First, following Martin Luther's path, we affirmed the individual in his or her individual relationship to God, Torah, and Israel. Catholic Israel was no more. Slowly, we have learned that "individual" interventions, that working with individuals, especially kids, has failed to generate enough new Jews. Philosophy, Identity, Consciousness—all that stuff—even Spirituality, are great tools; they however, are not the penicillin of Jewish survival. (Remember, bacteria learns ….) Moreover, individualism stands in dynamic tension with the centrality of family—that is, the story of ego development. To be a rebel, to be a hero, you have to leave home—even if you eventually return. Individualism demands space—you can't do it when five people have to get through the bathroom every morning. Moses didn't take his family up Mt. Sinai and let the kids enjoy the experience. Revelation isn't a family vacation.

Emphasize individual identity and personal need—and you destroy family. Family is inherently balanced on uneasy compromise and self-effacement. Family, so goes the developmental tale, is only the beginning, a necessary evil which like all beginnings, must be left behind. An adult has grown up, declared his independence, and his life and liberty are dedicated to the pursuit of his own happiness...Psychoanalysis has swallowed whole the myth of the individual development away from family. Everyone who buys an hour of analysis buys into this myth called "strengthening the ego." (James Hillman, *A Blue Fire*, 196-7.)

David Elkind clarifies the progression of family from modern to post-modern and beyond. **Around the '50s, most of us lived in nuclear families. We operated under the assumptions that women should stay home, men should be the providers, and the children should be protected...** Since then, that image had been broken down...**couples used to believe in romantic love—that there was just one person in the whole world who was for you...second there was the notion of maternal love, the belief that women possessed a maternal instinct to be with their children at all times...to make a nest, and that if they didn't, something was wrong with them...a third sentiment of the nuclear family was domesticity and the idea that the home was the center of one's life. That really grew out of the movement into cities and industrialization. The factory was a cold, hard place, and the factory worker was a cog in the machine. In contrast, the home was a warm, welcoming place in a heartless world. And in that home, mother was the center...**Then came the transformation...**The industrial revolution robbed women of their creative outlets. Women were told not to grind their own coffee because they could buy vacuum packed...Women were turned into consumers, which eventually contributed in a very important way to the women's movement.**

In this economic transformation, other values changed, too. Among other things, virginity lost its value. **The implicit contract based on an exchange of virginity for commitment no longer exists. The basis of the contract has become consensual. Marriage is an agreement between two equals, with the idea that we'll stay in this relationship as long as it serves our purposes and needs...**As marriage changed, so the family changed...**Parents today have to protect themselves first, much as in an airplane, they must put the breathing masks on themselves before they** put it on their children. To make sure that their children are provided for, they devote tremendous time to working and refurbishing their skills. So, too often, parents are focused on their own activities, forcing their kids to be autonomous as well—to be much more independent, to be home alone, to get their own meals, to organize their own time…This has big fallout. **The family meal has gone by the board. It used to be a gathering place for the nuclear family. Today, soccer practice or a business meeting takes precedence over dinner because personal needs are more important than the family…**

In this book we have often pointed out that every truth and its opposite are often simultaneously true as each over-reaction invites the next pendulum swing. So Elkind points out: **Statistics show that young people are marrying later and are having fewer children. They are trying not to make the mistakes in their own lives that their parents made. They don't want to go through divorce. When they get into a relationship they want to make it work. This bodes well for the family.** (M. Scherer, "On Our Changing Family Values: A Conversation with David Elkind." *Educational Leadership 53, 7:4-9,* April 1996.)

Some families now "abandon family" in order to participate as "individuals" in communal activities. Some families have now returned to nesting—devoting almost exclusive time to the family—and shunning outside involvements. Strong families eat away at community. Ask the Hatfields and the Capulets. Families breed nepotism. It is definitional. Community demands equality. Think about it. It is the same issue. The naive vision that strong individuals join together to create families which breed new strong individuals is indeed just a naive vision. It is a small part of a larger pathogenic truth. Adding the demands and tidal pulls of community involvement only complicates the picture. We live in an age where community is eroding from just these forces.

Consider this Truth: There is striking evidence that the vibrancy of American civil society has notably declined over the past several decades…It is not just the voting booth that has been increasingly deserted by Americans…number of Americans who report that "in the past year" they have "attended a meeting on town or school affairs" is down by more than a third…both religious service groups and church related groups have declined modestly (about one-sixth) and while more Americans are bowling today than ever before, bowling in organized leagues has plummeted in the past decade or so (40 percent)…The traditional form of civic organization whose decay we have been tracing has been replaced by vibrant new organizations (like the Sierra Club, the National Organization for Women, and AARP)…where the only act of membership consists in writing a check…" (Robert D. Putnam. "Bowling Alone: America's Declining Social Capital." *Journal of American Democracy*, January 1995: pp. 65-78.)

To a large decree, this is just what Christopher Lasch describes in *The Culture of Narcissim:* **The new narcissist is haunted not by guilt but by anxiety. He seeks not to inflict his own certainties on others but to find meaning in life… Superficially relaxed and tolerant, he has little use for dogmas of racial and ethnic purity but at the same time forfeits the security of group loyalties and regards everyone as a rival for favors conferred by a paternalistic state…** Why would someone join a synagogue with 3,000 members, a swimming pool and sixteen rabbis on staff? Lasch argues that such institutions are a perfect narcissist's choice because (1) they have the resources to meet needs on demand, yet (2) provide great anonymity. He argues, that like some trained in karate, the narcissist knows that his own "leanings" can be used against him. Therefore, being known, belonging in reality and not just on a membership list, means that demands can be placed on her/him. That is why, today, much which looks like affiliation and membership, is really just the purchasing of services from a vending institution. He (the narcissist) **extolls cooperation and teamwork while harboring deeply antisocial impulses. He praises respect for rules while secretly believing that they do not apply to himself. Acquisitive in the sense that his cravings have no limits, he does not accumulate goods and provisions against the future, in the manner of nineteenth century political economy, but demands immediate gratification and lives in a state of restless, perpetual unsatisfied desire.** Recently, a Reform Rabbi found one of his Bar Mitzvah students wearing a cross during a Torah reading rehearsal. He asked for an explanation and the boy, from an intermarried home, explained that he was to be confirmed in his church a few weeks after his Bar Mitzvah. When the Rabbi asked the father for explanation, the father replied: "We wanted our son to have the protection of both religions." Often *what looks like belonging is just paying dues.* **The narcissist has no interest in the future because, in part, he has so little interest in the past…Impending disaster has become an everyday concern, so commonplace and familiar that nobody any longer gives much thought to how disasters might be averted. People busy themselves instead with survival strategies, measures designed to prolong their own lives, or programs guaranteed to ensure good health and peace of mind.** (Christopher Lasch, *The Culture of Narcissism, American Life in an Age of Diminishing Expectations.* New York: W.W. Norton, 1991, p. 4.) In other words, while some new people have gotten really excited about joining bowling leagues—more people are bowling alone.

Home Alone is one of today's myths. It is the story of the competent child who is forced to raise himself. He is the suburban and urban ferral child—king of the latchkey. He or she is the child of lessons, carpools, and quality time. That is one new American Myth, Linda and Richard Eyre are another. They are Mormons who are family educators and who have made it to the best seller list (*Teaching Your Child Values, Teaching Your Child Responsibility,* and *Teaching Your Child Sensitivity.* New York: Simon & Schuster, 1993, 1994, 1995.) by suggesting intensive family processes which literally take five to ten hours of "family-work" every week. Included on their list is a family night, a family court, a family bank, a repentance bench, a family "value of the week" which is studied, a unique and different birthday celebration for each and every family member, and parent's night out weekly (to review and log the family plan for each child). All but absent parenting and hyper-parenting coexist.

But in general, we are in the midst of an era of nesting and comfort food. We live in a post-Einsteinian reality where time is collapsing—not so much from traveling faster than the speed of light, but from down-sizing. We are at a moment were the dissipation of the myth of "quality" time is generating a new gaggle of stay-at-home mothers who shun baby sitters, where professionals are refusing to move for promotion so that their children can know their grandparents. Having pushed family to the brink—having seen its impending destruction—we have backed off. We have recentered ourselves in home and family. We have invested in couch-based-memberships and participation in virtual community. This is a

224

moment when Martha Stewart is big time. Still, the reaction formation is growing, formulating, and on the rise.

Since Lakeville, since Marshall Sklare's first lists of Jewish behaviors, we've wanted to reduce Jewish identification to a series of observable and reportable actions and attitudes. At first we tried to influence individuals to perform more of these behaviors—now we believe the Jewish future can best be served by modifying or at least reinforcing family performance of these symbolic factors. Over-simply put, but not untrue, we see the Jewish future directly connected to the number of Jewish Families who light Shabbat or Hanukkah candles. We assume that Shabbat candles are a direct step toward in-marriage. The numbers have already proved those assumptions wrong, but understanding why is important. It is a "black-box" problem.

Jeremiah Johnson was a great early Robert Redford character. He was a mountain man who inherits an Indian wife and a deaf and mute son. They build a life together. They transcend the cultural issues. They overcome communications difficulties. They build a common life, common accomplishments, and common life rituals. For Jeremiah Johnson it ends by attack from the outside—his family is killed by marauders. But it would have ended anyway. Mythic marauders would have eventually disrupted the isolated mountainside. The *Wilderness Family* always returns home. Ultimately, the kid would have run away—with or without permission— the log cabin becomes claustrophobic and the sirens of outside beckon. Often, family education strives to create Jewish families which light their candles and say their blessings and feel their identity alone on the mountainside. When the kids age, they must leave home to reproduce. Families, except for incest, are sterile—it takes outside blood. Only the active and meaningful involvement of the family in the Jewish community dramatically increases the odds of in-marriage. Family is clearly a desirable condition for Jewish survival, but it is not a sufficient condition. In other words, as Vicky Kelman teaches in the name of the Torah of Africa, "**It takes a whole village to raise a child.**" She was quoting it years before Hillary Clinton.

Each of us needs a collection of peers (to pressure us differently than our family does) and mentors to help us reflect on our family condition. The growth curve of the human soul requires breaking with a family in order to achieve enough independence to then return to that family as an adult. The rabbinic tradition always balanced the mitzvah of marriage and home with the insight: "**Get yourself a teacher and find yourself a _haver_** (a best friend/Torah partner)." For home to work, there always needs to be a place away from home. You can learn this lesson from Dorothy. You have to leave Kansas to realize "**There is no place like home.**" That is something you can never see from Kansas. But, for Jewish life to be a closed environment—to keep our futures from the demographic truths of the _Little Mermaid_—a community relatively confluent to our family values must be the place we go to escape our family when the pressures build. "**The grass is always greener in the other fellow's yard**…unless they are part of the _eruv_ (those who live within the Shabbat fence), not the _eruv rav_ (the wild hoard/mixed multitude)."

Davar Aḥer:

Thomas Moore writes: "**Loneliness** (and God knows we are all lonely) **can be the result of an attitude that community is something into which one is received. Many people wait for members of a community to invite them in** especially after they have paid the dues, **and until that happens they are lonely. There may be something of the child here who expects to be taken care of by the family. But a community is not a family. It is a group of people held together by feelings of belonging, and those feelings are not a birthright. 'Belonging' is an active verb, something we do positively.**" (Thomas Moore, _Care for the Soul_. New York: HarperCollins, 1992, p. 94.) His message is clear and significant, community is not one big happy family (because we have already learned that no family is ever just one big happy family). Community makes different demands. Community requires different skills. Davening in a minyan is far more dynamic and takes a much higher skill level than lighting a Ḥanukkiyah. Just as pre-school takes a lot more education to actualize its full potential, so, too, family education must lead to a yet undefined process—Community Education. And, we must remember that community skills are more complex, less obvious, and harder to just "amass" than are family skills. Ducklings don't imprint on board meetings. Robert's Rules of Order are not natural law!

Adrianne Banks reads and asks: "Are you equating 'community' with your previously alluded to 'pseudo-family?'" No, but yes. While there can be aspects of "pseudo-family" that emerge from participation in community (Havurot being a good indicator), community is of a different scale. Communities don't fit in living rooms. Communities can't be moved or influenced by a single dining table conversation. Communities are public domains—families (real and pseudo) are private domains. Communities and families wear different outfits and different masks.

The two-fold conclusion of this article is therefore:

1. To be a true Jewish family educator, one must always paint a realistic, rather than romanticised, vision of the family.

2. To actualize Jewish family education, one must always educate toward community.

So much for praxis, now back to theology.

[3] Toward a Redemptive Vision of Dysfunctionality

Tom Bodett (the Motel 6 guy) is actually a brilliant storyteller whose Alaskan tales convey a deep sense of the mythic as manifest in modern American life. I use several of his stories as focal points—texts—in my teaching of the life-cycle. He introduces his new five part audio novel with these words: "That's what the...odyssey is all about—leaving home and coming home—and trying to understand the difference." (Tom Bodett, The Free Fall of Webster Cummings. Grand Haven: Nova Audio Book, 1995.) This is another expression of the family tango—the dance that we all do, moving toward and away from family simultaneously. We are always Jacob fleeing from family and envisioning ladders reaching to heaven. We are always Jacob, finding our way home and wrestling with dark angels at midnight. A pro-active theology of family needs to include both moves. And, the roots of that theology are present in the actual origins of the bibical text itself.

William G. Dever is a leading figure in Biblical archeology. In a series of lectures glossing the work of Lawrence Stager, he speaks of the unique difference between late Bronze era Israelite and Canaanite settlements in the land of Israel: "A typical peasant farmhouse can be related to the Biblical *bet ha-av,* usually translated literally as "the house of the father," but in sociological terms a descent group or "NUCLEAR FAMILY." (Emphasis

227

added.) **And clusters of these houses at the sites we have surveyed then reflect the Biblical *mish-pah-ḥah,* to be understood as AN EXTENDED or MULTIPLE FAMILY. This approach yields the best evidence yet that the new archeology can deal with ethnicity…Modern archeology begins to give Israelite "ethnicity" a real definition, both in terms of distinctive material cultural traits and in terms of the patterns of behavior they reflect.** (William G. Dever, *Recent Archeological Discoveries and Biblical Research.* Seattle: University of Washington Press, 1990, ibid, p. 171.) Based on this archaeological evidence, he implies that what made the Jewish people unique (and different from other people in the land of Canaan) was their sense of family. Their living space was designed to enforce and establish a sense of "family connection."

Let's compare Dever's reflections on Stager's insights with the work of Mark S. Smith: **Early Israelite culture cannot be separated easily from the culture of Canaan…Canaanite and Israelite material culture cannot be distinguished by specific features in the period of the Judges** (the same time frame Dever is discussing). **Items such as the four-room house, collared-rim store jar, and hewn cisterns, once thought to distinguish the Israelite culture of the highlands from the Canaanite culture of the coast and valleys, are now attested on the coast, in the valleys, or in Transjoran…(however) from evidence that is available, one may conclude that although largely Canaanite according to currently available cultural data, Israel expressed a distinct sense of origins and diety and possessed largely distinct holdings in the hill counties…Israel inherited local cultural traditions…and its culture was largely continuous with the Canaanite culture of the coast and valleys during the Iron I period. The realm of religion was no different.** Smith argues that Israel was intially monolatrous (worshiping only the One God but not denying the existence of other gods). Early Israelite culture tolerated (and ocassionally participated in) the worship of minor dieties, while holding that their God was the central and most powerful force in the universe. Smith argues that only later, in the period of the monarchy, did this ethnically unique monolatry shift into monotheism (as more of a political than religious process.) (Mark H. Smith, *The Early History of God.* New York: HarperCollins, 1990, pp. 1-3.)

What seems to evolve as Israel's monotheistic theology can be described as "mono o'mono," *monotheism* engineered to protect and sustain the *monarchy*. The one true God protected and sustained the one true king. The worship of the One was an act of feality to the other. Both benefited from the elimination of competition. Monogomy came as an interesting side-benefit to this process—one that prophets like Hosea exploited to the hilt (2.21-22): I (GOD) WILL BETROTH YOU (ISRAEL) TO ME FOREVER, AND I WILL BETROTH YOU TO ME WITH RIGHTEOUSNESS, JUSTICE, KINDNESS, AND MERCY. I WILL BETROTH YOU TO ME WITH FIDELITY, AND YOU SHALL KNOW ADONAI." Here, Hosea and many prophets use the metaphor of marital fidelity as an expression of Israel's relationship with God.

Hosea's story is this (Chapter 2): WHEN ADONAI FIRST SPOKE TO HOSEA, ADONAI SAID TO HOSEA, "GO AND MARRY A HOOKER AND ADOPT THE WHORE'S CHILDREN—AS A METAPHOR FOR THE WAY THE LAND WILL STRAY FROM FOLLOWING ADONAI...HE WENT AND MARRIED GOMER....He has three kids with her, whom he names (1) *Jezreel* (for bloody deeds at Jezreel), (2) *Lo Ruhamah* (I show no mercy), and (3) *Lo Ami* (not of My people). Then he breaks out in prophecy:

REBUKE YOU MOTHER, REBUKE HER
FOR SHE IS NOT MY WIFE
AND I AM NOT HER HUSBAND—
HAVE HER STOP BEING A WHORE—IT SHOWS ON HER FACE
TAKE AWAY THE ADULTERY FROM HER BREASTS
OTHERWISE I WILL STRIP HER NAKED
AND LEAVE HER AS ON THE DAY SHE WAS BORN....
THUS I WILL PUNISH HER....

Hosea goes on ranting and raving for awhile...then comes the reconciliation....

AND WHEN THAT DAY COMES—SAYS ADONAI
YOU WILL CALL ME YOUR ISH (Husband)
AND NO LONGER YOUR BAAL (Master/Husband/pagan god)
FOR I WILL REMOVE THE NAMES OF THE BAALIM (pagan gods)
FROM HER MOUTH
AND THEY SHALL NEVER BE MENTIONED BY NAME ANY MORE....

Hosea then describes a covenant made with birds and beasts and people...

I (GOD) WILL BETROTH YOU (ISRAEL) TO ME FOREVER,

AND I WILL BETROTH YOU TO ME WITH RIGHTEOUSNESS, JUSTICE, KINDNESS, AND

MERCY.

I WILL BETROTH YOU TO ME WITH FIDELITY,

AND YOU SHALL KNOW ADONAI."

Then comes the final reconciliation . . .

I WILL ANSWER FROM THE SKY

AND I WILL ANSWER TO THE EARTH

AND THE EARTH WILL ANSWER BACK

WITH NEW GRAIN AND WINE AND OIL

AND JEZREEL WILL BE ANSWERED

I WILL SOW FOR HER THE LAND AS MY OWN

AND RETURN LO RUHAMAH TO FAVOR

AND I WILL SAY TO LO AMI, "YOU ARE MY PEOPLE,"

AND HE WILL RESPOND, "YOU ARE MY GOD."

Here, the saga of family becomes metaphor for the relationship with The Divine. Hosea tells us that dealing with God is also the family tango—Tom Bodett's **"Leaving home and coming home."** Just as our story, of a people of faith struggling with fidelity to the one God, a story of failure, forgiveness, and reunion—a story of exile and return—is a family story. So to, the struggles to be family, with its moments of creation and corruption, revelation and rebellion, redemption and destruction are issues of theology as well as therapy. It is a rich irony that David (who's lack of fidelity is legendary) had a political agenda of monarchy which made Hosea's theology of family monogomy desirable. Both in the biblical text itself, and in the probable reconstruction of its origins, we find the same eternal duality.

Dever, in his argument, doesn't suggest what is *cause* and what is *effect*. But to us, the possibilities are interesting. What is the connection between monotheism and a strong sense of family? Especially in the tales in Genesis where we see an emphasis on fidelity and monogamy. Each of the stories where monogamy does not happen is seen ironically as exceptional. We explain why Abraham takes another wife; it is not an obvious action. It is infertility, not lust or greed. We justify Jacob's multiple partners because of family politics and find a way to understand that strange practice. Etc.

There is an active apologia going on relative to polygamy, and this apologia, in the long run, teaches a monogamist ideal—long before Rabbi Gershom's *tahanah*.[35] What is the connection between monogamy and monotheism? Which is the chicken? Which is the egg? I suspect monogamy is at the core. Jews have always lived with the ideal of family, all the time knowing that, like the speed of light, the sunlit ideal vision of family can be approached but not attained.

That echoes precisely one of the dual truths with which this proem began, taught by Theo in Arthur Miller's play. *Lyman*: **Oh.— Actually, though, why do we think of monogamy as a higher form of life?...***Theo*: **The family disciplines its members; when the family is weak the state has to move in; so the stronger the family the fewer the police. And that is why monogamy is a higher form.** *Lyman*: **Jesus, did you just make that up?** (Arthur Miller, *The Ride Down Mt. Morgan,* 1992)

Families, despite their weaknesses, tend to move us toward higher values (and in turn find the confinement suffocating and ocassionsally regress toward their perversion). David, who established monotheism in the name of monarchy, is a big abuser of human rights. We know that the "God's Image" piece which is big in his public theology doesn't play out in his interpersonal relationships, despite Natan's bedtime counting of sheep. In community as in family, as in any psychologically true theology, we can't forget that every castle has a dungeon. Every *Yetzer ha-Tov* (good urge) has a *Yetzer ha-Rah* (evil inclination). Where there are giants, dwarfs will also be found. Nothing is absolute—except the eternal duality of bipolar paired truths. This is the teaching of Rabbi Tarfon (*Pirke Avot* 2.16) **"You are not expected to finish the job—but you can't give up the ghost, either."** (Something like that!) One is always leaving home. One is always coming home. And, Adrianne Banks would add, one is always building or remodeling the home from which others leave and return.

Thomas Moore teaches: **To care for the soul of the family, it is necessary to shift from causal thinking to an appreciation for story and character, to allow grandparents and uncles to be transformed into figures of myth and to watch certain familiar family stories become canonical**

---

[35] A tahanah is a "fix" or improvement in the Jewish tradition. Circa 1000, Rabbi Gershom issued a ruling that Jewish (Ashkenazim) men could no longer have more than one wife at a time.

through repeated retellings....If we were to observe the soul in the family by honoring its stories and by not running away from its shadow, then we might not feel so inescapably determined by family influences. (Ibid. pages 28-30) This is, indeed, the universe of Genesis—the deep process of Truth we should acquire from all those wonderful stories of strong families in stress and dynamic tension. We need to learn to do the same kind of exegesis of our own family stories—to live family *aggadah* and make family midrash. I'd love to do a midrash on the time Nana dragged an iron bunk bed home on her back on the MTA (Poor Old Charlie!). And such is a path toward a workable family education—and a workable community education—one which deals with light and with its shadow.

A true theology of family is therefore a study in quanta. Functionality and Dysfunctionality are not actual places, but probable instances which can be recalled. They are wave and particle in the struggle to become family. A true theology understands that "being a family" is simultaneously something we are (without escape) and something we approach (without being able to reach).

Davar A̲her: The other side of the duality: Hillman: The measure of a family's magnanimity is not measured by what it gives to charity, but rather its capacity to shelter the shadows of its members. Charity begins at home. Hillman, who is a Jungian, attacks the Freudian fixation on the battle between ego and family. He suggests that the psychoanalytic myth blames the family for everything. It believes that the "child is father to the man," and that our upbringing tends to be a kind of psychic-predetermination. He suggests that it is much more important to view family relationships archetypally, to relish their ambivalence. He says: **We go back home because it is a regression and rejects the independence which is the heroic thing. The purpose of family is to provide shelter for the regressive needs of the soul. Everyone needs a place to crawl to and lick his wounds. A place to hide and be twelve years old, inept and needy. The bar, the bed, the board room and the buddies do meet the needs which always limp along behind the myth of independent individuality. Families are unreal, he teaches, because they live in the fantasies of each of the individual members. Families are creatures of myth,**

not of rational reality or even direct causality. Homelife is always lived in mythical proportions. (James Hillman, *A Blue Fire*, 199, 200.)

In other words, the very shattered and stretched families we are keeping in the closet are real Jewish families. Jewish families struggle with Hagar and don't always reach a perfect accommodation. Jewish families hate the little snot-nosed brat Joseph, but still find that they need him. Jewish fathers, like Jacob, split their emotional loyalty, but still seem to manage to hold together a vision and process of family. Jewish families have always done the best they can. They don't live in Mayberry. Norman Rockwell didn't paint Tamar in action. Kids always want to keep the coins their fathers believe that they need. The family path to redemption is a balancing act— a tightrope if you will—always stretching between the idealized vision of the "adoptive" family, and the stuckedness of the "actual family" in which we find ourself confined. Our walls have hearts—and hearts do bleed as well as beat. The family path to redemption also lies at *le grange* points, at a syncronous orbit between the needs of the individual and the demands of the community. Family not only enables and confines, supports and burdens, but also mediates and mitagates—providing shade, sometimes in its walls, sometimes in its shadows.

A theology of family is very useful. It allows us to tell tales of how our hearts can point in two directions at once. It let's us know that when we leave home we can always return. And, it let's us know that when we return home we can always leave. Our own life experience, and our own tradition, provide us with both stories. The need, á la Tom Bodett, is **"trying to understand the difference."**

Epilogue: We know that family is not the instant cure to the Jewish future. Even if family was all that Louis B. Meyer hoped it was and wasn't, it couldn't do it alone. *Little House on the Prairie* isn't Jewish, it takes *Walnut Creek* and the Olsons to make a shtetl. Individualism, Family, and Community will always be involved in interrelated dynamic tension—simultaneous attraction and opposition. Now that we've reinvented the Jewish family, we need to think about jump-starting our sense of community as well—otherwise it will be another all-or-nothing dead-end.

We also need to know that family is a fantasy. It is a construct made up of the perceptions and projections of each of the participants—it is a mythical reality, not a state of fact. Rationality has nothing to do with it. Family is a midrashic realm—it goes way beyond the *p'shat* (the literal meaning) of any of the interactions. We need to broaden and deepen our vision of family back to what it always ways: chaotic tensions dreaming of an ultimate monotheistic monogamy. When we do this, we will validate all kinds of interdependent psycho-economic living units and good and authentic *baytim*—Jewish families.

A Family Midrash: Once I saw Sonny and Cher on the
Mike Douglas Show. They got into a disagreement on camera. This is back in their "*I Got You Babe*" days when the beat still went on. Sonny looked at the camera and said, "**And you thought it was all Sunny and Cher**?" It was a great moment. Families are stuck together, their histories are inescapably bound up together. Jarod Barkey is right: **Whatever trouble he's in, his family has the right to share it with him. It's our duty to help him if we can and it's his duty to let us and he doesn't have the privilege to change that.** But Arthur Miller is right, too; family is only a "socially" useful manipulation—a lessening of police power—unless its vision empowers fantasies that we can realize. We have to bring the *Addam's Family* up from the dungeon and take them to Club Med once in a while.

My mother called today. She was worried about me in the latest earthquake. We had to settle-up bills from the Palm Springs vacation. It wasn't an easy conversation. Everything wasn't Sunny and Cher. But, we'll talk again next week. Families are like that.

Fragment D

Wet Moses
Conversations with the Angel of Death about Mortality and Middle Age

This last essay in this collection weaves together my relationship with my father with a serious spiritual statement. Here again we stare loneliness in the face and make sparks.

Pre-Text: We inquire about the living space we have in our head for our own father. What sort of rooms have we made up for him? If we have the grudging, stingy respect for him suggested by Geoffrey Gorer and the sitcoms, the chances are that room will be in a rundown neighborhood with sagging doors, plastic curtains and a smelly refrigerator with rotten food in it. The demons of suspicion, we can be sure, have visited this place. They throw out the sofa one day without opening the windows. They put up paintings of Pinochets and Jesse Helms and tie little black dogs to the radiator.

The son's first job, then, in a country like ours, is to redo the room, clean it, widen it, refurnish it, honor the father's clear and helpful side. The men who love their fathers simply and completely—and there are many of them—will find this work easy. They can put up paintings of George Washington. Some, of course, know consciously only the positive side of their father, and don't have a clue to his dark side.

I remember a young man, about age twenty-five, who appeared at a small men's conference in Alaska. His father was a policeman who had been killed while on duty. In order to keep a positive father image for the child, his mother had lifted the father up on a pedestal, so the father wasn't quite human. A few years later some of his father's old police friends took one look at the young man and invited him over for a night of talk. Soon they began to tell stories of how his father had cheated at cards, how good he was at it, and stories of his drinking, then stories of women. The old men gave that son a gift through stories.

Men with such an ideal father in their heads need to build an entire room for the father's twisted, secretive, destructive, vulgar, shadowy side, even if he was a hero to others. All of us in that situation need to add a room onto the apartment to house the Destructive King and his relatives.

By contrast, the son who always knew about his father's cruel and destructive side will find it easy to furnish one of these dark rooms. Perhaps a coffee table would be good, with Kafka's *Letters to My Father*, bound in leather, some poison darts on the wall, walls papered with Jim Beam labels, and a bed whose headboard is elegantly carved with scenes from the life of Cronos, the son eater.

But that very same son needs to build a second room to house the generous and blessed side of his father.

If we haven't yet made two rooms and furnished them, we can't expect our father, living or dead, to move in. Those men who have made both rooms inside their souls could begin to think of inviting a mentor in. He will also need two rooms.

Robert Bly, *Iron John: A Book About Men*. Reading: Addison-Wesley, 1990, pp. 118-9.

My Opening Meditation on Dying: This

week, for the first time, I lit my father's yahrzeit candle with certain knowledge that I was going to die. The doctor says that my heart is busy rusting away the same way his did. This Shabbat, as I gathered and kissed the fringes of my tallit during the *tzitzit* paragraph of the Shema, the movement of the kiss in my jaw again set off spasms of pain, pain left behind by reconstructive oral surgery. Again, I've re-learned that the mitzvot are indeed a burden. And again I've confronted my own fragility. Ironically, the shooting pains in my head are my version of my mother's decaying gums, which are literally at the root of this problem. I have seen the Angel of Death often in my life, both in real life and on television, but it is only in the last few weeks that we've begun to talk in earnest. I am now unequivocally middle-aged—the Angel of Death and I have begun our relationship; she and I now have regular conversations.

I say "she" because my angel of death is no grim reaper, no dark shadow out of a Bergman film. My angel of death is not John Huston's green smog, either. My angel of death is more Victorian, more Gothic than that—and certainly more erotic. This is, after all, my dream, my future

236

nightmare, my eventual final coming to rest, and I'll take the prerogative to cast it any way I want. My angel of death is one who will come with a kiss, not a scythe, because I hope to die the way that Rashi says that Moses did: not with my boots on, not *in flagrante delecto* with my heart giving out after one final orgasmic climax, not mangled after a car chase, not robbed of my dignity by tubes and electrodes pushing my body past my soul's allocated number of days, not violently, out of frustration cut-off by my own hand, not in some dark urban mini-drama, not through Dr. Kevorkian's well-intended help, nor by drinking elderberry wine, but with the *Shehinah's* gentle kiss.

She and I talk a lot these days. Eddie loses 17 inches of intestine to colon cancer and will do a fearful year of chemo—she and I meet in a corner and empathically wonder how I would hold up under the same anxiety. Kyla's biopsy comes back negative; her breast is still pure, we share our relief. With Yosi we talk about Exercycles and pills. With Uncle Seymour we lament about his spine that is too far twisted to support the stainless steel hip replacement—it is too late for his Teflon miracle. Yes, the Angel of Death and I take our daily walk on the treadmill of life; all the time I wonder secretly how much of my heart is flaking away as rust and dust, how deeply into my soul the black hole in my jaw is burrowing. I ask the question of everyone who talks to the Angel: "How many days do I have left?"

Our Torah Verse comes from the Torah's final death scene, the last chapter in Deuteronomy: AND MOSES WAS 120 YEARS OLD WHEN HE DIED, HIS EYES STILL SAW CLEARLY, AND ALL HIS JUICES STILL FLOWED. If you open up most translations of the Torah, you find "juices still flowing" politely stated as "nor had his strength abated." Rashi's Victorian cover-up of this image is his life-sap did not depart, and decomposition had no power over him." Rashi evidently thought Moses was spiritually embalmed, but it was my Rabbi and teacher, Mordechai Finley, who pointed out that the Torah was literally saying that Moses's spirit still felt physically well-endowed, even if his heart was rusting away, too.

I only really understood this when I read OUR **PROEM VERSE**, in an essay by Robert Fulgum: **Some tangible evidence of the secret life is often close at hand, or in the case of men's wallets, close behind. I was asked to conduct a seminar for the senior members of a department of the federal** government in Washington, D.C., held in the solemn marble atmosphere of one of those classic Greco-Roman office buildings. The participants came in wearing facades as serious as the building …. The message to me was clear: this seminar had better be worthwhile. "A simple request, gentlemen: please take out your wallets and place them on the table in front of you." And out of the niche on their sterns came the fat old leather hamburgers—molded and moldy from years of use. They laughed. Their covers were blown. "Now, please take everything out of your wallet and spread it out on the table in front of you." In the meantime, the men had, of their own volition, loosened their ties and taken off their suit jackets as they opened up their private lives without me. Not everyone was willing to share everything. One man—the oldest and most respectably dressed of the lot—a man who, I learned later, was within a week of retirement—had not opened his wallet or relaxed enough to remove his jacket. He had not eliminated himself from the group discussion, but he was not sharing. His colleagues teased him into emptying his wallet. For openers, he took out three brand-new condoms. There was a razzing cheer from the group. They gave him a standing ovation. He held up his hand for attention and said, "You're never too old, boys—never give up hope." And the ovation continued."(Robert Fulgum, *Maybe (Maybe Not) Second Thoughts from a Secret Life*. New York: Random House, 1993, pp. 123-127.) This much I now know. After facing forty years in the wilderness, after so much exhaustion, so much exasperation, so great a sense of failure, with so much more left to do, and after battling with God to stay alive long enough to cross one more river, when Moses finally gave in and went up the Pisgah to kiss his Maker, three brand new condoms were in his wallet.

Commentary: Now that I know that I am dying, the flashbacks start. It is time for my montage of death. Before my eyes the projection booth of memory starts rolling the old black-and-white footage, clips that are scratched and worn out from too many screenings, from too long in storage.

A Story: My mother says that I was five the time I know I first heard the Angel of Death. It was late one night in the spare bedroom at my Nana Grishaver's house on Atherton Road. Death called from Chicago.

Grandma Lurie was dead. My parents would stay another couple of days for the funeral. I didn't hear the conversation, but I did hear the phone ring, and I knew instantaneously that death had called. The room got colder and darker, but I didn't know what to think or feel; I was just cold. Then I went to sleep. The next morning Nana woke me and confirmed as truth everything I already knew; death had remained on the other end of the telephone. A few years later Nana died, but my mind is blank. I remember nothing. I went to the vault and looked for some footage to play back, but the canisters are empty. The Angel of Death sometimes works that way.

Another Story: Five or so years later, the family went to Chicago. A visit to Grandma Lurie's grave was part of this return to my mother's roots. We went to the cemetery. I got sick. Then we went to visit Hank Skirball and family. I don't remember the cemetery, just a flash frame: a glimpse of lawn and a tree backed by the sun (maybe a real memory, maybe a fabricated place holder). I don't remember the visit. I just remember rolling around on a spare bed in a back room (a white camp blanket with a single red stripe and a single black stripe). It felt like food poisoning. My mother said that I was sensitive. She felt sure it was the visit to the cemetery. That day I had "cemetery poisoning" and learned that I was allergic to death. The Angel of Death was hiding somewhere that day, but I didn't look into her eyes. We didn't nod to each other, and we certainly didn't talk. I wasn't yet ready.

Another Story: I was fifteen, at a six-week summer Hebrew-speaking program in upper New York State, when Bobby Corkin flipped his convertible somewhere back in Massachusetts and ended his too-short life. Death came in the mail. I spent the next day or two looking for her by the lake, in the weeping willows, in the mist, in long walks long after curfew, under the stars, barefoot in the dew-soaked lawns—but she wasn't there. I was chasing my fantasies of death, my projections of the emotions I should be feeling—not her. Bobby Corkin was the first person I knew who died, not someone I knew about, not someone old whom parents knew. I went looking for death because I wanted to get to know her, and I'd never really thought about her before. The problem was, I didn't actually know Bobby Corkin. I used to see him around high school. I talked

239

to him a couple of times. I once played basketball in his driveway. The problem was that he wasn't a friend of mine, wasn't ever in my class, didn't go to my elementary school. He was just someone who lived down the street from Dicky Fishman, someone who was in the advanced class, which I wasn't considered smart enough to join. Those days were my own Bergman festival of depressed moments. I was chasing death everywhere, but I was faking my emotions, trying to churn up feelings that weren't really there. The best truth I can reconstruct is that I spent a couple of days obsessed with the idea and imagery of death, not her reality. Even my "Zipruder film" of a blue Chevrolet convertible, white leather splattered with blood and a headless Bobby, is a fake. I know nothing about the actual death—and I suspect that the image came much later as I retold the story, not in the confrontations with the news. It was my version of black lipstick and black fingernails, my own little tribute to Roger Corman.

Another Story: The summer of the death watch over my

father, I was angry. I was just twenty-three, and this was just too young for "me" to have to face all of "this." I blamed him for being "an old father," for not being responsible enough to have birthed me when he was young enough to still want to play catch. I had been in Israel for the first heart attack, and perhaps a second. They weren't telling me the whole story. They weren't spoiling my first year of rabbinical school when there was nothing I could do. They weren't sharing the burden of the details with me. They thought I was too young. I thought I was too young. We all thought death could wait a while. That summer I came home and took my rotation, being with my father. He was home, not working, but up and dressed every day. The doctors, then afraid to do a single bypass, were playing around with medications and hoping. Some days my father was there and we had good times. Some days I talked to the medication. Mostly I went to work at a day camp and spent as much time there as I could. I was home, but not home. There, but not there. After all, I was allergic to cemeteries; everyone knew that.

Near the end of the summer came the single most precious moment in my relationship with my father, the moment for which I will never forgive him. It was almost the end of the summer. Gail, my then-wife, was already in California finding our next home. It was late at night, and I heard

Dad walking around. He was lost, disoriented. Not a light was on in the house. Mom was asleep. It was my turn to be on duty. I took him back to bed—his twin bed, in a fifties bedroom made for the Cleavers. Mom snored with the sinuses she and I share. I tucked him in. He seemed scared, and in my memory, at least, he was crying a little. It was then that I did for him just what he had done for me so many times: I held his hand and sat with him till sleep came. It was the perfect opportunity to repay all the love and kindness. I know that. It is a beautiful image, the idea of being able to do for my father that which he had done for me. I have told it that way many times, yet it masks a lie. The truth is that deep somewhere inside I am angry and sick. That night took me too close to the grave, too near death, and at twenty-three I wasn't yet ready to talk to her. I went back into my bedroom and tossed and turned the way I once had on Hank Skirball's bed in Chicago.

Another Story: The doctors later got the drugs under control, and my father came back. Everything seemed well. A brighter future seemed certain. I drove off with Don Rossoff to see the Grand Canyon and then meet our destinies by becoming Rabbis. In November the doctors laid the odds on the table, and my parents opted for surgery. Dates were scheduled, plane tickets were purchased, anticipatory (but certainly "unneeded") good-byes were prepared. None of this ever happened. A week too early, on a Friday morning, Stuart Kelman, now friend, then teacher, pulled me out of class and somehow got me to the airport. Stáph infection. My father died in the hospital before I could change planes in New York.

This was the "death" semester in rabbinic school. We had been rehearsing funerals and eulogies. We had been mapping the stages of dying and mourning. We had been given all the right truths, the best truisms, all the laws and practices—and had been coached into perfecting a good graveside manner. I arrived home in the midst of the already organized procedures and hit the ground running the "tapes" of all the things I was supposed to "do" and "go through." One of my delegated tasks was to drive the clothes to the funeral home. Everything else to do with the body and the grave) had been done for us by someone else. The undertaker met me kindly, with his best graveside manner, and we said our well-rehearsed truisms to each other. He invited me through the swinging doors to view the body. I knew without thinking, because I had been told by my teachers, that was something I should not do. I went home. Since that night, those swinging doors have often become the doors to a meat locker—their found glass is frosted over. Each time I dream my way through them, my father is hanging naked from a big hook, not bloodily, just cold and white and dead. It is not a place to say final words. I just repress a scream. Somehow I know in some inner recess that had I walked through that door that day, she would have been waiting. We would have talked, and the meat locker would never have entered my life (though other and different dreams were probably ready to haunt me in its place—I am, after all, allergic to death). I was still too young to die, too young to really know about death. The nervous breakdown came a year later.

Another Story: Almost fifteen years go by. I've now learned all the funeral dance steps, and I've gotten good at my *shiva* hug—I've had a lot of deaths to practice on. I've gotten good at doing Clint Eastwood calm, at the Hoss Cartwright "I really care" hug, in voicing Rod McKuen's hoarse whisper of meaningful and caring truism—and I've learned to go home before I get sick. Then my friend Joel started to die. I flew to Seattle to share the tubes and electrodes, to help wipe away the indignities. I was there for a piece of the dying, but missed the death. It came for me one Sunday afternoon when I was home watching *Star Trek*. It came for Carol when, home from the hospital, he died mid-sentence that morning in their bedroom. I packed my best funeral practices in an overnight bag, and my friend Rabbi Stuart Kelman once again got me on an airplane. It was the one and only time I will ever be Rabbi Joel Grishaver. I was there comforting Carol. I was there for her. I was there for my loss. I was there for my memory of Joel. But I hid from death. Each time she entered the room, I hugged Carol and hid my eyes. It was like a Marx Brothers movie, the scenes where people keep walking in and out of doors, the *I Love Lucy* where she and Harpo play hide-and-seek with the mirrors. Sometimes our eyes met anyway, we were closer, but I still would not talk to her. Deep in my heart I knew that Joel's luck had run out, but it would be hard for Carol, hard for me, to live forever without him. Death was still something that happened only to others, even if they were close.

How I Finally Met the Angel of Death:

Three months ago I got this cold. It went straight to my sinuses, exploded into an infection, and then dripped down into my throat. Kleenex® in hand, I called my doctor for the usual over-the-phone prescriptions of antibiotics and decongestants, then decided to give in and have the long-overdue "expensive" checkup. I suffered the indignities of all the tests and then got invited into his office for "the chat." The doctor held up my EKG and said flatly, "I wouldn't insure you." The verdict was "cloggage around the heart." Then came: "No fat! No oil! No sugar! Half an aspirin every day, anti-oxident vitamins—and EXERCISE." It was a doctor's visit written by Edgar Allan Poe, my version, or perhaps my father's version of "The Telltale Heart." I could hear my heart rusting—lub-dub, lub-dub. The bad news: because of my HDL's, I will have to live forty or more years without prime rib, forty or more years without a real dessert. God bless cheesecake, especially the lemon one Nick sometimes serves at Off Vine. Sadly, my next hamburger and fries will have to wait for the Messiah.

A week later, my gold crown was loose and rocking, again! The gum under it was bleeding. Hot foods began to cause pain. The visit to the dentist couldn't be put off. Two years ago, my dentist, the High Holiday _Hazan_, sent me off to have my mother's gums scaled by the periodontist. They never got there. Instead, I waited for my bank balance to improve, just as I had waited for the inspiration to really diet more than three months at a time, just as I waited for the _kavanah_ to actually exercise all year round and not just in the convenient months. While waiting, I brushed well, really used my Water Pik®, and hoped. Now it was too late. Pain meant dentist, and dentist meant periodontist. I went. However, it wound up meaning much more. A root canal gone bad, hidden under a gold crown, means two teeth pulled, sterile bone tissue grafted into my jaw, thousands of dollars, new implants, and weeks of unexpected pain. Somewhere, nerves have been damaged, and while everything is clinically healing well, two months later I was still living with chronic pain.

Life was now just perfect. In my mind, I am the second-rate Irish poet in _Reuben, Reuben_. My teeth are falling out one by one. I will never chew again. My life is over; I can look forward to non-fat, cholesterol-free, sugar-free gruel for the rest of my life. I contemplate the English sheep dog, the chair, and the rope.

A couple of weeks of living this way and death becomes a reality, not a joke. I am keeping my diet like kashrut, better—if truth be told—than I ever kept kosher. And every night, honestly five or six a week, I walk my walk of life on my newly purchased home treadmill. Every night the Angel of Death walks with me. She is my coach; she tells me I can make the extra five minutes each time I want to stop before the doctor-prescribed thirty is achieved. She reminds me, "I want to live." The lessons begin to sink in. Not just "no red meat." Not just learning to read all the labels. Not just what I can eat in which restaurant. But "My body is no longer a renewable resource." "I am indeed mortal." "Prices are always paid." And, most importantly, I am going to die—someday. In the process, I decide that my life, with all its failures and unachieved dreams, is somehow worth extending. I chose to nightly walk the walk of life and hope that whatever I taped off the tube is interesting enough to numb this spiritual pursuit enough to allow it to continue.

Commentary: I try to tell my friends about the joys of feeling older. I don't think I'm rationalizing. To my way of thinking, something spiritual has happened now that I am doing my version of "living each day—one day at a time." But most of them laugh. If they've talked to their angel of death, they deny it. The ubiquitous response to my celebration of middle age is, "**I don't think of myself as old.**" Or "**I still feel young.**" Perhaps the most powerful and moving denial comes from Stuart Maitlen, the owner of Jewish Lights, another Jewish publishing house. He says, "**My mother died a couple of years ago. She was seventy-eight and still could remember everything she did on a given day when she was eleven. Yet she said to me, just a couple of weeks before she died, 'When I get up in the morning and look in the mirror, I still expect to see a seventeen-year-old girl.'**" Old woman that she was, her soul knew from Moses, her juices were still flowing, and I suspect she had condoms hidden somewhere.

This much I believe I now know: admitting that you are dying is one important spiritual truth. Raging against the darkness is another. As with most opposite things in life, we need both.

Davar Aher: **Another aspect:** Dov Gartenberg is a rabbi in Seattle and another friend of mine. Often he is my teacher. He just turned forty. Honoring that truth, he gave a High Holiday sermon about it. The following texts are all stolen from him. I, however, did my own spiritual spin-doctoring, so the meanings attributed to them are all my own.

First, the "birthday mishnah," the one everyone quotes when they have to do a Jewish speech about anyone who has lasted another decade: Rabbi Yehuda ben Teima taught: At five one should study Torah. At ten one should study Mishnah. At thirteen one should be responsible for the mitzvot. At fifteen one should study Talmud. At eighteen one should marry. At twenty one should seek an occupation. At thirty one enters into full strength. At forty one achieves understanding. At fifty one gives counsel. At sixty one is old. At seventy one's head is white. At eighty comes a special gift of strength. At ninety one bends under the weight of years. At one hundred one is as good as dead (*Pirke Avot*, 5.24). Our quest for understanding middle age has to start here, because forty and understanding somehow do go together, even if none of the other ages seem to really fit their prescriptions today.

Robert Bly, in *Iron John*, says that same thing differently. Bly is a self-defined pagan who begins with one of our truths: **We remember the Baal Shem Tov, the genius of the spirit in the early eighteenth century in Poland, would not let his young men read certain spiritual texts until they were thirty-five. Some say that the man's task in the first half of his life is to become bonded to matter, to learn a craft, become friends with wood, earth, wind, or fire. When Jung established a training center in Zurich, he would not accept a person who was not already a success in some other career. It was a way of saying thirty-five or older.** Later, he expands this notion of maturity and says: **Despite our Disneyland culture, some men around thirty-five or forty will begin to experience the ashes privately, without ritual, even without old men. They begin to notice how many of their dreams have turned to ashes.** Now here comes the punch line. **At thirty-five his inner stove begins to produce ashes as well. All through his twenties, his stove burned with such a good draft that he threw in whole nights until dawn, drinking parties, sexual extravagance, enthusiasm, madness, excitement. Then one day he notices that his stove doesn't take such big chunks anymore. He opens the stove door and ashes fall out on the floor. It is time for him to buy a small black shovel at the hardware store and get down on his knees. The ashes fall** off the shovel and onto the floor, and he can see the print of our boot-soles in the ashes. (Robert Bly, *Iron John: A Book About Men*. Reading, MA: Addison-Wesley, 1990, p. 59, 81.) Robert Bly meets Rabbi Yehuda ben Temia and sings a duet about the spiritual benefits of having to live with no fat! no oil! and no sugar!

Jewish tradition teaches the same lesson: that **a person cannot study the Kabbalah, the mystical truths of Judaism, until he or she is forty.** That was a boundary against which I always rebelled. It was a place where I called the tradition parochial and patriarchal (and a lot of other big words). My high school notebooks were filled with Kabbalistic doodles and po-etry attesting to my rebellion. I was saying, "I can read, you can't stop me." And like any good *puer* with my manhood emerging, I believed that my father's mysteries held the secrets of flight, and I was ready to fly, even if he thought I was too young.

Now, as a forty-plus-year-old man with a rusty heart and a black hole in my mouth, I affirm the tradition differently. I say to my rebelling teens, "You can study the Kabbalah any time you want, but you won't really under-stand it until you know with profound simplicity that you are dying."

Davar Aher: Another aspect: *Genesis Rabbah (100.10 on Genesis 50.22)* tells us this story, via Moses, this way: **Moses lived forty years of denial in Pharaoh's palace,** *his childhood*; **forty years of reflec-tion and redirection in Midyan,** *his time in the ashes*; **and actualized his mission with Israel for forty years.**

Hillel matured in Babylonia for forty years, apprenticed to the Sages for forty years, and then led the Jewish people for forty years.

Rabbi Yohanan devoted himself to his business for forty years, studied Torah for forty years, and then served Israel for forty years.

Rabbi Akiva was an ignorant shepherd for forty years, studied Torah for forty years, and then served the Jewish people for forty years. The sim-ple message; a full life takes a long time. Forty is just the first part—mid-dle age, the first achievement. Now I think I know that an honest conversation with the Angel of Death is the door to middle age. One Moses is on the edge of forty. He kills out of anger and flees everything he has ever known. He is a man who spends time in the ashes, who lives with

246

death. The other Moses is 120, the man who has faith in his fluids, and the one who will not die. My simple truth; we need to be both of them.

Davar Aher: Another aspect: And What of Angels?

Because I love *The Horn Sounds at Midnight*, I never believed in angels as real—I knew all about dry ice, lenses and mirrors. I never took angels seriously. I have this conversation with the guy sitting next to me on the way to Cleveland. He says, "**I believe in angels—even though I've never knowingly seen them, but I do feel protected.**" I laughed it off. I imagine Senator Joe McCarthy ferreting out hidden angels everywhere, starting in Hollywood. Besides, Cleveland is no place to expect angels. Then four conversations come back to me; they had all happened in one week.

First, my rabbi, Mordechai Finley, taught in the name of his teacher, Jonathan Omer-man: "**What are angels? Angels are packets of Divine energy.**" It was a wonderful explanation. Rashi teaches that "**each angel can only do one thing.**" Jonathan's explanation says, "**Angels are when God directs Divine energy toward one single task.**" In other words, angels are encountering God, one truth at a time. I liked the idea. It was cute. Then I promptly forgot it.

That was Shabbat. On Sunday I was teaching my twelfth-grade students, and I asked, "**What is an angel?**" It was a Socratic question, I was looking for a right answer, namely, "a Divine Messenger, not wings and a halo!" But Cheryl Klein gave me a great answer instead of my correct one. She said, "**Angels are when we don't want to blame things on God!**" It took a second to understand she was saying the same thing that Tikvah Frymer-Kensky does; "**Radical monotheism has never been truly tried; [humanity always]…peopled the heavens with a multiplicity of divine beings. Periodically, all of these lesser spiritual beings have passed out of favor…but they have never permanently succeeded in leaving God as the sole inhabitant of the invisible world.**"(Tikvah Frymer-Kensky, *In the Wake of the Goddess, Women, Culture, and the Biblical Transformation of Pagan Myth*. New York: The Free Press, 1992, pp. 217-8.) At that moment, Jonathan's "bundles of Divine energy" re-entered my memory. The two views were simultaneously opposites and the same. It was a cute insight. It had nothing to do with my life. It was filed for the next time I had to teach a biblical text or a midrash with angels in it. It still had no place in my experience.

Next day, a new friend, Jeff Salkin, called on the phone and said in the middle of a looping conversation, "**Someday I want to write a book about all the things people 'know' are true that they don't 'believe' are true. For example, no one sitting in a funeral home before the burial doesn't accept a working notion of eternal life; and everybody in some ways knows that there are angels out there.**" I had to think about that, but angels were now indeed everywhere.

On Wednesday I get a fax from Kerry Olitsky suggesting that I write an article on Meeting the Angel of Death. My first reaction was: "Stupid, I don't believe in angels, I am a radical monotheist." Then it sat with me for a few hours, and the other conversations came back to haunt me. I found myself dancing on the head of a pin, me and Tailgunner Joe. I said, "Damn the dry ice," and I realized that in a very real metaphoric way, I'd been talking to the Angel of Death for three months.

Davar Aher: Wings and ashes: The kid is fifteen and a half. His father is not well, but the kid doesn't really know it. The doctors are doing all the tests, Torquemada is probing, extracting, and analyzing, looking for the "death sentence." The kid just knows that at this moment he hates his father, because every time his wings begin to grow, his mother, at his father's urging, takes out a nail clipper and cuts them off at the root. (The non-metaphoric translation: every time he is scheduled to get his learner's permit and start driving, his parents postpone it because of grades, attitude, responsibility, or some other abstract adultism.) Every time I try to explain the tension in the household, he just says in one way or another, "I am angry. They won't hear what I need." He is perfect *puer*, almost manhood on the edge of flight. He is boy Icarus who doesn't know death, who only knows he must fly. When I try to deal with the medical reality, he says plainly, "I don't want to know that." He stops me; he, too, is too young to meet his angel of death, too young to consider that his father might have one.

A week later, after a couple of well-placed interventions, we go out flying in my convertible. I am willingly sacrificing the future good health of my Synchro-mesh in order to watch and aid his adolescent Kitty Hawk. With great joy (and a lot of personal fear of flying) I watch him stall the car. Then, never quite understanding the nature of bodies at rest, he jerks the car; he can't quite get the hang of going from a dead stop to first gear. Once he is moving, second, third, fourth, and fifth are a slam-dunk. Once he is moving, this kid knows how to go. I feel privileged to be his mandatory adult training pilot.

A few nights later, I sit with an old friend. He, the bravest man I know, is finally losing the battle he has fought all his life. For as long as I have known him, he has fought the results of childhood cerebral palsy, walking his way though life on atrophied legs, a cane, and raw guts. He managed to do it all, just like anyone else, and thought he would succeed in dying with his boots on. Now, after years of twisting and straining, the chassis is worn out. No one will operate. Everything is just too mangled. With great pain he moves from bed to scooter, scooter to chair, chair to scooter, in slow and painful rotation. An undiscussed wheelchair is out of the question. We spend a wonderful night together. We talk surgeons and pills, politics and life. A pretty good time is had by all. He gives me lots of advice I now take seriously. The new subtext we hold in common is that none of us want to die, and that we are willing to work to hold on to all the life we can. That is the deep meaning of all the discussions about good and bad oils, about how many milligrams of what each of us is taking. I secretly learn that before you meet the Angel of Death you take pills; afterwards your life is measured in milligrams. Even though life offers no solutions for my favorite relative, even though there is nothing I can offer, the sense of connection seems to be enough for both of us. The next morning, because I am expected elsewhere before dawn, I have my no-fat, no-oil, no-sugar breakfast, and I leave on my wonderings.

As I board my flight, the ironies are wonderful. The old friend who has always flown the way the kid wants to, is rejecting the wheels the kid is seeking. The deeper irony, though, is that these days, I seem to find it easier to identify and relate to the aging relative than to the kid. That scares me. That thrills me. I go home, pick up my electric guitar, turn my distortion box up to ten, and thrash it around for awhile.

I get to this point in writing this article when Ben Merins calls. Twenty years ago I was his youth advisor. Twenty years ago I took him out for his first driving experiences the way that I had just taken out the kid. It was easier for me then. He calls, essentially, to tell me that on one of those drives I had told him what he should do with his life—"talk to people, because that's what you are good at." Today he does a talk show on public radio and heard my name mentioned at a study group at his synagogue. Twenty years ago it was also much easier to be right. Somehow Ben's call fits into the end of this story, too.

This Much I Know: My mother named me Joel because of a biblical citation: **"Your youth shall see visions and your old men shall dream dreams."** These days, like Moses, my corrected eyesight is still clear, but I spend more time dreaming of my success in the days of Ben & Co. than I do believing that I can actually change the kid's or the relative's world. No longer do I expect to fly, even though I still dream of it. Slowly, my visions are indeed turning into dreams, less focused, aged by pragmatism, but no less powerful. In the words of my friend Carol—words she throws at me all the time when I challenge her to push past the realistic—**"I know who I am—I know what I can do."** That, too, has become part—not all—of the blend that is me. Then again, Neil Young did say it all: **"It's better to burn out than it is to rust!"** This much, however, I now profoundly know; someday, in thirty or forty years, when I do feel old, not just aged, I will carry purple Day Glo condoms in my wallet, look in the mirror, and expect to see seventeen, too.

Coda: A week later this letter comes from Ben Merins:

Dear Joel,

I'm glad we spoke recently. While we haven't done much staying in touch, I think of you often…and very fondly.

I haven't lit a yahrzeit candle yet with the knowledge that one shall burn for me someday. I have a father obsessed with staying "young" who looks five years older every time I see him lately. My younger brother and I frequently discuss him and the day he dies and how it won't matter to us. But I can't help thinking that his death will rock me in a big way—I just don't see it coming.

Unfortunately, I do light a y.c. for my mother. She became ill in the Florida Keys in March of 1989. My brother called me to say, "Mom keeps falling down." "What does that mean?" I asked. "She keeps falling down." He said he didn't know, but that he was worried about her.

Two days later she came home. My aunt and uncle rushed her to an MRI clinic on a Sunday afternoon. (A sign her problem must be serious.) I began to accept the fact that we were losing her…I didn't know why or how…or how much longer she'd be with us. There was a hazy, slow motion to that week. When we saw her, her face was sagging on one side…as if she had had a stroke. Some medicine cleared the problem up for a short time, and we had "Mom" back. But within a few days she was in Highland Park Hospital. An out-of-control brain tumor was growing in the center of her brain.

I knew we were losing her and began to resent friends, family, strangers telling me that it would be all right and that the tests they were conducting might find out how to cure her. I knew it wasn't so. The last week of her life my two brothers lost it. Our family and my mother's friends kept a daily vigil in the visitor's lounge, across the hall from her room. I drank a lot of coffee and smoked pack after pack of cigarettes—just wanting the wait to end. I seemed to keep calm because I had begun to grieve her death weeks before she died.

And through all of the pain, I found that my mother had prepared me for her death. She taught me how to take a deep breath, then another, then a small step, then another…and eventually I would go on. Even though she wouldn't be there.

It was my worst nightmare come true.

When I was ten, my brothers and I spent the weekend in Chicago with my dad. Every Saturday night for years I dreamt that we would be driving home to Glencoe and come around the curve on Green Bay Road to find that the townhouses we lived in would be gone, along with the gas station which stood next to our home. And the worst part of the nightmare is that my mother would also have disappeared. Everything would just go black after that…and then I would wake up.

Well, the nightmare came true about four and a half years ago. My mother left. The gas station is no longer there, and the townhouses were sold and fences constructed to give them a different look. Years from now my childhood home will have no physical traces left.

And yet, while I overcame the loss of my mother and the living out of my worst childhood nightmare, I read your Proem 9: We, like Moses learn that. While I survived those two crises…I won't survive or beat the inevitable. I will hit a stage where mortality isn't just a threat of "some-day" but a reality. It isn't something I think about much…nor do I want to. It seems fitting that I have been doing so lately. You have a history of getting me to think about my life in ways I try to avoid thinking about it. In the past, this redirection of thought was good for me—I think my contemplating your Proem and my life lately has also been good for me. And, like twenty years ago, I just don't know in what ways it has been good for me.

I think the most important question one can ask when contemplating one's life and the fact it will end…is, what are you doing? And why are you doing it? Are you making a difference? Are your moments spent living worthwhile ones?

I don't necessarily like the answers I come up with, but I know I am doing what I wanted to do years ago. Now I wonder whether there is value in it or just the satisfaction that I climbed the mountain I sought to climb, and now I can say, "I did it."

So much for the inner thoughts of Ben. I thought somehow you'd want to read them. Maybe not. I wrote this letter this morning as I ran on the treadmill I run on every Monday thru Friday morning. They moved the equipment to a new room this week, and I now run looking out of a window that reflects back at me until the darkness becomes light and I can see the forest outside.

While I ran today, I started the mental game of What Are You Going to Do Today. If I think about this down to the most minute detail, the fifteen-minute run goes much quicker, and my day has an organization to it that seems to allow more to get done.

Somehow I have a hard time seeing you on your walk of life. Physical activity never was one of our long suits. Two weeks after my mom passed, I lit and smoked my last Marlboro®. I was wearing jeans and rubbed some of the ashes into my jeans. Just to spite Dr. Nate Beraha, who always told me that when I died, someone should rub my ashes into a pair of jeans. Well, I have stayed on the tobacco wagon for four and a half years…and been exercising ever since.

Ben Merins

Copyright Acknowledgments

Recent Archaeological Discoveries and Biblical Research by William Dever, University of Washington Press, Seattle, WA, copyright © 1990.

The Culture of Narcissism, American Life in an Age of Diminishing Expectations by Christopher Lasch. Copyright © 1991 by Christopher Lasch. Reprinted by permission of W.W. Norton & Company, Inc.

"Bowling Alone: America's Declining Social Capital" by Robert D. Putnam, from *Journal of Democracy,* Johns Hopkins University Press, Baltimore, MD, copyright © 1995).

The Savage in Judaism: An Anthropology of Israelite Religion and Ancient Judaism by Howard Eilberg-Schwartz, Indiana University Press, Bloomington, IN, 1990, copyright © 1990.

Maybe (Maybe Not) Second Thoughts from a Secret Life by Robert Fulgum, Random House, Inc., New York, NY, copyright © 1993.

The Resilient Self by Steven J. and Sybil Wolin, Villard Books, Random House, Inc., New York, NY, copyright (1993.

The Torah: Genesis by Gunther W. Plaut, UAHC Press, New York, NY, copyright © 1981.

Cornhuskers by Carl Sandburg, Holt, Rinehart & Winston, Orlando, FL, copyright © 1918 & 1948.

Miriam's Well by Peninna Adelman, Biblio Press, New York, NY, copyright © 1990.

Scherer, M. "On Our Changing Family Values: A Conversation with David Elkind." *Educational Leadership* 53, 7:4-9, copyright © 1996 by ASCD. Reprinted by permission. All rights reserved.

A Little Book on the Human Shadow by Robert Bly, HarperCollins Publishers Inc., New York, NY, copyright © 1988.

Care of the Soul by Thomas Moore, HarperCollins Publishers Inc., New York, NY, copyright © 1992.

King, Warrior, Magician, Lover by Robert Moore, HarperCollins Publishers Inc., New York, NY, copyright © 1990.

A Blue Fire Selected writings by James Hillman. Edited by Thomas Moore, HarperCollins Publishers Inc., New York, NY, copyright © 1989 by Thomas Moore and James Hillman.

Our Fathers' Wells by Peter Pitzele, HarperCollins Publishers Inc., New York, NY, copyright © 1995 by Peter Pitzele.

The Early History of God by Mark S. Smith, HarperCollins Publishers Inc., New York, NY, copyright © 1990 by Mark S. Smith.

The Memories of Earth by Orson Scott Card, copyright © 1992 by Orson Scott Card. Reprinted by permission of Tom Doherty Associates, Inc.

Reprinted with permission of the publisher from *In A Different Voice*, by Carol Gilligan, Cambridge, MA: Harvard University Press, copyright © 1982, 1993 by Carol Gilligan.

Moment Magazine, February 1992. David J. Meyer, "Doing It Myself."

R Bly, IRON JOHN: A BOOK ABOUT MEN, (extracted from pages 118 & 119) copyright ©1990 by Robert Bly. Reprinted by permission of Addison-Wesley Longman Publishing Company, Inc.

Myths of the Family by James Hillman, Sound Horizons Audio Video, Inc., New York, NY, copyright © 1991.

The Dancing Wu Li Masters, An Overview of the New Physics, by Gary Zukav, New York: Bantam, copyright © 1980 by Gary Zukav.

You Just Don't Understand by Deborah Tannen, Ph.D, New York: Random House, Inc., copyright © 1990 by Deborah Tannen.